TONIKA RINAR

JOURNEY HOME

A TRUE STORY OF TIME AND INTER-DIMENSIONAL TRAVEL

BOOKS

Winchester, UK
New York, USA

Copyright © 2005 O Books
O Books is an imprint of John Hunt Publishing Ltd.,
Deershot Lodge, Park Lane, Ropley, Hants, SO24 0BE, UK
office@johnhunt-publishing.com
www.O-books.net

Distribution in:
UK
Orca Book Services
orders@orcabookservices.co.uk
Tel: 01202 665432 Fax: 01202 666219 Int. code (44)

USA and Canada
NBN
custserv@nbnbooks.com
Tel: 1 800 462 6420 Fax: 1 800 338 4550

Australia
Brumby Books
sales@brumbybooks.com
Tel: 61 3 9761 5535 Fax: 61 3 9761 7095

New Zealand
Peaceful Living
books@peaceful-living.co.nz
Tel: 64 7 57 18105 Fax: 64 7 57 18513

Singapore
STP
davidbuckland@tlp.com.sg
Tel: 65 6276 Fax: 65 6276 7119

South Africa
Alternative Books
altbook@global.co.za
Tel: 27 011 792 7730 Fax: 27 011 972 7787

Text: © 2004 Tonika Rinar

Design: Jim Weaver Design
Cover design: Krave Ltd., London

ISBN 1 905047 00 2

A CIP catalogue record for this book is available from the British Library.

Printed in the USA by Maple-Vail Manufacturing Group

Contents

Be Your Own Garden

Be the still pool; Let your face reflect the glory, the wonder.

Be the dragonfly; silent but joyful.

Be the bud; prepare to blossom.

Be the tree; grant shelter.

Be the butterfly; accept the riches of the moment.

Be the moth; seek the light.

Be the lantern; guide the lost.

Be the path; open the way for another.

Be the wind chimes; let the breeze flow through you, turn the storms into song.

Be the rain; wash away, cleanse, forgive.

Be the grass; bounce back when you are trodden on.

Be the bridge; reach in peace towards the other side.

Be the moss; temper your strength with softness, with mercy.

Be the soil; bear fruit.

Be the gardener; create order.

Be the seasons; welcome change.

Be the temple; honour the divine in you.

Be the moon; shine through the darkness.

Be the pebble; let time shape and smooth you.

Be the sun; let your warmth and light touch everyone.

Be the leaf; fall gracefully when your time comes to let go.

Trust in the cycle; to end is to begin.

Tonika Rinar

Dedication

This book is dedicated to my husband, whose endless supply of support and encouragement made the writing of *Journey Home* possible.

To my children – Lucy, James, Toby and Atlanta-Rose – for just being themselves

Acknowledgements

Acknowledgements and thanks to:

Valerie Wood – for all your priceless support in the early years

Mary Elizabeth Hoffman – whose words I both honor and respect

Sue Cameron – for your strength and calmness

Bill Dawes – whose belief in me enabled
the completion of this book

And finally, many thanks to John Orr

Preface

After the birth of Toby, my third child, I thought that my life was complete. But under the surface of my life's activities remained this constant niggling doubt. I knew that deep down I was lying to myself – my life most certainly *wasn't* complete. I was living a fulfilling life but something was missing. I had the feeling that there was more to be done – there was more to *me*. I was not fulfilling my true destiny, whatever that may be. I tried to suppress the feeling; I did not have time to do any more with my life! I had three children to look after, with no help from any family and a husband who was distant and very rarely at home.

Nevertheless, the pressure inside me began to increase; pressure to stop fighting against myself, pressure to face up to the reality that there was something more that I had to do. I began to get very confused – I didn't know who or what I was meant to be – so how could I be someone or something I didn't know? And why *should* I succumb to this pressure? After all, I liked myself and the life I had – I didn't want to change it. On the surface I was still the same. I could chat and laugh with everyone I met – I loved being with others. The pressure inside me felt as if it was being released when I was with people. Yet the moment I got home the pressure began to build again. Intuitively, I knew that there was more to me; some new side to my self that I had yet to discover, but I had no idea as to the future that this "complete me" would find. Throughout my childhood I had felt very alone, and now – just when I had so many friends that I loved being with and I knew they all were fond of me – the last thing I wanted to do was turn into someone else, and perhaps lose everything I had gained! But still the fight in me, against myself, grew ever stronger. And it was destroying me; I was gradually becoming weaker and weaker inside. I was burning myself out with my constant fight against myself. My constant denial of my destiny.

Eventually I realized I could fight it no more. Spiritually, physically, mentally and emotionally exhausted, I had come to the end of the road. I was very, very scared by what it all might mean – I didn't want to say goodbye to the life that I had. But I knew that if I didn't accept my true self and my destiny my life would somehow end anyway. The choice was simple; stop fighting and fulfill my destiny, or deny it, and die. Put that way, it seemed pretty simple – I had to find out what my true destiny was. And the moment I made that decision my life was transformed. Completely surrendering, with no more fight left in me, I stepped into my true self, which opened the door into oneness and **wonderment**. In this book I will share with you my voyage of discovery, and the lessons I have learned about the important things in life along the way.

———

Tonika is available for personal guidance and growth.
She can be contacted at TonikaRinar@yahoo.co.uk
or www.angels.gb.com

———

I

The Awakening

My journey home begins on a grey morning in
March 1991. I had reached the end of my tether
– I had to find out what I had been put on this
planet for, even though every cell in my body was
shaking in fear as to what that destiny may be.
I was prepared to fully surrender myself to my
destiny, even if I was to die during this process of
acceptance. Even if my true calling was something
that I really didn't fancy doing for the rest of my
life – cleaning public toilets perhaps – if it was
destined and brought me a sense of fulfillment
and peace, then I would do just that ...

I checked on baby Toby, lying in his cot. As I peered into his bedroom
I could see he was fast asleep. His afternoon nap often lasted for
just over the hour, which would hopefully allow me enough time to
begin my journey. I was ready to listen to the Universe.

At many times during my life I had experienced a very frightening
negative force. Just at the point of semi-sleep, I could feel myself
being pushed down into the bed. It was horrible, but I never

told anyone about it. I did not know what it was. Eventually, on one occasion when it happened I called out in my mind to God, Creation, whoever's in charge: "Please, please, please take this away from me." I repeated this over and over again in my mind. Within a few moments, a wonderful presence responded to my calls. Whatever this "negativity" was, it was lifted from me, and then what I can only describe as liquid gold bliss swept right through me – calming me beyond words. I then relaxed into a peaceful sleep. I subsequently found that I could call this wonderful calming energy to my aid whenever I needed, and have since discovered that he is familiar to many people as a protecting Angel, and is known as Archangel Michael. So I was aware that there were good forces at work in the Universe, and it was to these forces that I had decided to turn for assistance on that cold grey March morning. My surrender was absolute; I was prepared to do anything the Universe inspired me to do.

The first encounter

I made myself comfortable in my bedroom, and asked for Archangel Michael to be with me. I had total trust in his benign presence and protection. Intuitively, I knew that he would be aware of how scared I was feeling, and that he would be absolute in his efforts to help bring out the courage inside me, to finally listen to the Universe and walk my path in truth and light.

Almost immediately after my call to Archangel Michael, I could sense his presence at my side. As my heartbeat began to quicken, I took in a deep breath and simply said to the Universe, "Okay, I'm listening." I sat repeating slowly; "I'm listening, please inspire me, show me my destiny so that I may feel fulfilled." I wasn't necessarily expecting an answer straight away, I figured it may come the next day, the next week, the next month, or even the next year. The simple act of ending the fight within myself, and withdrawing from the internal battle I had created, was enough for me at that moment. To cease feeling tormented inside as a result of opposing my own destiny, and to allow the act of total and absolute surrender to whatever lay ahead.

So there I sat, repeating in my mind those words, "I'm listening – please inspire me, I am ready to do whatever it takes to feel at peace with myself". Within minutes, I felt a tremendous power fill the room. This was utterly unlike anything I had ever experienced before – my heart began to pump fast and hard – fear of what was happening filled every part of me. I didn't dare open my eyes. Part of me thought of getting up and running out of the room, but I told myself with immense determination that I would not run away. "I'm not running any more."

While firmly asking for Archangel Michael to stay with me, the room felt as if it was shaking with the incredible power that filled it. My heart beat furiously, I was absolutely petrified. Although I trusted Archangel Michael implicitly, I felt my body could not take much more of this terrifyingly powerful energy. Mentally I accepted the possibility that I could die during this process. If I had opened my eyes and looked down at my body, I am sure my heart would have been beating out of my chest wall. But I knew I could not live as I had done previously, I could not survive that way any more. So with one hundred per cent conviction, I decided that if I did die in this process, then this was how it was meant to be. Standing next to me was Archangel Michael and my trust in him and the unknown outcome of my surrender gave me the strength to face whatever was in the room.

Very slowly, my right hand began to move. It seemed to have a will of its own. I was really petrified – what was happening to me? But despite my fear I knew that I did not want to go back to the existence I'd had previously. If my hand had a will of its own then so be it – I wasn't going to fight this.

To my astonishment the fingers on my hand curled back, so that my index finger was in a pointing position. It then began to draw on to the carpet – first a circle, then a figure eight on its side and finally a triangle. I now began feeling a little calmer – I realized my hand wasn't going to attack me, it seemed too preoccupied with the three symbols it had just drawn. I hadn't a clue what they meant[1]. My body took a gentle breath and the energy left the room, my hand returning to normal. I did not in any way understand what had just happened, but was incredibly relieved that I had survived it! Mentally I thanked and thanked Archangel Michael for staying with me. My heart was still beating furiously – I felt as if I had just been through a fast spin cycle in a washing machine.

During my pregnancy with Toby, I had met a brilliant astrologer and wonderful lady called Sue, who kindly mapped out my birth chart. One particular detail in the chart had really surprised Sue. She cautiously explained to me that: "It's an aspect that I have only ever seen once before – an aspect of great power. The only time I have ever seen this aspect was when the atom bomb dropped on Hiroshima. Power is power, and you can use power for good or destruction. Unfortunately, for Japan it was a power to destroy. Your chart has the same astrological configuration – Uranus in Leo in mid heaven. You have access to great power!" She finished by saying: "You are a power house. But with that comes great responsibility."

At the time this didn't really mean anything to me. But after experiencing this immense power in the room, Sue's words were coming back to me. Was this the power Sue spoke of, I wondered? I

---

[1] As far as I understand it, the circle (the most pure, perfect 2-D shape in the Universe) indicates wholeness, while the infinity sign (the figure eight on its side) indicates the Universe, and Universal Flow. The meaning of the triangle is slightly less clear, although in nearly all religions there is an important three-cornered reference, whether it's the Holy Trinity (Father, Son and Holy Spirit) or Father, Mother and Child. The ancient Egyptians placed huge importance on the pyramidal shape.

decided to telephone her straight away. Breathlessly, I told her what had just happened; about the symbols and that I hadn't any idea what they meant. I was almost begging her to explain to me what was happening, I was so frantically confused.

Sue spoke in a calm, soft but firm voice, which reassured me immediately. "This is something very special – see if you can connect with this energy again, and ask for a name, you must get a name."

So, still more than a little scared but by now extremely curious, I sat back down and asked once more for Archangel Michael to be with me. Taking a deep breath, I calmed myself as best I could. I felt the energy return and again my hand began to move, this time with greater ease. My fingers curled back, leaving my index finger once more in the pointed position. My finger began to draw the same symbols again on the carpet. When it had finished, I firmly asked for a name. Writing on the carpet as if my finger was a pen, the answer came back, "I am you, you are me" It then continued to draw the three signs. I thought the energy didn't understand my question, so I rephrased it; "What's your name? – because I know you are not me."

The answer was a drawing of a circle again, the figure eight on its side and the triangle. Feeling somewhat braver, I said; "What was your name the last time you had a body on Earth?"

It then spelt out my name and then my maiden name which was Lenk. Well I'm not having that, I thought: "Unless you tell me who you are, I'm not going to continue this connection."

The answer continued to be my name, followed by the symbols.

"Okay," I told the energy, "I'm not talking to you any more." And off it went. I telephoned Sue back – she had been waiting eagerly for my call. I explained what had happened; how I had asked for a name, but all that come back as a reply was my own name, followed by the three symbols. Reassuringly, Sue once again reaffirmed that what was happening to me was very special.

"Don't be afraid, you are communicating with a very high and pure energy," said Sue reassuringly. I trusted her words completely, I had great respect for her. When she had explained so many things within my birth chart, for the first time in my life I felt that someone understood me. So after hearing her reassuring words, I agreed to see if the energy was still around. Returning to my bedroom, I felt regretful that I had been so abrupt with the energy. Settling myself down again, I asked for Archangel Michael to calm any fear I had. Once again the energy connected.

The energy told me once again that, "I am you, and you are me." It then went on to explain that, "I am soon to bring to you many more energies that resonate as 'I.'"

"Who are these energies?" I asked.

"We are the energies that you call Angels. Some refer to us as their higher self; this is not a term we are comfortable with. Angels is a more acceptable term."

As I received this answer I realized how incredibly tacky and limiting the word "angels" was in reference to such an awe-inspiring and magnificent energy. Well, I can tell you I was bowled over and excited beyond words. But, back on the Earthly plane I had run out of time. Toby was waking up, and the school runs had to be done!

At the school, I met my friend Jan and told her what had happened.

"Come back to my house and watch!"

Jan was intrigued and excited, so after collecting the children we all returned to my home. Whilst her two children and mine played downstairs, Jan and I carried Toby up with us to my room, and I made the connection to what I realized now was my "Angel". Jan, needless to say, was amazed. She saw my head go back and my hand do the writing, but most of all she felt the huge energy presence. When I finished the session, opened my eyes and looked over at her, hers were as wide as saucers.

Learning to communicate

The transition from my Angel communicating via my hand to my voice took around four weeks. It was something I never expected. During this time I discovered that I could connect with absolutely anyone's Angel. Meeting all these different Angels showed me how they all have an individual personality. The connection to the Angelic Kingdom slowly manifested from using my finger to write, to using a pen and paper to write. The handwriting would vary and was as individual in character and style as the Angelic energy that was sharing my body at that time.

Before each connection, I always asked for Archangel Michael to be nearby. When I felt his reassuring presence, my head would be very gently eased back and slightly twisted from side to side. It was a bit like pulling a corkscrew out of a bottle of champagne! This was my will[2] leaving my body, my will being that part of me which has the hands on the steering wheel of the car (my body). I simply step out from the car (my body) and take a seat in the back of the car. I am fully conscious at all times, only now I cannot steer the car. The Universal Essence now in my body takes over the driving. The wonderful thing is that everything the Essence says or writes while it is in my body, every memory and every emotion it has – I feel also. But the feeling is magnified tenfold – and that's a pretty awesome feeling!

After becoming comfortable with the Angels using my hand to write with a pen through me, my awareness began to heighten.

---

[2] Our will is actually the combination of the ego and the fragment of our Angel that resides in our body. Ideally these two elements should be in balance. However, if a person is very opinionated, domineering or overpowering it indicates that their ego is eclipsing their Angelic self – they are out of balance. Whereas in someone who is unsettled and not very realistic, it's likely that their Angelic self is dominant.

Mandala is Sanskrit for "whole world" or "healing circle". It is a representation of the Universe and everything in it.

My own Angel would connect with me and begin to use my arms in movements that were graceful and poetic. It felt as if she was creating some type of *mandala**, at the same time moving and clearing energy from me. It was as if I was having *Feng Shui* on my energy field. My Angel would make certain movements with my hands around my throat area, as if she was clearing congestion. She would then very gently begin to move my jaw up and down. And then, eventually, her first words came through my voice box. She was very gentle, to ensure she didn't frighten me.

For the following three weeks, she would softly sing her messages, and these would always be in rhyme, which would absolutely fascinate me. Her timing and spacing of her gently sung words were impeccable. This mesmerized myself, and others who came to listen. After another three weeks she began to speak. To begin with, she spoke very slowly and gently. The communication process developed in this way so as to build up my confidence in my connections to the Angelic Kingdom. My Angel told me I was going to begin to receive information that would assist mankind and his growth. She also told me that it would be wise not to read any books of a spiritual nature, explaining:

"You have to remain free in your mind of another's words and experiences, so that the information you receive will not have to pass through another's thought form."

This made sense, and ever since then I have never been able to read any books of a spiritual or esoteric nature, even if I wanted to. When I *have* tried to read them (and I have on many occasions, ignoring the wise words from my Angel and allowing curiosity to get the better of me), I have found that after reading just one sentence my bowels become really loose and I have to rush to the bathroom! This is absolutely true. Having this reaction in my bowels can actually be quite useful – whenever I get constipated I just go to an esoteric or spiritual bookshop, relief beckons and off I go to the toilet!

Encountering other Universal Essences

One day my Angel told me an energy that was not from the Angelic Kingdom wanted to speak. She also said that she would stay right by me when this happened, so there was nothing to worry about. My head gently was eased back and my Angel stepped out. And then an essence entered, which felt more physically grounded than all the Angels who I had previously communicated with. I was shaken when the Essence explained to me that it was the energy of the planet Venus. This was certainly an insight – it had never occurred to me that a planet would have a consciousness. Venus had popped by simply to open my awareness to the fact that everything in creation has a consciousness. This was a really exciting time for me.

As well as connecting consciously with the Angelic Kingdom, I now found I could connect with the planets. This progressed in time to connecting and talking with different stars, the sun, the moon and our own planet, archetypes of animals, unborn children, the fairy kingdom, divas, spirit guides, the many different gods and goddesses indicative to different cultures. To date, I have communicated with over four hundred different Universal Energies. Some have come to communicate only once, others have been quite a few times and are more familiar to me. The visitations are always different in character and voice. Sometimes strong, sometimes weak, sometimes gentle, sometimes booming. (Some energies don't communicate at all – the "etheric" operator which I will tell you about later never says a word). I always taped the sessions, and have also kept everything that was written once we had graduated to pen and ink. Again, these show a variety of different handwritings and styles.

I love sharing my body with a universal Essence. Any aches or discomforts I have in my body disappear completely as the Essence enters. When eventually my will slips back into my body, I feel as if my whole persona has had a spring clean. It's brilliant; I have so much energy and my will arrives back to a body totally free of stress.

Encountering the animal archetypes

The archetypes of animals have been a particularly fascinating voyage of discovery. On my own one evening, after the children were tucked up in bed, I switched my tape recorder on and asked for Archangel Michael to stay close to me whilst I communicated with any Universal Essences that may be around and wanted to talk with me. I felt an energy draw close and my head was gently eased back, allowing my will to step out. In popped the archetype energy of the gorilla. I got the impression as this gorilla presented itself that the name gorilla was rather limiting in comparison to the actual energy of this species. This energy resonated more with the title Great Ape.

As the Great Ape sat in my body, I felt his great body of energy sway me from side to side. As he did this, he created a rhythm in me as he knocked my knuckles against the sofa that I was sitting on, alternating beats between the left and right hands. As I was getting used to this great energy inside me, I became aware that the best form of communication between man and ape is to look directly into each other's eyes. However, I was sure that I'd read somewhere that the last thing you should do is look directly into the eyes of an ape. The Great Ape, sensing my confusion as to what to do, explained that when eye contact is made, the ape can immediately sense if there is any fear in the other party. Since fear usually heralds huge negative energy, the ape will attack. However, if no fear is within the eyes of the human, then acceptance and love will flow between human and ape.

After the Great Ape had departed from my body, a universal Essence entered my body and we chatted about the connection that I had just experienced. The Essence told me that soon my consciousness would be expanded enough to be able to communicate freely with the archetypes of all creatures from the kingdom of animals, including the archetypes of sea creatures and the archetypes of creatures that inhabit our skies. "Wow", I thought, "This will be brilliant!"

Experiencing these animal archetypes was indeed a wonderful time. Each of the animal spirit's physical form would be projected through me, so I could feel their physical strengths and movements. The archetype is the blueprint, or design formed from creation. It is the mass consciousness that runs through that particular species. You could say that it is similar to when Ford motor company creates a blueprint design for a new car. Then from that one blueprint, thousands of cars with that particular design are created. So for example, when the archetype of the Leopard was in my body, it wouldn't be the spirit of a particular leopard, either in captivity or living freely, that would enter – but the whole essence of the leopard species.

By having the archetype of the leopard in my body, I could tell its main strength was in its powerful shoulder blades. As the archetype leopard sat in my body, I could feel my shoulder blades rise in strength. The leopard archetype's awareness did not relax for one moment. Listening to the sounds within the silence, sensing the slightest change in energy, always ready to pounce instantaneously. His awareness was present at all times.

Power animals

Learning about the animal archetypes also enabled me to understand how they function as "power animals" for people. At the time this was all happening, lots of people were going on workshops to find out about their personal animal helper or totem. The Native American people believe that spirits of different animal species are around us at certain times in our life. They have qualities in them that they can ignite in us, to help us through a situation or time span in our present life period. The problem for most people who were going on these workshops and meeting their "power animal" was that they hadn't a clue what the animal actually signified. The workshop leader would often tell them "it's whatever it means to you". This seems to me to be avoiding the issue! If these animals' spirits have presented themselves to the person, it is to help them discover strengths in themselves that they were not aware of. So if they were not aware of those strengths in the first place, then how would they know why the animal helper/spirit was with them? (Just to clarify one thing; deceased cats and dogs or other domestic pets can be around someone to bring comfort in spirit form, but they are not seen as power animals/spirit animal helpers. Power animals come from the spirit and kingdom of the wild and free creatures.)

As I learned from my experiences with the animal archetypes, sometimes a power animal will be around you to wake you to changes that are occurring in your life. Sometimes a power animal can bring healing to a pained spirit of a person. The black swan for example, is brilliant for this. She has an incredibly velvet soft energy, capable of immense compassion and strength. The black swan says:

> When I show my energy it is so the child may take refuge beneath my wings. Often the child will have become somewhat disillusioned and distraught with life. They will have a feeling of unworthiness, of solitude and often of despair. When I come it is to show the child they are on the path of great mysteries that can only be experienced through the emotions of despair and unworthiness and dissolution. The child must experience these most deep of emotions, before they can climb once more the golden thread to oneness.
>
> When I appear to you, or when you feel me around you, know you will never ever hit the bottom of all existence; for I hold you in my wings and calm you and remind you there is only one way, and that way is up."

At the time when my consciousness opened up to fully take in and understand the many archetypes of animals and such like creatures, I was pregnant with my fourth child, Atlanta-Rose. During the middle three months of my pregnancy, over a hundred and fifty animal archetypes entered my body to share with me as to why they would place their essence in guidance around a particular person. It did not occur to me at the time that this might have an effect on my unborn child, but a few years after Atlanta-Rose was born, she began to take on many animal characteristics – the list is endless! If I want her to do something in particular, for instance; tidy her bedroom, I just have to say something like "let's see how this great big bear that's so strong, can clear this room of rubbish." She'll squeal in acknowledgment and bounce off like a bear to sort her room out (I hope she doesn't get wise to what I'm doing!).

Even four years later, the room in which I had met these animal archetypes was still filled with their presence. A few years ago, an international Medium who was doing a performance of his abilities in our home town came to stay overnight at our home. My present husband Adrian (not the one who was never around who I mentioned in the introduction!) had met him a year earlier and had offered to put him up, should he ever need accommodation on his travels.

After having spent the night in my back room I enquired as to whether he had a good night's sleep. He looked tired and a bit confused. "Well" he said, "It's a lovely room, and the energy in there feels so pure and calm, but ..."

He scratched his head in puzzlement. "I couldn't sleep – all night long I kept seeing lions, tigers, elephants, rhinos, giraffes, buffalos, eagles – just loads and loads of animals coming at me!"

To calm his confusion, I told him about my experiences and what had occurred in that room four years ago. He was taken aback! And I was elated – so very happy the animals hadn't left my home.

I continue to this day to experience, from time to time, archetypes of different animal species. It's really great, since I get to know what they are really like, their movements, their breath, their response and ultimately their spirit.

First lesson

It was in the early days of encountering the animal archetypes that I learned an important lesson about the meaning of truth, and the nature of communication with these universal energies. I had decided that I would like to speak with the energy archetype of a dolphin, as I was due to visit Windsor Safari Park, outside London, the following day, with my three children Lucy, James and Toby (I hadn't had Atlanta at that time) along with my friend Jan and her two children. Jan's daughter was uncertain whether she wanted to go, as she was upset by the dolphin's existence in captivity. She felt she would be somehow betraying the dolphins if she went to see them in such a place.

Although I do not agree with how some zoos and parks house animals, I would not refuse to visit these places in protest. In my view, I feel if one of my children were innocently placed in a prison, I most certainly would not in protest refuse to visit them! Yes, I would do everything to get them out and into freedom. But, I would go to the prison – to be with them and support them as much as I could.

I also knew that the dolphins at Windsor were fine, since I had already communicated with them on a previous visit to the Safari Park. Such was the joy that emanated through these beautiful creatures when the spectators' hearts opened to appreciate the performances they gave. There was certainly very little room in their sense of pure joy for feeling imprisoned,[3] I explained to Jan's daughter what the dolphins at Windsor had shared with me, but she remained unconvinced that they really were fine.

So, during a communication session with a Universal Essence, I thought I would ask if I could speak with the energy of a dolphin. My thoughts were that if I could connect with the energy of a dolphin, maybe it would be able to put Jan's daughter's concerns to rest. The Essence said "I will make this so" so I expected the next essence to be the energy of the dolphin kingdom. At this point in my learning I had not grasped the difference between third dimensional timing (i.e. the understanding of time that we humans have in our daily lives), and universal timing (where time actually means very little![4] Because the Universal Essence said "I will make this so" I took that to mean it would happen right now. So I was waiting – my head had been eased back so the being of light could slip out. "The next one" I thought excitedly, "would be a dolphin energy".

As the next energy began to enter my body, I immediately began to feel strange. I knew that this wasn't a dolphin. I asked who it was. The energy told me, "I am the Angel of Toby" (my baby son). Well, I had communicated a number of times with Toby's Angel and so I knew this most definitely wasn't it. The vibration of this energy felt

---

[3] However, I cannot say the same for the whale I met there. Her name was Winnie, a big girl she was and she lived and performed alongside the dolphins. When I tried to communicate with Winnie, all I got back was an apathetic response. In fact, it wasn't until four hours later that I picked up any signal from her. When I finally did, I realized the reason for her state was that she had no mate and therefore no reflection, and no one to behave similarly to and communicate with. She didn't know who she was. She didn't feel sad, happy or even confused. She was like a zombie. She performed her tricks for the audience in a mechanical manner and that was it. In her energy and its movement, she was very still indeed. I tried to get through telepathically as best I could, but it was very tough. Fortunately, a year later Winnie, in a blaze of publicity, went to Florida to be with other whales like her.

[4] Universal timing is held within each moment. It is not us, it is the Universe that creates the moment – we simply fit in to it.

very different. This energy felt like astral energy. (Spirits within the Astral Realms – and this does not include Angels that work within these Realms – have a denser vibration. They sound as if they are knowledgeable, but they don't give direct answers to questions and will often tell you simply to "love the world", "heal the world" and all that sort of thing. So they will use a name that's familiar or even sensational, to get the attention of the person whose body they have entered). Well, very firmly I told that one where to go! Composing myself, I wondered what had happened, and continued to wait for a dolphin energy to communicate. But the next energy to enter my body was not the dolphin energy either – it was another deceptive spirit. I told that one where to go too! In shock, I decided that it was best to finish there and then.

I was now feeling greatly troubled and confused. I had asked for protection, and had felt Archangel Michael draw close to me as I asked. He was there, as he had been with me throughout all the other communications I had experienced. So what had gone wrong? I now began to doubt whether I had ever been protected. I did not doubt all the vibrations of the Angels and the wonderful universal Energies and Essences that had spoken through me on previous occasions. I could not deny their existence, but felt I could not trust I would be protected again from false energies. The last two energies had tried to be loving, but I knew they were fakers. If this is how communication with other dimensions was to be, then I wanted no part of it. Since I could not trust that I was being protected from deceptive forces during my communications or healing sessions, then I decided I would never be involved in communicating with the Universe again. I felt let down, and very alone.

During the following week, I had quite severe pains around my heart and at times my breathing would become stifled. I knew this was because I had closed out the truth of the Angels. Even though I had great trust in them, the trust in myself to be clear had gone – in other words, I couldn't even trust myself. It was a horrible feeling. By the end of the week, such was the urge to communicate once more with the Angels and light beings that I put my pain and distrust to one side, and once again surrendered myself and my confusion to whatever the Universe wanted of me. A beautiful Essence came through and explained to me what had happened the previous week. Here is an extract from our conversation:

You were never protected through all your communications. We stood by you to encourage your confidence within yourself to grow. You have grown so much, but you still doubt yourself and in your doubts you have asked for protection. You were like the child, ready to explore, ready to let go of your mother's protecting hand, but you doubted yourself. We stepped aside from you momentarily to allow these lower entities to enter your persona, to help you understand that in expecting to speak with a dolphin at that precise moment, you were limiting yourself – and by your own limitations you brought upon these lower entities. In your limitations you could not fully acknowledge our presence, our existence. The Universal Essence told you they would make this so, when you asked to speak to a dolphin energy. But they never said when. Your assumption in thinking the next energy to enter your body would be a dolphin blocked your light and your connection to Divine Will.

Sometimes it is fearful to let go of the hand that you feel has been protecting you. But that hand simply guided and encouraged you to firmly commit with strength and courage, to walk your path in truth. Why feel the need to be protected when you come from Divine Will? Divine Will knows only purity and absolute truth. Remember always – if you feel the need to ask for protection, then you do not have the connection to Divine Will and Oneness.

A great burden lifted in me as my spirit rose in understanding. I had not really appreciated the truth behind my connection with these universal Essences before. To connect with Universal Flow or Divine Will, one must be completely open and clear in one's mind and body. To become clear, one first has to confront their own reasons and attitudes for being an open channel for healing energies and universal truths to come through. We cannot be protected from negative or deceptive energies if we haven't opened and cleared ourselves completely to connect to Divine Will.

Our spirit knows no boundaries; it is part of an infinite energy. It does not need proof or acceptance. It is still and knowing and alive. It does not struggle with life – it is balanced and pure. It always has connection to Divine Will, but it is so often swamped by our ego-based desires and needs.

Whenever we think of these emotions, no matter how slight and unassuming the thought is, we can be certain at that point we are **not** connected to Divine Will. My hoping that the dolphin energy would come through was simply because I wanted to reassure Jan's daughter. But by creating an outcome to the hoped-for connection, I had also created a block in my connection to Divine Will.

As I began to look more at the energy of truth, I realized the head, the mind, the ego, will all tell you what you want to hear. You have to go deeper to be true. Our blood and our bones have no ego – they are our basic building blocks; rooted to the Earth. They are free. So, I figured I would only now communicate with the Universal energies and the information they bring when I had the correct sensation filling my blood and my bones, confirming that I was connected to Divine Will. I vowed from that day never to do anything of a spiritual nature without feeling and sensing fully my blood and bones responding.

Second lesson

My second lesson in understanding came in the form of a walnut cake! A lady came to me for a self-empowerment session, performed using very ancient Native American Indian teachings. For a whole hour we moved in and out of the elements, washing the spirit in the hottest fire, bathing in the silver crystal waterfalls, riding on the wings of the air, and dancing in the heart of the Earth. At the time of performing the session I was connected in oneness to Divine Will. As I had a few of these sessions booked throughout that day, I had decided it would be really good for me to consume only vegetables, fruit and water throughout the day, thinking (naively, as I now realize), that this would make me even purer, or clearer.

After the session was finished with this lady, we both felt really good. Many beautiful things happened during that hour and I felt like celebrating.

"Would you like a hot chocolate and some walnut cake?" I asked her.

"Yes please!" she eagerly replied.

As I was cutting her cake a very small thought ignited in me. It was only small; one of those niggling thoughts that begin just inside the back of your head but doesn't quite make it all the way to the front. "I really fancy some of this cake too!" But I quashed the thought before it could fully surface, and reminded myself that I was only going to consume fruit and vegetables that day – no stodge. "You are going to be a very good girl!" I thought to myself.

But, the walnut cake became more and more appealing. Finally I thought, " So what!" and succumbed to a piece. And I thoroughly enjoyed it, although I did feel somewhat disappointed that I had not kept with my idea of eating vegetables.

Around three months earlier I had acquired a beautiful Native American drum, on which I found I could drum a person's true beat, rhythm and sound. For the person hearing their true beat, it was like looking in a mirror for the first time. There is much energy carried through sound and to hear one's own beat is very empowering.

The energy of the drum, when drumming a person's true sound, can sometimes create a second tone in the drum. If I turn my head to the side whilst the drum is drumming, I can sometimes hear a whole orchestra of sound behind me. It's a pretty incredible feeling, and I love it when it happens. However, I didn't really understand why I should be able to work with the energy of the drum in this way; able to drum out the participant's true sound. Surely they should be able to do it for themselves? Eventually I realized that if a person is so deep in their own social conditioning, limitations and belief systems, they would find it very difficult to access their true rhythm. So I would hand the drum to the person and ask that they let the energy of the drum beat for them. The person would then drum. Usually, I have to say, the effort they put in was quite fierce or on the other end of the scale – extremely pitiful. I would then take the drum back and give a verbal translation of the beat they had just done. Then after checking I was connected to Divine Will, waiting for my blood and bones to respond in confirmation, I would begin drumming their true beat, and very empowering results were achieved.

Anyway, back to the cake. After enjoying our cake, the lady asked me if I would beat her son's true beat. (Despite her son not being physically present in the room, I was able to tune into his frequency, via his mother). Always one to oblige, I got my drum and stood up.

Although I had previously spent the past hour connected fully to Divine Will, it was not for me to assume I still had that connection – since for the past fifteen minutes I had been back in the physical reality. So I checked to see if I was still connected to Divine Will. Usually it takes me around thirty seconds for my blood and bones to respond, but two and a half minutes later, I was still waiting and my head was desperately trying to mimic the sensation I was waiting for. It became a fight of wills between my heart and my head. Struggling with this fight, I decided not to drum and placed the drum back onto the table, not understanding why I could not regain that connection. All of a sudden a little voice said, "The way you viewed that cake was not in light."

My heart leapt as a greater understanding enveloped me – whoosh, my blood and bones responded. It was not the cake that took me off Divine Will; it was my own feeling of failure for succumbing to it. It showed me a thought as small and as innocent as that can pull one off Divine Will!

Understanding discernment

My experience with the walnut cake revealed to me how any attitudes and limitations that we may have, however small and insignificant, are enough to pull us off centre, and away from our connection to Divine Will. Along with these lessons in discernment – the understanding of the Energies and Essences I was dealing with – I also learned about the illusion of protection and feeling the need to be protected, which supposedly enables us to comfortably open up to the Universe.

Many people who try to connect with greater understanding ask for protection from a divine source. Indeed, there have been many books written, sharing the insights and experiences of others in their search for enlightenment. These books supposedly offer spiritual guidance, describing messages that have come from other dimensions. However, as I very quickly learned after beginning to open to the Universe, these guides are not as straightforward as we all think (see Chapter 4 – Spirit Guides). This is because they are usually operating from the Astral Realms, so they are not operating in complete understanding and Divine Will – they have lessons to learn and transcend from. All energy comes from creation, but the ego of the channeled can unwittingly mould certain energies within creation into identities that sound plausible and recognizable to us. The only way this can be avoided is if the channeled/receiver is, at the point of connection to a universal being or astral spirit essence, totally free of any ego based needs, concepts, belief systems attitudes and desires.

My experience with the misleading energies during my dolphin-at-Windsor session was a vital lesson for my own greater awareness, in learning how to tell the difference between the energies from Divine Will, and other energies which were there essentially because I was **not** connected to Divine Will.

The truth as to what these energies really are can only be found within yourself. There is no such thing as protection from false energies. You can't be protected from whatever is within you in the first place! And it's really hard to be sure that you are completely without judgment or preconditions when you open yourself to other energies. There's actually much deception and invalid information being passed through mediums and suchlike, and I did not want to be part of that, consciously or unconsciously. There are no guidebooks for this – no one else can help. The only help is relying on truth. If a person cannot discern for themselves whether they are coming from Divine Will, then it seems a touch irresponsible to ask some spirit to do it for you! The head is very powerful, it will tell you what you want to hear, so to have confirmation via your *head* that you are connected to Divine Will is not a reliable technique.

The blood and the bones on the other hand are really simple. The ego has no access here. Wants, needs and desires cannot get into your bones and blood. Your blood and your bones cannot lie – they do not have the capacity. When Divine Will, God, Creation at its most pure, runs in full consciousness through you, your blood and bones will respond, confirming your connection. Never will I enter into spiritual 'work' without my blood and bones confirming to me at that point that I am connected to Divine Will. I never ask guides, the Angels or any universal essence to tell me I am connected to Divine Will. It is only my blood and bones that can confirm this for me.

Experiencing Universal Flow

This Divine Will / Universal Flow, call it what you will, is within us all. If a person can physically access this power for themselves, then they will have the ability and ease to heal and transform into who they really are. Yet the connection to Divine Will is more easily accessible than you might think. The understanding of it can come from the simplest – and most unlikely of sources.

Ten years or so after I had surrendered myself to my destiny, I received a painful letter of rejection from my stepmother. Finally I got the message that she really wanted nothing to do with me. Having something in writing like this really hit home! Later on that evening, I watched a program featuring the skills and disciplines of the Shoalin monks. The monks, who are from China, are able to control their *chi* energy; the life force that flows through them. It fascinated me how the monks could manifest that energy. They performed a number of incredible feats including balancing their naked torsos on razor sharp swords, without getting a single mark on their bodies. It was amazing to watch.

The following day, my eldest child Lucy was to report to a local holiday village for her week of work experience. She was to work as a children's entertainer. Lucy thinks she is on this planet simply to party, so being an entertainer was right up her street! Adrian and myself, along with Toby and Atlanta-Rose, took Lucy to the village to settle her in. She was to share a chalet with a school friend who was also doing work experience that week. While the two girls got comfortable with their surroundings, Adrian and I took Toby and Atlanta-Rose to the swings and climbing frames in the nearby park.

We all sat on the swings, and had a bit of a swing, then Toby and Atlanta asked Adrian to chase them on the climbing frame. I sat on my swing and watched Adrian and the children laughing and playing. I still felt numbed by the letter my stepmother had sent me, yet alongside this feeling of numbness I was also still intrigued at the feats of the Shoalin monks witnessed the night before. My thoughts wandered back to my stepmother and the rejection she projected towards me. As I began to feel this rejection more deeply, I wondered whether this is how Divine Will feels when, individually or en mass, we reject its energy. I wondered if, when we separate ourselves from Creation, feel that we are in control and ignore the universal force that flows through us – does Divine Will feel as pushed aside, as I do now? I thought deeply about this. But then my thoughts were broken by the swing, which had suddenly began to rock more firmly. "That's odd", I thought – I hadn't done anything to make the swing rock faster. My feet were tucked neatly under the base of the swing seat, and my hands held onto the swing at shoulder height.

My thoughts froze and my eyes widened as the swing changed from its gentle rocking movements to increasing speed and energy – I was swinging without doing anything. I was speechless – this was not my imagination, the swing was swinging all on its own with me on it! What on Earth was happening? By now it was swinging really hard. I sat frozen and without motion on the seat, my hands gripping the chains as hard as they could. Maybe a ghost or a negative spirit was pushing me? I couldn't feel hands or a force pushing the swing. Instead, there was a sense of exhilaration all around me. But I was still fearful. I decided to call Archangel Michael – if there was anything present that is out of balance with Universal Flow, he would sort it out. So, I asked and I asked. All the while the swing was reaching higher and higher. I called firmly, but he didn't come. So, I knew the fear I was feeling was self created – this was not a situation I needed to be fearful of. But how do I deal with it – what do I do? It was getting to the point where if I didn't stop soon, I was going to go over the top of the swing frame!! The chains that I held so tightly onto were beginning to buckle against the lack of gravity. Not knowing what to do – except that I certainly did not want to fly over the top of the swing's frame – in my mind I shouted "STOP!" To my amazement the swing suddenly slowed down and began to stop, in a pendulum type fashion. It didn't seem to waste any energy in stopping. I was completely surprised by the response of the swing stopping so immediately.

I reasoned to myself, "This situation was obviously not negative, as the swing stopped when I asked. So, maybe it will start up again if I say 'push' 'swing', or something!" Still very unsure as to what was happening, firmly I said in my mind "push!" – and sure enough, off the swing went again; exhilaration filling me once again as the swing gained motion, swinging higher and higher. In a state of complete wonderment, as the swing again started to get beyond a height I wanted to be at I called out loudly "STOP". As before, the swing stopped clearly and positively. Two more times I repeated this experience. It seemed I could control how fast and how high I wanted the swing to go, and yet my body wasn't swinging the swing at all. Realizing by now something incredible was happening, I shouted out to Adrian and the children

"Adi – come over here quick! Watch this, you'll be amazed."
Adrian and the children rushed over to me at the swings.

"Watch this," I shouted, "I'm not going to move my legs, and my hands are just holding on."

In my mind I said "push." A knowing ran through me as I said that word, a knowing that I was already swinging the moment the word left my thoughts. Off the swing went – I sat as still as possible, keeping my focus on the swing's gradual incline. Within moments it had reached the top of the swing frame.

"Look Adi, I'm not doing anything!" I shouted down in sheer excitement.

Adrian looked at me, his mouth wide open – the children were speechless.

"How can you do that???" Toby called up.

"I'm not doing anything," I shouted back. "Look, I'm going to say stop – watch what happens." I took a deep breath, and clearly in my mind I said "STOP". The swing began to slow down as it had done before – like a weighted pendulum, rather than the usual slowing down motion of a swing that had been propelled by the use of one's body and weight.

Gathering himself together, Adrian said in disbelief, "That's amazing, how does that happen?"

By now I had realized that the energy propelling the swing was the same energy used by the Shoalin monks – what they call *chi* energy. The original questioning thoughts about God feeling rejected by us humans and the *chi* energy of the Shoalin monks was answered and shown in the action of the swing. It was my own connection to Divine Will – the same thing as *chi* energy – that created the power to move the swing without trying. This ultimate force in the Universe; God force, Divine Energy, *chi*, Great Spirit or whatever you want to call it, feels so, so pushed aside and ignored when we deny its existence. The force is the absolute source of all Creation, and if we can detach our self from own self-created way that ignores this Divine Energy, we can step into a way of living created by Universal Flow. Then life and understandings become a whole lot easier. And more exciting!

This was a wonderful experience, and it also gave me further food for thought. If I could do this, maybe other people could too – without necessarily having to have experienced everything I had on my journeys into other dimensions and encounters with Universal Light Beings. I realized that if people could swing like this and experience this *chi* energy for themselves, then it may open the door to allowing them massively more self-understanding and self-empowerment. It would teach them to trust their instincts and free themselves of concepts that were restricting their growth.

I told Adrian what I was thinking – he was desperate to have a go and jumped onto a swing. To his disappointment nothing happened. The children tried also, but without success.

"You are all trying too hard." I told them. "Just remember how you feel when you swing. When you can remember the sensation of the swing you stop trying; and then simply know you will swing."

They all gave it another go, but were still trying too hard in their minds. If you try to will the swing to move, you will get nowhere. The only involvement one's mind has with swinging effortlessly is the simple words of push, or swing, and stop. You have to step away from your mind and into your feelings, and call upon the memory of what it feels like to swing.

It can be done. I have since taught many people how to do it, although it takes a bit of patience to start with. On one session I took a number of people to the local park (park swings are best as you know they will take your weight, so you don't have to be concerned as to whether the swing may collapse!). The adults claimed the swings before the children in the park could, and followed my instructions. After about ten to fifteen minutes of coaching, half could swing without swinging! They could feel the exhilaration running through them but didn't know where the energy came from, marveling at the ease at which the swing built up momentum. They had no reasoning at all for what was occurring. Interestingly, the ones who were having difficulty were the ones who either meditated or had quite fixed ideas and beliefs on spirituality. I could see they were trying from their minds and couldn't quite grasp the simple instructions I gave – it was almost as if they were afraid to let go.

Adrian managed to swing within a day or two. Watching a fourteen stone ex-rugby player sitting perched on a park swing, and moving through the air without using any body motion is a real sight to see! Interestingly, the children have not yet managed it. I guess it's because they don't understand when I tell them to recall

the feeling of what it's like to swing, to feel the air passing through
and around you, and to remember the relaxed flying motion when
swinging. But I know they'll do it one day!

The Energy of Truth

To finish this chapter, I want to look at understanding truth in a bit
more detail, by sharing with you the contents of a group session,
when I was visited by a particular Universal Energy. The sessions
are shared by people from different backgrounds and walks of life,
so that there is a range of different questions put to the Divine
Essence that is borrowing my body at the time. In this instance, it
was a very fluid type of feminine energy that entered my body, and
announced that she was the Energy of Truth. While this Energy was
in my body, she constantly used my arms in a graceful and flowing
manner to clear my energy field, assisting my energy to move more
freely in and around me.

This is how the session went:

QUESTION: You said you were the Energy of Truth. Could you
explain what truth is?

TRUTH: To answer such a small question would only lessen the
strength in truth. Beings often talk of one truth. The one truth that
beings talk of is simply creation, but many have misunderstood
this truth. Truth can come in many, many ways, all leading to the
centre of creation.

Truth is real and truth is unreal; but truth in its whole energy
can touch the hearts of many. When truths are sounded without
the whole energy, then they are mere shallow words, for the energy
of truth does not need words. Truth is merely an energy that leads
to oneness, and yet as mere mortals you feel, to know truth must
indeed bring you enlightenment. But enlightenment *is* truth.

QUESTION: So how do we begin to start to feel that truth and work with that truth in our lives?

TRUTH: Now you speak shallow words. Often you are shown the whole picture and yet you choose to break down; 'this is not so and this is so', but in the process', truth is lost. In all your situations in your daily life and the lives of others, truth is all around. It is by dissecting and analyzing that truth is lost.

And so to answer your question, how can you begin to answer this truth? I say:

Do you feel from your heart or from your head? Your head breaks down all and your heart stays whole; and yet people on this planet are conditioned to use only their heads.

Many people say, "Begin to feel with your heart", but to begin to feel with their heart they use their head and so the cycle repeats. The heart just *is*, and truth will touch you when your mind is still. And your mind does not become still through trying, or by saying, "now I shall be silent." This is not the way to truth.

QUESTION: Just to ask about stilling the mind. It is written that the way to still the mind is very often through meditation?

TRUTH: You must be more specific.

QUESTION: Certain meditation practices, such as mantras, attempt to slow the mind down?

TRUTH: But this is *trying*. To still one's mind is to bring the mind within the Universe, to create a vastness. The mind will gradually become much more open. But often many beings attempt to hide their wants and desire through these certain practices. But wants and desires become stronger if you try to hide them.

To allow your mind to become still is to constantly look at all these wants and desires, and to begin to understand how they can change or benefit your life. Then you become the judge of your life.

QUESTION: It seems as a species mankind places emphasis upon logic and using logic, reasoning and analysis. What place does the mind have – it must have some use?

TRUTH: The mind is indeed a very powerful creative tool for mankind. But it is a creative power, and unless the power is directed for the highest good it shall turn downwards. Often beings do not see results from their creative mind energy, and so they begin to place that energy elsewhere. Because, quite simply, they do not trust their mind is so vast.

So they lose the trust, and look for confirmation of their mind power from others. They create tools and all such objects and they become so in wonder at what they have created; yet that creation was a small part of what the mind is capable of. But for me to tell you would only lessen your own faith in your creative mind power. Man always looks for results, and yet the Universe is changing in many ways.

QUESTION: Many people tend to exaggerate their words (I know I do) and many people may also speak untruths and false words. Sometimes they may think that it is for a good reason, to hide things from others; but how important is the spoken word?

TRUTH: The words that man speaks with his brothers are so powerful, for the words man speaks can influence the mind power of his fellow man. Man knows this consciously and this is why he chooses to elaborate. He feels by elaborating or falsely speaking, he feels his mind power will grow, and he will hold a place of power within all Universes.

And so quite simply if you are unsure, then silence is the best option; and yet many choose to listen to false words, because also it enhances their own false words.

QUESTION: Could I ask, and I do not expect to be told the 'divine plan', but often beings talk of the divine plan – what is meant by this?

TRUTH: Divine plan is a plan brought forth from many beings from many galaxies. These beings are, shall we say – enlightened. But that is a description that holds so little light, for these beings have a light and presence that is beyond all man's understanding.

Divine plan often moves and changes. It is never one structure, for it grows and grows all the time; and so one can never know fully its extent.

QUESTION: I've been told that out of the many, many planes of existence and the many, many dimensions that exist within the Universe, that the Earth is one of the finest learning grounds. How important is our life down here on Earth for our learning?

TRUTH: Man's life here upon this planet is as important as it is in other dimensions, but it is more important when man has a physical body. When man walks with a physical body upon this planet, then it is more important than when he does not have a physical body. Man exists within many dimensions without a physical body, and is still man.

Man has been created to move in and out of many dimensions. But upon your planet the structure is very solid; it is very heavy and very vast. So man needs much of these learning lessons to help him move freely around this planet.

If man cannot move freely around this planet, then he will find difficulty moving around the other dimensions. Discernment is of great value upon this planet; it is not a tool used for other dimensions, and so discernment is indeed a most powerful tool for man to learn whilst he is in the physical body. This planet is his anchor, for him to be able to move freely in and out of other dimensions.

And you may ask, 'Why does man need to do this?' and the answer is: as man is becoming more solid and is able to move in and through other dimensions, he is able also to assist with creation within different galaxies. This happens often through Sleep State.

New galaxies are always being formed. And so, as I have already spoken, the divine plan changes all the time. But if man is not flexible and changes as divine plan changes then we get... [*a long silence. At this point the energy of Truth's hands that previously had been moving continuously with grace and light suddenly dropped down by her side motionless. Her energy stopped. A short moment after her energy began once more to flow, as her physical answer to divine plan was absorbed.*]

TRUTH: Do not search for only the occasion, more is wasted when you search; grasp what has been said, do not try to analyze.

*   *   *

At the start of this chapter – the start of my journey – I was desperate to find my true role in life. I now know that I have been given this insight into the other energies and essences that inhabit our Universe, the ability to learn from them and hopefully pass on some of the understanding that they have shared with me. I have no idea *why* I have been chosen for this role (and who am I to question or try to comprehend the divine plan?!). Buddhist monks deprive themselves of every comfort and submit to a life of abstinence to try and reach the unconditional surrender state required to reach enlightenment. But I wonder if perhaps even just that desire to reach it is enough to prevent it happening. For me, I sometimes think that the reason I can do it is because it isn't actually ever something I have strived for or desired. I was never looking for anything in the first place, other than to end the struggle I was experiencing within myself. At least I now know that I am doing what I am meant to be doing, and living to something much more close to my full potential. And I am now getting a good night's sleep!

The contents in this book come from the central source of truth. They are not aspects of the truth. They are not fragments of the truth. Using a metaphor; think of the central source of truth – truth in absolute wholeness – as a light bulb. When you switch the bulb on, beams of light touch different parts of the floor. The beam that shines on the right side of the floor is not the same beam that shines on the left side of the floor. They are both fragments of the light that is emanating from the bulb. As aspects of the light, as aspects of the truth, they are all valid. But, they are only aspects, only fragments. The beam of light that shines on the right side of the floor is received in acknowledgement by that part of the floor, but the right side of the floor does not acknowledge the beam of light that has landed on the left side of the floor. Now, the two parts of the floor could get into a dispute as to which beam, which truth is brighter, which one is real. Well, they are both real, they come from the same light bulb – the central source of truth. As your gaze travels to the beam of light that is touching, say the right side of the floor and you move your gaze up the beam, the truth becomes brighter, eventually it becomes so bright that we shy away. So bright is the light, so bright is the truth, that it becomes harder to face it. Nevertheless, the most important challenge facing humanity is to begin to face and accept truth in its wholeness. Over the next few chapters I will be trying to shed some understanding on how by embracing this truth, this Divine Will, we can find answers to the questions, which have troubled humanity since its first existence.

2

Angels, Archangels, our Soul, Negative Entities and God

There is so much to write on the subject of angels that it is difficult to know where to start. My understanding of these wonderful "light beings" is by no means complete; each new experience that I have with them enables me to understand their essence a little more. It is this voyage of discovery that I will attempt to describe in this chapter, along with my discoveries and increased understanding of our soul, Archangels, negative energies, and at the other end of the scale – the ultimate creative energy that we call God.

I   Understanding Angels

Although I refer to these pure energies as Angels, I am constantly aware of the inadequacy of this label. As I have already said, it feels tacky to encase their energy within such a mundane title. We are unfortunately a race that so often limits our expression by the use of words, so I ask you to try and see beyond the restrictive title of Angels as you read further.

Our relationship with our Angel

As described in the previous chapter, when I first began my communications with these beings of light, I was told that the Angel I was communicating with was actually me, which I did not at that time understand. Despite many people referring to their guardian Angels as their "higher self", the Angels themselves do not actually see it this way. The term higher self suggests that the Angels are already evolved and are all-knowing. Whereas Angels are actually still growing, still evolving, and very much dependent on what we do here on Earth. It is through our life's experiences and learning to trust and integrate our Angel into our physical bodies that both our Angel and ourselves grow to the highest. Of course, that's just a small part of the many reasons why we are here – nevertheless, it's a really important part of the picture.

Our belief systems place Angels on a pedestal higher than ourselves, yet my experiences have shown me that Angels are actually just like us. They have personalities, they know how to have fun, they have concerns, and yes, they can get mad! Angels are our divine blueprint, there to guide and steer us through this human dimension.

The more I understand of our existence here, the sufferings and lessons we endure through life, the more I can see that we each grow through our individual trials. As we learn through life experiences, our Angel (since each of us has an individual Angel) is able to integrate with us more and more, and in so doing we move ever closer to becoming a balance of light and dark. Not in the good versus evil sense – what I am referring to as "dark" is more our physical grounding, essential to our being able to survive on this planet. Dark is the mass, the mind, the body, the blood, the bones, the Earth, the rocks etc. Light is our consciousness, our energy. Light is what enables new life to grow, whether in plant, animal or mineral form; you do not see this energy, because it does not have a form.

Angels, because they are pure Light, do not have a form, yet so immense is their energy that it is not difficult to understand why historically they have been depicted with wings. Once, while lying on my bed, I seemed to be lifted into what felt like a vertical position by Archangel Michael's energy. It felt as if his wings were lifting me. So blissful was the experience that I didn't dare open my eyes in case I lost the connection. I knew Archangel Michael didn't have wings, yet here I was in the heart of what felt like the most fabulous wings imaginable. But it was not his wings that wrapped around me, but his immeasurable power. His energy enveloped me, flickering and wavering like ripples riding on the top of the sea. The power of the Archangel caressed my skin, taking all my cares away and filling me with serenity.

Angels have feelings too

Up until I met the Angel of my four-year-old son James, I had assumed that Angels were immune to emotions such as anger and frustration. James was a very happy and peaceful baby, sleeping right through the night at just two weeks, eating well, and when awake he was very responsive. However, as a child he did not seem comfortable with himself; he found it difficult to mix with other children, often preferring his own company. As his mother I could always sense when he began to feel uneasy, in situations that most children would sail through. In a nutshell, after James had been in the company of a lot of people, he would start to become irritated and a bit of a pain! The best solution I found to cope with this was for him to spend about half an hour in his room – he would resurface calm and happy. I wondered about the reason for this and began observing his reactions when he was with people, to see if certain situations bothered him more than others. Sure enough, he was particularly affected by people rushing around or who were at all unsettled, people who were heavily opinionated, people who were aggressive and sharp, people who were indecisive and slow. It seemed that these people's disharmonious energy was causing disturbance to his own energy field. Consequently, being on his own for a short spell seemed to re- energize and centre him.

One day James seemed particularly irritated. At first I didn't take too much notice, hoping that whatever was causing his sense of frustration would pass. Unfortunately, it didn't. He slowly became more and more fractious and irritable. I knew all he needed was time in his room, but I'm his Mum; I thought *I* could make him better – I didn't want to put him in his room, since that gave me a sense of failure as a Mum. Although I knew what was best for him, my ego wanted me to feel successful as a Mum and cope – succeed in calming him down.

Of course, it didn't work. Instead, James's behavior pushed me over my limit. I felt so frustrated, so mad towards him – I just wanted to shake him, make him as mad as he'd made me. I grabbed him, stomped hard up the stairs and flung open the door to his bedroom. My hands were stiff with rage; mentally I was fighting to control myself. I looked at his bed, wanting to throw him onto it – well, I did drop him six inches onto it, shouting at him not to see me until morning. I slammed his door shut and then went into my bedroom, feeling as if I had failed and was the worst mum in the world, I sank to the floor and cried and cried. How could I feel so much anger towards my child? He should feel safe with me, he should feel nurtured and loved. How could I behave like that? I absolutely detested myself. Why did the Universe give him to me – he should have gone to someone who could respond to him and not be affected by his behavior. I felt I was the pit of existence!

As I sat mentally and emotionally rebuking myself. James's Angel came by.

He told me "My child frustrates you, but he frustrates me also!"

Those words stopped me in my tracks, I was stunned – a

frustrated Angel? I didn't know Angels *could* get frustrated. James's Angel continued explaining to me; "My child comes from a place so distant from this Earth, he knows he is not like others yet he tries to be like others and in this trying he loses his identity, he becomes lost in the crowd."[1]

His Angel reassured me as a parent and as a mother that I was doing well, and then expounded about James and his origins so that I could understand him a little more. Re-energized and uplifted by the experience, I looked into James's room – he was fast asleep.

He awoke the next morning, bright and cheerful and his behavior from that moment on improved dramatically (it certainly needed to!). It was as though he had been understood, and in this he could understand and accept himself more fully. It was a great relief for me, too! Many of us struggle at times to understand our kids or try to get them to conform in behavior as to what we see as acceptable.

---

[1] As I now understand it, a lot of people on this planet don't actually originate from here – their spirit comes from somewhere else in the Universe. (Don't ask me where!) And so their natural frequency is not initially resonant with this world. Perhaps as a result of this – maybe his spirit had been sent to this dimension against its will (see chapter on Past Lives, John's regression) – James has an unusual and extremely large aura. The full picture emerged during a holiday to Greece with the family, when James was eight years old. He'd got me so mad on that holiday and frustrated me right to my core. Adrian suggested I ask James's Angel why he so easily gets angry. I really wasn't ready to take that short cut though, I wanted to try and understand and accept him in my own way. Fortunately, despite my stubbornness I was telepathically shown an image of James and his aura – it turned out to be absolutely huge; very stretched out and transparent, with a small line of foggy mist at the boundary. As I was shown this it was explained to me that the fogginess in the aura entangled with other people's auras, so that James 'picks up' energy of a confusing nature that is projected from weaknesses in other people's auras. If someone is heavily opinionated for example, they will create holes and weaknesses in their aura. The holes and weaknesses will contain bad energy and it's this bad energy that James was picking up, causing his discomfort.

Yet what results is a distance created by the struggle and our inability to understand them.[2]

When and why our Angels arrive

Further understanding of Angels and their place in the greater picture followed very soon. Adrian and I had often seen (psychically) a little girl running around the family home. Intuitively, I knew she would join and complete our family in the near future. Sure enough, I soon conceived a child. At approximately seven months pregnant, I felt the spiritual essence of the child I was carrying around me. I told Adrian of this, and we both sat down on the living room floor and hoped we would be able to communicate with her essence (i.e. her Angel). It was difficult to spiritually connect with the fetal part of her growing in the womb, as it was still forming.

Atlanta-Rose is the name we had chosen for our new daughter-to-be. We sat in stillness, open to Divine Will, and ready to accept that we may or may not experience Atlanta's Angelic essence. My head was very gently eased back and loosened from side to side. I felt my will leave my body. Then I found myself filling with a calm and graceful energy that settled comfortably into my body. She, (the essence felt very feminine) began to dance, using only my arms, creating and moving energy with each intricate and graceful arm movement. She did this for about four minutes before announcing herself. The angelic essence told us she was "the Angel of the child I carried." Adrian asked her if she visited often. She said her form (the babe in my stomach) moved each time her essence (the energy

---

[2] After this experience I decided to make myself available to help parents who were struggling with their children. By talking with the individual child's Angel, the parents were able to gain insights into the mental and emotional make-up of their children. They also were shown issues in themselves that they could work on to help their children. The results were brilliant.

of Atlanta's Angel) entered into the developing form, in response to having been energized with life force from the Angel.

Actually, when an Angel checks on their new form it is a bit like how a person wiggles their toes when trying on new shoes – checking that they fit OK! Interestingly, Atlanta's Angel did not choose to use the words *me*, *I*, or *baby* to describe the fetus (her form inside me).

Talking with Atlanta's Angel provided me with a clear understanding of the relationship between an Angel and what would be her Earthly vehicle. An Angel sees the physical body as we would view a car; something that can get us from A to B. At this stage the Angel has no emotional attachment to the developing fetus. Which led me to wondering when we stop just being a visible shape? When do we start to be who we are, capable of giving and receiving different emotions, being creative, being destructive, and being part of the human race? What is it that makes us live, makes us learn, makes us wonder?

Like a jigsaw puzzle the answer started to take shape. After experiencing many different encounters with various beings and energies from the other realms, I began to realize that the human spirit – which enters the body at the point of birth and leaves at the point of death – is a sort of metaphysical photo album. Our spirit is, through life and life experiences, collecting and storing memories. Our spirit that enters at the time of birth is a combination of a fragment of our angelic self (our personality), and our aura. (More on the aura later in the book).

When we leave the physical body our spirit departs with a full album; a full collection of memories contained within our aura. Our Angel, enriched or burdened with the memories and experiences from our spirit depending upon our Earthly life experiences, passes over to the Astral Realms to reflect on these memories. (More on this in Chapter 3.) The memories that weigh heavily on our spirit will become issues for us to face on our next incarnation to this planet.

Much of our spiritual progress and soul expansion is spent learning how our human dimension works. It appears that for our Angel to grow and expand through an infinite Universe, this dimension must be understood and experienced. This Earthly dimension is essentially just a piece of the jigsaw – indeed a very tiny piece – but without that piece there would be a gap in the whole. We cannot therefore avoid being here. To be whole, to be complete, we must experience all aspects of Creation within the Universe. It is because this is not actually our natural dimension that many of us lose our way and begin searching for home, searching for who we are. We become addicted to alcohol, drugs, lifestyles, belief systems, thought forms, and this does seem to be because we are all looking for ourselves.

Our personality is a fragment of our Angel, sealed into the physical body at the point of birth. The Angel then guides and steers this small fragment of themselves as safely as can be through this human dimension. So there lies the answer to my question. An Angel's love begins at the point of birth.

*   *   *

Back to that first encounter with the Angel of Atlanta-Rose, who continued creating these amazing rhythmic movements with my arms during our conversation. Adrian asked Atlanta's Angel how she viewed us all. She referred to me as "my Earth Mother" which caused me to feel "Oh! She could have flattered me a bit! Is that all I am – an Earth Mother?" But in Atlanta's Angel's eyes that's exactly what I was, a vehicle for her to enter into this human dimension. She sensed my disappointment and said: "She gives herself a hard time, she is hard on herself. She doesn't need to be."

This hardness I understood to be because I still hadn't fully accepted myself (something which so many on this planet struggle to do) and what I do. I was confused about many aspects of my personality; everything from why on Earth the Universe had felt the need to give me a really rough London accent (which was most strange, since none of my family spoke in a similar fashion), right through to why I had been given these abilities to access all areas of the Universe. I felt the forces of pure light and creation had got it all wrong by giving me this task. Adrian, who could always see the hard time I gave myself but felt powerless to help, asked, "Will she always be so tough on herself?" Atlanta's Angel replied, " She won't always, she will soon be free of her battle."

"I hope so," I thought.

We then talked about all the other members of the family, and Atlanta's Angel gave us her insights on all her brothers and sisters to be. It was fascinating how the Angel appeared to know already how she would be fitting in to the family. For example, when asked about Lucy, her answer was filled with fun.

"She needs to learn how to play – she is too serious, soon she will have fun and learn to play. She won't be able to be serious with me."

This has since become true – Lucy certainly is playful with her and since Atlanta was born, she makes Lucy laugh and is capable of lifting Lucy's depressed mood during those times when being a teenager becomes too confusing for her.

After Atlanta's Angel had shared with Adrian and myself her observations of her new family, she felt she would like to share insights of her own personality with us. She explained, "At times I will wander."

At the time I thought she meant that she would literally wander off down the road, without telling anyone where she was going. So we had large gates erected on our driveway to ensure her safety when she was playing in the front garden! But as Atlanta grew I realized what she had actually meant was that at times her *mind* would wander. I suspect Atlanta's Angel knew this would be frustrating for those around her and so forewarned us, for which I am eternally grateful!

I would certainly otherwise have found it very irritating when Atlanta's mind wandered, as it so often does. Understanding this aspect of Atlanta has strengthened my relationship to her. Atlanta's Angel also shared with us that "at times my head will overrule my heart. When this happens, just let me be."

Great advice from Atlanta's essence! And Atlanta is indeed a very headstrong young lady. When in a situation that she wants to control, but is unable to because of her young age, she can become stubborn and a little raw with her choice of words. I remember the advice from her Angel and mutter to myself, "Just leave me alone," then reply to myself "I'm leaving you alone."... The saying *forewarned is forearmed is* most apt!

Atlanta proved to be an exceptionally swift developer. By the time she had reached two and a half years of age her vocabulary was vast; she could easily say everyone's name, she could name around twenty different animals, she could count to ten. I feel strongly that her vocabulary, her expressions, her freedom to be herself, is partly due to her being understood and accepted by Adrian and myself before she was born. In a sense she has not had to 'find herself' or adapt to the masses to fit in. She was accepted for who she was before she was born, and with that acceptance she had no expectations of who or what she may do or become – she was born with absolute freedom, and part of my role as a parent is to ensure she continues to be able to access that freedom.

During the first few days of Atlanta's life on Earth, she would intermittently move her tiny arms in the exact sequence that her Angelic essence had done when using my arms the day she communicated with Adrian and myself through my body. Neither Adrian nor I have ever witnessed such unusual arm movements in any other young babies.

II   Our angels are our inspiration

My understanding of Angels has been greatly increased by the insightful and deeply personal experiences I have had with them. Many have been quite breathtakingly beautiful in their responses. Possibly the most profound experience to date was with my own Angel during a past life regression session, which made me realize just how close we are to our Angels...

Introducing Sara

Sara, a lady in her late forties, had been coming to see me for some crystal healing. She had read an article about me in the local newspaper that had made a lot of sense to her, since it had touched on many aspects of spirituality that she herself had been looking into. She thus felt compelled to visit and see if I could help. She told me that she often felt low in physical energy and at times suffered severe anxiety attacks. My first impression of Sara was of a lady with a bubbly personality who naturally looked on the bright side of life. However, my examination of her energy field revealed that most of her energy centers were blocked.

Sara visited me for treatment on her energy centers, which I treated and balanced on a number of occasions. During our sessions Sara would quiz me about aspects of spirituality and I answered her questions in the best way that I knew. She would often get very excited about my answers, because they were very similar to the conclusions she had already reached. Eventually she told me that she believed the root cause of her anxiety attacks were due to a past life situation, and enquired whether I performed past life regression. I confirmed to Sara that I could, with the help of my Angel, regress her back into past lives. But I advised her to be very clear in herself as to the reason why she wanted to be regressed. I needed her to be sure that she felt the regression would benefit her and was not simply a desire, out of idle curiosity, to discover who she was in previous lives. Even though she *thought* her anxieties were linked to a past life, she had to be able to react to those instincts, and not use her head to say they were due to a past life incident. I explained to Sara that although her anxiety attacks may well be because of some past life incident, she must also be prepared to discover that there could be a deeper reason for them – if so, was she ready to face that reason? At the same time I reassured her that she would be, at all times, totally protected by the Angels. I reiterated that she would remain conscious and completely aware of her surroundings throughout the regression, and she would only go back as far as – and experience as much as – she could handle safely without fear.

Strengthened by my explanations. Sarah convinced me she wanted the regression very much indeed, and had done for a number of years. But up until now she had not felt that the time was right. She now wanted rid of her anxiety, and she wanted answers as to why it was occurring. We made an appointment for her regression session.

When my Angel could go no further

The day for the regression arrived. I always used my Native American drum, acquired a year earlier, to clear any stagnant or negative energy from the room that the regression was to take place in. Whilst drumming I would sense the room was clear when my bones and blood responded – telling me I was connected to Divine Will. Candles were then lit for each energy and Universal Essence appropriate to assist the person who was to be regressed, always including a lighted candle for the "Keeper of past lives and existences".[1]

After the room preparations were completed and I knew everything was safe and ready for the sitter, I would then scrutinize my own attitudes as to why this regression should take place. Any expectations that I may have created, however small, would be let go of so that the Universe could flow unblocked through me. I would then know that if nothing actually occurred during the session, I would feel no concern that the sitter may consider me a fraud. (Fortunately this has not happened as yet – but one must always remain open to all possibilities!) After sifting through any expectant thoughts and clearing them fully from my being, then once again my bones and blood would respond, this time in a deeper fashion, as the room began to fill with all the beings that were appropriate to that particular sitting.

Well, on this occasion I knew the "keeper to past lives and existences" had not entered the room, but I hadn't a clue why not. It had seemed so right to book Sara in for the regression, so I was somewhat surprised, although intuitively I knew whatever happened during the session was to be for Sara's highest benefit.

Sara arrived and was clearly quite nervous. Apparently she had once been to a man who told her he channeled a discarnate being. She couldn't remember who this being was, but when the being spoke (via the man whose body the discarnate being was borrowing) the voice was so fierce and incredibly loud that it really scared Sara. Not surprisingly, this experience had discouraged her from attending

---

[1] In the early days, before I started regressing people, I had communicated with a universal energy who informed me that his role was the "Keeper of Past Life Existences". It is this energy that I now work with when regressing people. My introduction to this "Keeper of Past Life Existences" occurred after I had become uncomfortable with being able to tell people what their previous life existences had been. It brought with it too much responsibility, due to the eagerness and anticipation projected towards me from people curious to know of their past lives. I was becoming uneasy simply satisfying their curiosity. They should, I thought, be able to access a past existence for themselves. It was at this point that my Angelic contacts gently made me aware of the ease of accessing past lives, when one is working directly with the energy who holds the keys to past life existences.

any other sessions of this type – until now.

I did my best to calm her, and outlined what would happen during our session, explaining that my Angel would guide her through the whole process. My Angel's essence would enter my body and my voice would become softer and yet firm, and my Angel would say words and phrases that I would not normally use. "Don't waste energy on observing the difference between my Angel and me. Just remain focused on her words," I concluded. (At the start of any session I always like to explain this, as – accustomed to my London cockney twang – the sitter would otherwise wonder what was happening when my voice changed into softness and light.

Sara settled in the chair, and her nervousness began to evaporate as my Angel began the relaxation process. Every so often my Angel would ask Sara how she was feeling, searching for any doubts, fears or anxieties that might arise while becoming completely relaxed. If any such feelings arose my Angel would help Sara to go deeply within herself and face them, and by facing and understanding those feelings they could then be dealt with. My Angel helped Sara relax fully, and then started taking her back gradually through this present life of hers, observing traumas and pleasures along the way, and assisting her to access her own personal strength to overcome anything that may have suppressed her spiritual growth. Sara went back to childhood, and then to being a tiny babe.

Just before we were about to enter her mother's womb, Sara became quite anxious: "I can't do this, I can't do this!" My Angel asked her why she couldn't, and Sara told her there was a very dark figure standing next to her, very sinister indeed! Sara was clearly quite fearful. At this point my Angel went quiet, paused for a moment, took in a deep breath and said to a very unhappy Sara; "I will have to depart, I cannot go any further. A *Karmic* Essence of the highest order shall lead you through this pain and into your heart." And off my Angel went.

"Oh, great!" I thought. "Now Sara is really going to panic and maybe get one of her anxiety attacks." From past experience I have known the *Karmic* Essences to be pretty tough cookies. Their words are strong, their energy dynamic, and their voices are loud and clear. Very much the last thing Sara needed to hear in her already highly nervous – especially considering her previous bad experience with a loud-voiced being during a channeling session. Despite this though, I was also aware of the immense love that the person would be bathed in from the essences that governed Karma.[2] *Such* love usually calmed any fear or panic that may have been felt by the person, and with trust and strength – and the *Karmic* essence by their side – they could face any dark thought form or negativity that may manifest itself.

Into my body came a *Karmic* essence, one who I had not met before. To my astonishment his voice was actually very soft and reassuring – a voice of absolute trust that immediately made you feel at ease. It was if you were in the midst of the greatest hurricane known to man, but as you rode on that voice through the storm you knew no harm would ever come to you. Boy! Was I relieved for Sara.

As we then discovered, this dark sinister figure was indeed the root of Sara's problems.[3] It had placed a dark spell on her whilst she had lived in an ancient civilization thousands of years ago. The reason for this dark spell remained unexplained, since knowing the reason why would not have held any benefit to Sara. And with the assistance of this beautiful *Karmic* Essence, Sara was able to free herself of this spell.

---

[2] *Karma* is a type of judgment that the human spirit places on itself; a kind of what-goes-around-comes-around way of thinking that exists in this human dimension and the Astral Realms – it does not exist beyond these dimensions.

[3] You may wonder (as did I) why my Angel was not aware of this dark figure looming close by. My only guess is that this figure was operating on a vibration that our own Angels are not part of.

When the session was complete the essence of Karma departed and my Angel returned to bring Sara back into full consciousness. She opened her eyes and such a sense of peace filled her. She felt amazed by what had just occurred – a very heavy burden had been released from her and she felt great. Serenity exuded from her whole being.

Understanding just how close we are to our Angels

Although I was obviously very pleased and happy for Sara, this experience had a very profound impact on me, causing me to become really quite ill over the following week while my whole understanding of the Universe was reconfigured. For the first time ever I began truly to understand the physical aspects of Angels and their purpose. It was such a shock to my system to discover that Angels could only go so far, and that their own ability to travel within the Universes had limitations. (It was fortunate that this all occurred during a particularly beautiful summer. So while my cells moved to accommodate this new understanding, my being was surrounded by warmth, greenery, vibrant colors, birdsong, fresh sea air and the love and joy of my husband and children. It definitely helped!)

So what did it all mean? Prior to that experience with Sara, I had assumed that Angels can move freely through the Universes, through all the many, many dimensions. To discover they cannot was a complete shock to my system.

As I now understand it, my Angel could not go into the realms of Karma, which can be thought of as courts of judgment that you can only enter if you have reason to be there. As my Angel had no reason, a *Karmic* Essence from those realms took over the regression. (The *Karmic* situation Sara was caught up in was due to the negativity brought out during this past life memory of hers. This was being ignited by the presence of the sinister figure who seemed to have some control over her. A block in Universal Flow had been created – this block is what is known as *Karma*.)

It would seem that there are many layers, dimensions and existences in Creation, and each layer or dimension is a piece of an absolutely enormous puzzle. To understand the puzzle fully, one must experience every piece of the puzzle. If we decide that we don't want to experience a particular piece, that it doesn't look too appealing or that it appears somewhat difficult to experience Creation in that piece, then we will never be whole, we will never be complete. Our Angels are *us*, and our personalities are thus a fragment of them. Our life experiences enable our Angelic essence to gain a greater insight and understanding of this human dimension. When we have fully appreciated and learned of all the realities this dimension has to offer, we can then in Angel form move on to the next piece of the puzzle.

My experience with Sara showed me our Angels are actually closer to us than we could ever possibly imagine. We are inspired and guided by them through our intuition. Instinctively we all know this to be a very powerful form of guidance, but how many of us actually *respond* to this Angelic guidance? We are so controlled by our social conditioning that we constantly allow our thoughts to override our intuitive guidance. And when we follow our mind or social conditioning we weaken the link to our Angel – our ego becomes stronger and intuitive ability weaker. Whereas when we *do* act from our intuitive guidance we create a stronger link each time to our Angelic self and Soul.

Better and lasting results are always obtained by acting intuitively, contrary to whatever anyone thinks. Acting intuitively at times may not seem to be the correct course of action. But if you look back and observe the decisions you made from intuition – assuming you *have* made intuitive decisions (remember that intuition is *not* the same as impulse!) – and you compare those intuitive decisions with decisions you made based upon your social conditioning and logic

- ask yourself which ones gave you greatest strength?

When we act from intuitive guidance, for whatever reason, there is no room for guilt (a very negative emotion which immediately sits in the heart centre and blocks it). When we act intuitively, our hearts and souls become stronger and the link to our Angels becomes clearer. Angels are more physical than we realize. It is our own limited understanding of them that has elevated them to the God-like status that most people see them as having.[4]

The consequences of that session with Sara left me feeling numb with shock. With hindsight, I now realize that I was entering through a doorway into greater understanding. Any restrictive thoughts or beliefs had to evaporate; my new lightness of spirit would now allow me to access freely yet more of Creation.

III   Negative entities

In this section I will explain what I have learned with regard to negative entities – demons or evil spirits if you will – along with the further insight this has delivered as to the incredible strength and power of our Angels.

Encounters with the unpleasant

A neighbor had recently purchased a house with the intention of turning the upstairs of the property into a healing sanctuary, but he had encountered a presence in the upstairs rooms that made him feel uncomfortable. He asked if I could, perhaps with the help of

---

[4] The term *Godlike* is used here as a whole structure, since I have learnt that the energy that is God, great spirit, *prana* or *chi* or whatever one wishes to call it, is truly far greater than the human mind (without integration of our angelic self), can fully comprehend.

the Angels, check the house out before he proceeded with his plans. I had never attempted anything like this before, and neither of us knew what to expect.

When I arrived, the owner immediately led me upstairs. As I climbed the stairs I too began to feel uncomfortable; my back began to stiffen, like a defense mechanism. However, I was aware that my reaction could simply be because I had unintentionally allowed myself to become influenced by the concerns of the owner, so I tried to push my discomfort aside. We went into one room, which was to be the main healing area. This room felt fine, absolutely clear. This guy's imagination must be running overtime, I skeptically told myself. But then I entered the next room, across the hall. Whooo! The atmosphere immediately became cold, prickly and restricting. I felt my awareness become cautious and acute, my eyes widened, and my ears pricked back like an animal that had sensed something threatening. My breathing slowed, as I stilled my energy to allow myself to sense more deeply.

"Right!" I said to the owner. "Definitely something unpleasant in here."

I found a spot on the floor to sit down on and prepared myself to do whatever was needed, trusting in myself and the Universe. My head was very slowly eased back, my will stepped out and a beautiful light being entered my body. This presence was my Angel in her wholeness. As she entered my body, her energy seemed to contract inside me; strengthening her energy immensely. She sat my body upright and firm. As she took a deep breath in, I felt her strength pour into every part of my body.

Until now my communications with my Angel had been truly "heavenly". My Angel was so gentle, so soft; her essence flowed gracefully through me and she was unconditional in her love. So what happened next whilst releasing that deep breath was very unexpected. With immense power and presence she demanded that all entities come out and face my essence. My Angel's demands were fierce and focused; her words filled with authority and energy. If you imagine the loudest of thunderstorms and then triple that, you'd have some idea of the energy projected by my Angel. This turmoil went on for around five minutes.

Throughout this time I was petrified; uncertain as to what was happening and horrified at the prospect of all these negative entities surrounding my physical body. Yet at the same time I felt completely protected by my Angel, who continued her fierce crusade.

As I observed my Angel's actions I thought to myself, "I would not like to be on the wrong side of an Angel!" I realized that my Angel had to be fiercer than the most fearsome entities for the house clearing[1] to be successful; there was no room in her energy for lack of purpose and conviction. As I continued to observe all this commotion I sensed what I can only describe as an army of Light beings enter the room – these beings quickly took charge of the situation and dealt with the negative entities. How they dealt with them I have no idea – some other-dimensional procedure that us human beings could probably not comprehend anyway. However, I do understand that my body was needed there as part of the operation. Those negative entities originated in the human dimension, so I was there as a connector to allow the entities to be cleared, unconcerned as to their fate. I was just relieved that the entities had gone.

Silence settled, and absolute peace entered the room. My awareness during this beautiful calm-after-the-storm was drawn towards a half opened door at the back of the room, leading into a small box room. Inside this small room was a ghost, who seemed to be trapped between worlds. This ghost was so scared, so frightened, so alone – it had been hiding from all those negative entities and was absolutely

---

[1] I prefer to call it house clearing rather than exorcism, because the word exorcism conjures up a sense of heaviness and darkness. House-clearing feels a more comfortable phrase.

petrified. My Angel gently, softly tried to coax the little ghost out of the room, all the time reassuring it that it was now safe.

"Go to the light," my Angel said.

"I can't," replied the ghost, very timidly.

My Angel explained about the light and the peace that the little ghost would find there; tears of tenderness and of immense love fell from my Angel. Never before in my life had I ever experienced so much compassion – and all this for the frightened little ghost.

After a while the ghost came out of the room, reassured no one was going to harm it, yet remaining uncertain and apprehensive. The ghost was now blocking his own way towards the Light – his fear was keeping him trapped. My Angel once more gently encouraged the little ghost and reassured him that he was safe and everything was going to be OK.

My Angel said softly, "Go to the light, little one."

"But I don't know how," was the reply from the ghost.

"Open your heart – your heart is the key," explained my Angel.

Then I observed the small ghost opening his heart and finding the light and the peace. As he did so his whole energy expanded and he was able to enter into a dimension where beings that he recognized and loved came forward to greet him. I was absolutely overwhelmed with emotion; this experience with my Angel and the small ghost was the first of many similarly beautiful episodes I was to have.

About three days after this incident I was in my home washing up at the kitchen sink, when I felt a sudden surge of gratitude pour through me. It was a blissful feeling. I immediately knew this gratitude was sent to me from the little ghost, who had finally found his peace and light.

The house clearing experience showed me another side of my Angel (and I have since discovered that all Angels can behave in a similar fashion when required to do so.) I didn't realize Angels could be so fierce! However, I could see how perfect my Angel had been in her fearlessness, for her behavior enabled her to deal with an unbalanced situation that was creating a block in Universal Flow.

The difference between dark and light

The house clearing also gave me a much deeper insight into what negative entities are, something about which I had up until now been relatively uncertain. This experience led me on a journey of discovery into the darker side of Creation.

I have never bought into the theory of devils, demons and that type of thing, although I was certainly aware that incredibly negative, fear-creating energy existed. A simple defining word for all that fear-creating energy to which most people will relate would be "evil". Personally though, I prefer to refer to it as negativity – a word I feel more comfortable with and which is less fear provoking. So when I use the word negative in the following explanation you will know what I am referring to!

Over the years, since I began to try to understand the existence of negativity, I have observed many different situations and many different behavior patterns of individuals. Throughout my learning with the Angels and various universal beings, it has continually been explained to me that light and dark are both equal, and as beings in the human dimension we cannot survive without both light and dark, as I have already touched on in the previous section.

Dark is the mass; the solid form. For example; a tree in itself is dark; it is a solid form, a mass. Each year the tree produces blossom, and young leaves that grow into maturity. We see the beauty the tree offers with our naked eye. But what we don't see is the energy that flows through the tree, enabling it to look so beautiful to us. The energy contained within the tree is light. Without the light the tree cannot come alive every spring. Yet without the solid tree mass we do not see the beauty that Light creates. In autumn the energy, the Light, withdraws and the tree sleeps until spring, when the energy returns in accordance with the natural seasonal cycle of the Earth.

A healthy tree is an equal balance of both light and dark. A diseased tree does not have equal balance; it has a glitch in its system, a malfunction. Negativity lives inside the tree and is creating imbalance. If allowed to continue the negativity takes over completely and the tree dies. The negativity in the tree occurs because too much dark and not enough Light in the tree's existence occurs, or vice versa. Light and Dark are out of balance.

The same is true of humans. And, while the imbalance sometimes occurs through natural causes, there are many other possible reasons for an imbalance to occur. We have complicated our existence looking for answers to the meaning of life, and in the process, we have forgotten *how* to live. When we truly live, the Universe flows freely through us. But, our need to create and sustain life for ourselves is blocking the hand that feeds us, which is Universal Flow / Creation – whatever term you give it.

The negativity that occurs in all our daily lives is not the work of demons or devils, but collections of unproductive thought forms. Every day, each of us thinks, and a vast amount of these thoughts are absolutely unproductive. A thought however, does not disappear just because a person is now not thinking it. When we create a thought it has to go somewhere – so where does it go?

A thought form homes onto similar thought patterns created by other individuals. For example, if you think you are not worthy, then that thought latches onto a pocket in the ether of similar thoughts. When that particular pocket of thoughts of unworthiness becomes full, it will have formed a large enough mass to create some type of energy that enables it to manifest. It will manifest at the first opportunity or outlet, and can appear in many ways; through illness and disease, atmospheric changes, Earth disruptions or manic behavior from individuals.

Negative energy born out of this dimension cannot be transferred to any other dimension; it lives in our physical dimension, as this is where those unproductive thoughts were first created. The consequence of these negative thoughts can cause suffering to many individuals. In other words, any thought, attitude or belief system that causes separation from our fellow man will create a blockage in the natural flow of the Universe.

Preventing negative energies and entities

I'm not saying that we should never think *anything*, in case it's negative. That would be a ridiculous scenario, and a terrible waste. We have a fantastic brain, a brilliant mind, which should be used to its full extent. There are in fact only two things to understand so our thoughts can be free and productive.

Firstly, practice non-judgment. The mind itself has no conscience; it loves to judge, since doing so creates a sense of my-way-is-the-right-way. The mind houses wants, needs and desires, all of which make living in our human dimension relatively comfortable. And unfortunately these wants, needs and desires, when coupled with feelings of greed and wanting more, become unbalanced within the mind. It is the mind that dictates belief systems; social conditioning, the false need to be accepted by others.

When out of balance with conscience, which is an aspect of light, the mind begins to act egotistically. ego is important; it is our grounding into this dimension. Without ego, our spirit would not be able to exist in our earthly bodies. Ego is as important as the air we breathe to sustain our life here. But out of an unbalanced mind grows an unbalanced ego.

The mind when out of balance can be the most destructive tool known to man, both personally and globally. However, in contrast, the mind is the most powerful component of the dark and – when in equal balance with the light – can access freely all corners of the Universe. We can experience a way of living that we never felt was possible. No longer will we feel fettered to this dimension, instead we will see and experience this earthly reality as it truly is – a wondrous and glorious part of Creation.

The mind can easily trick or deceive itself. We are experiencing a tug of war – dark pulling against light, light pulling against dark. This is how we have created our earthly existences. But the reality is, for us to understand and transcend this earthly dimension the two forces within the Universe must be equal and complimentary – leaving no room for negativity to enter. To be judgmental restricts Universal Flow immensely.

Secondly, aim to have complete freedom in your life. It's OK to use or have a belief system – religious or otherwise – but every religion or organization adheres to some type of ruling, no matter how flexible or subtle those rules may appear to be. The Universe is not bound by rules, it does not have restriction – it is infinite. If you tire or move on from a particular belief system, religion or organization, then realize that it was a helpful stepping stone and has helped you move further on in your journey. It is wise never to see anything as having *all* the answers, and always allow your spirit (your intuition) to guide you.

Negative energy, and healing

In the early days of my journey, when my persona was still opening up to many possibilities in the Universe, I was occasionally finding that the experiences and insights I was gaining were not always welcome when I shared them other people at talks or seminars. One memorable example of this was with regard to spiritual healing, and the reason I mention it here is because it sheds more light on the issue of negative energy, which can often actually be mistaken for positive energy!

The friction occurred at a series of seminars I was giving, the audience for which contained people comfortable with their own view of spirituality and the Universe that they understood and worked from. Many were healers and were of the belief that *all* healing energy was positive. They were getting results in what they were doing, and that was good enough confirmation for them. Then suddenly I come along and share with them my understanding that *not* all healing energy is positive. It is all too easy to 'tap into' negative energy which will heal, but at a price. And that price would be at the expense of the healer, the person receiving the energy, the Earth and humanity as a whole. The healer or patient could become ill or drained and if the Earth absorbed that negative energy it would have to release it some way. Energy is energy, it cannot be brushed away under the carpet. (Indeed, the conservation of energy is a concept which scientists have been comfortable with for years. Energy cannot be destroyed; it simply manifests itself in other ways). So if negative energy is used to heal, it will need to manifest or erupt in some other form. One way negative energy can manifest is by feeding off a person's own energy and draining their life force. This may sound implausible, yet nothing is impossible in an unlimited Universe.

Yet Divine energy is absolutely pure and empowering, and when a person works directly with this energy unconditional healing takes place. But to tap into this energy one must realize they are simply a plug or receiver; they do not have any outcomes of the healing session in mind. A bond must be created that runs through both the healer and the recipient at the point of healing; a complete sense of equality that they both are experiencing something wonderful. The healer has enough trust in the Universe to understand that if the patient's symptoms worsen, then this is still for the highest good for the patient. Even if the patient dies during this process, then this is the most potent growth experience for them.

In most simple terms, a healer needs to step aside from himself. They should not feel the need to ask for protection from any negativity. If a person is able to access Divine energy then no negativity can enter. But if they hold onto any type of attitude or belief system they cannot access Divine energy, and the energy they are using is actually destructive. True universal energy does not flow through belief systems, it does not flow through restrictions, control and limitations. Belief is not the same as *knowing*, belief conjures up a sense of physical restrictions. The two may appear similar, but they carry with them a different energy.

Anyway, as a result of sharing these insights I unintentionally 'stepped on a few toes' and upset a few people, which caused me great concern. I had never intentionally set out to upset anyone, and I was confused as to what it meant. Fortunately, a powerful Angelic essence (an Archangel) visited to reassure me; "The truth can never upset, but what *can* upset is what people *thought* was the truth." And the truth is that there is a lot of negative energy out there, and it can deceive even those people with the best of intentions.

The manifestations of evil

Historically, various religious texts, dogma and belief systems have portrayed evil as being represented by the Devil, demons and entities that are said to exist as separate creatures to that of mankind. These demonic entities are believed to prey on supposed innocent and vulnerable humans. As I have explained, my experiences with the Angels and other universal light beings has taught me that this is not actually the case – negative entities are actually formed from man's negative and destructive thought forms. Demons and similar harmful entities are therefore merely different pockets of collective unproductive thoughts, opinions, attitudes and beliefs. A collective amount of negative thoughts can manifest in the guise of an evil form that we recognize as negative – i.e. demons, devils, etc. Unfortunately though, it isn't as simple as just trying never to have negative thoughts. Even if a person does a good deed, if the reason for doing the deed is because they think it will save them from the Devil or some similar type of evil outcome, they are still subconsciously giving power to that image of the devil. The more fear you put in to an image, the stronger that image becomes, just as the more paint you apply to a canvas, the more well formed the picture becomes. The more colors you add, the more alive the image. Thus there is actually more fear created by doing what might appear to be the right thing – the person is working only according to their head. A person who can work from trust and intuition, operates without fear, without conditions and in wholeness.

In understanding the destructive nature of emotionally charged and judgmental negative thoughts, we can also then appreciate just how incredible and important *positive* thoughts are to the Universe. If we accept that it is our own unproductive thoughts – individual or collectively – that produces the negativity that we call entities/demons etc, we have more freedom to understand how we can all assist in the positive and productive flow of the Universe.

IV   Etheric operations and the electronic gem machine

As a result of my introduction to an incredibly powerful healing therapy technique, my connection with and understanding of the Angelic realms was further increased by a series of profound incidents. To explain these in more detail, I must start by outlining the principles of this therapy, and where it took me.

Jon Whale and gem therapy

Around the time I was introduced to the Angelic realms, I also had a far-reaching encounter with someone very much of this Earth. Jon Whale – a man I would describe as a genius; eccentric in nature and scientific by profession – had developed his own technique of gem therapy after recognizing that every gemstone (such as rubies, sapphires, emeralds, diamonds, carnelian, gold topaz, yellow sapphires, etc), had its own subtle but unique light frequency, which could be used in combination with other gemstones to accelerate recovery from injury and illness. He designed and developed an Electronic Gem Machine that stimulated different gemstones to produce light of specific intensities and frequencies for use as a healing tool.

The therapeutic benefits of precious and semiprecious stones have been recognized for thousands of years, right back to the days of the ancient Greeks and Romans. The electronic gem machine follows a similar principle of stimulated emission to that used with lasers. The gem machine works with subtle variations of light frequencies controlled by electrical technology. A small electrical input is used to excite the electrons in the atoms of the particular combination of gemstones placed into the head of the gem machine lamp heads. They are then further stimulated by an external light source to emit the stored energy within each gemstone in the form of photons, which are directed on to the patient's body. These photons enter into the body, flow through the system and initiate a rapid healing response, clearing blockages caused by a trauma to that particular area of the body. Light from the gems stimulates the damaged cells at an atomic level, instigating a very fast healing response. The machine works incredibly well – but initially I have to say that I was as skeptical as anyone about its abilities!

I was first introduced to Jon as a result of suffering two years of recurring tonsillitis. The doctor had asked me to consider having them removed. As an adult operation, I had heard it was an incredibly painful procedure, and I wasn't convinced my throat problems would be cured from the surgery.

A friend told me about Jon. "See if there is anything he can do before you decide on the operation," she suggested. So I traveled to her house when Jon was visiting with a friend. As I walked into my friend's lounge I saw a very serious looking man in his late twenties holding a Perspex tube filled with rubies an inch or two away from his head. My ignorant reaction was to burst out laughing in disbelief at what I was seeing.

"Er, what are you doing?"

"I'm trying to get rid of my head cold, he replied.

Whatever makes your clock tick, I thought. In walked another man, about thirty-eight years' old, quite thin in stature, and softly spoken.

"Hi, I'm Jon," he told me.

My friend excitedly told me of Jon's machine.

"I hear you've had a lot of tonsillitis – lie on the floor and we'll see what we can do."

I have to say I felt an absolute fool! I couldn't believe I had gone along with my friend's idea of seeing her somewhat eccentric friend. But I did as I was told, as I knew this chap meant well.

Jon began checking out my energy centers[1] and balanced them up using the gems. He got to my crown centre, which was spinning very fast. If a centre spins too fast another centre /chakra will be weakened by it. On this occasion it was my throat centre that was weak. Jon's attempts to calm my crown centre using his gem machine with blue sapphires had a direct result on my eyelids – they began to flicker like crazy.

Jon was intrigued. "Never seen that before," he told everyone.

He found if he slowed the right side of my crown centre, the right eyelid slowed, and then the left side of my crown centre was treated and the left eyelid slowed. Finally Jon had them both slowly flickering simultaneously. After about twenty minutes and having re-balanced my throat, Jon told me to stand up. I stood – and to

---

[1] These energy centers are often referred to as *chakras*. In eastern tradition there are seven main *chakra* within the human energy field. I refer to them simply as energy centers, since that is exactly what they are! If these energy centers become blocked or unbalanced, then the human body doesn't function as it should.

my absolute amazement I could not feel the floor; it felt as if I was hovering about six inches above it. But the best bit was that I felt absolutely fantastic; so clear, so energized, so full of life. I don't think I'd ever felt so well in my life before.

I could not believe what had just happened – and my tonsillitis never returned! I asked Jon to let me buy one of his Electronic Gem machines, which I began using to treat people at my home town. The word soon spread about my success with the crystals and gem machine, and patients would travel long distances to visit me.

Jon has since updated and improved on the design, and I am currently using the later more powerful machine at a chiropractic clinic in Sussex, UK. From this clinic, Adrian sends me patients suffering with chronic and painful injuries that his treatment hasn't been able to fully alleviate. The results are incredible. However, it has been the assistance of the Angels that has produced the most impressive results.

Angelic assistance in healing

In the early days of using the machine I would often be unsure of what combination of gems to use for the many varied conditions that people presented me with. I never offer a diagnosis on a condition, not having had any medical training or detailed understanding as to how the human body functions. My intention was always to assist the pained area using this form of energy medicine, to the best of its potential. Having no pre-conceived ideas about how to treat medical conditions allowed me a clean slate to work from.

It soon occurred to me to try and seek some "higher" guidance on how to do things, asking an Angelic source what mix of gems to use. (Sometimes it is necessary to mix them, a bit like making a cake, so that you would achieve the right mix of photons entering the body). The Angels always gave a successful answer. With this guidance I discovered that different gems assisted different conditions. If for example, someone came to me saying they had arthritis, it was important to ascertain which type they had (the two main types I treated were osteo- and rheumatoid-arthritis). With osteo-arthritis, rubies and diamonds worked brilliantly and the patient would gain flexibility and pain relief in the joint by up to eighty per cent. However, this mix did not work for rheumatoid arthritis – it actually made things worse. I would treat these patients with a mix of emeralds, gold topaz (also known as Mexican topaz), diamonds and yellow sapphires. Again relief from pain and inflammation, reduction in swelling and flexibility occurred by up to eighty per cent.

Etheric operations

I was excited and encouraged by the results that were occurring using the gem machine, and I also found my connections to the different dimensions opening further. It was during a gem session for someone with a frozen shoulder that I became aware of a "higher" essence beginning to surround me. Whilst the patient lay relaxed and comfortable, her shoulder being stimulated by the chosen gems, I sat down and made sure I was connected to Divine Will. Gently my head eased back, my will stepped out and a tall, very upright, higher being entered my body. He told me his name and touched my heart in acknowledgement. He explained to me that his essence comes from the highest healing temple in the Universe, a place for spirits that have died traumatically. As he explained this to me, I could sense through his words a place of absolute peace and nurturing. He was and is a being of very few words, he works in silence and serenity. I have learned much about the human body through my observations of him working. I shall not disclose his name as that is personal to me, so I shall give a pseudonym. As I can't think of anything relative to him, I shall call him Scorpio – my birth sign.

On that first encounter with Scorpio, working through my

body he held out my arms and began pulling towards me (him) the energy field of my patient's body, laying there in front of me. This quite astounded me – I didn't know what to expect next. He eased the energy field around until he had access to the area where the damaged shoulder would have been. He then proceeded to do an operation on that part of the energy field. It was amazing! I could see all that he was pulling apart, cleaning out and stitching up. He would receive from beings standing to the right of him the instruments he needed for the operation. He would simply put my hand out and a tool would be placed in it, and off he would go, working away with minute accuracy – sometimes using his fingers, sometimes using the instruments. Each operation would take about ten minutes or so. When he was finished he would seal the area he was treating by using certain hand movements. Then Scorpio would scan the energy field for any more malfunctions or blockages. He would work on them until he became aware of me becoming bored at his activity. If he felt I'd had enough he would seal the energy field in a protective layer and gently encourage it to slide back into the patient, who was resting three feet or so away. Not once would my hands, guided by Scorpio, have contact with the patient.

It may sound odd that I should get a touch bored watching an "etheric" operation, but once I had seen the block in the energy field and had observed its intensity, I had only a small amount of attention left to observe the operation. Scorpio quickly got to recognize when my boredom threshold was reached and he would work very quickly. He would then depart from my body and I would quietly creep out of the room, leaving the person to rest peacefully for another fifteen minutes.

On my return the patient would slowly open their eyes, stress free and energized. They would often relay different sensations they had experienced during the time they had been experiencing the gems and the "etheric" operation, describing strange sensations which usually correlated with the areas that Scorpio had been working on –

even though I had not told them what he had done. Indeed, to begin with I never used to tell the patients about the "etheric" operations at all, in case it scared them in some way. Eventually I did start telling people, since the strange sensations they experienced were so much due to what Scorpio was doing. Practically all patients felt their body was being turned around, which is what Scorpio would do to more easily access the areas he needed to get to.

The patients were often astounded that I knew there were slight problems in some areas that Scorpio had been treating. They hadn't previously mentioned these to me – I was only made aware of these by observing Scorpio's activities. Any advice regarding the health of the patient that I telepathically received (via images) from Scorpio, I passed on to the patient in a diplomatic and undiagnostic way.

Operating on Emily

Rather than list all the many amazing results we have achieved with the gem machine and these "etheric" operations[2]. I'll just describe one particularly pleasing case study. One day Emily, a lady in her late sixties, asked if I would treat her. (I had previously treated her builder who had injured his knees, and he had told Emily about me and the gem machine.) Emily explained that she had a blood clot in a vein on the right side of her neck. As a result of the clot, she had had about

---

[2] There isn't actually any direct connection that I am aware of between the gem therapy and the "etheric" operations. Indeed, it's impossible to say objectively which is having the greater effect. Jon Whale and many other practitioners have also achieved great results from the gem therapy, without any recourse to assistance from angelic realms. Nevertheless, the environment of a gem therapy session provides a very convenient and comfortable way of allowing "etheric" operations to take place – if it's appropriate for it to occur. I should stress that I do not ever offer to facilitate these "etheric" operations – it's not for me to offer it or even say it will happen. If I did I would not be working within Universal Flow! I'm just there as the conduit.

twenty-six mini strokes (transient ischemic attacks), and she was seeing a specialist at Harefield Hospital, outside London. Harefield is an outstanding heart hospital with respected consultants.

Emily told me she had been advised to have arterial "balloon" surgery to release the clot. She had reservations about the operation as she was told at the time that it only carried a fifty per cent success rate – i.e. a fifty per cent chance of leaving her in a worse condition than she was already in. Since Gem therapy is non-invasive, she wanted to give it a go. After talking with Emily I told her about Scorpio, explaining that I had no influence over whether he came, and that he would only pop by and do an "etheric" operation if it was appropriate. I explained to Emily how disease first occurs in the energy field before showing itself in the physical body, and that the energy field is like a blueprint of the physical body. If a malfunction or imbalance occurs in the blueprint, unless it is dealt with it will manifest itself in the physical body. Often just simple things like diet and an examination of one's attitudes can resolve the block in the energy field, and if caught early enough will prevent its physical manifestation. Still, Emily was prepared to try anything, so – with resolve and confidence in her voice – she declared that whatever I felt was necessary was fine with her.

I asked the Angelic realms which gemstones to use for the clot in Emily's neck. The advice was to use blue sapphires, with a very high frequency shooting through them. Emily lay down and I placed the gems on her neck as close as I could to the clot. I checked my connection to Divine Will, and then in came Scorpio. Scorpio very rarely acknowledges me, unlike the other universal beings who have taken over my body. His vibration is very focused and direct; he likes to get straight on with the task in hand. Scorpio drew Emily's energy field towards me, and began to work very quickly around the neck area. I was aware of the amount of detritus that he was clearing from Emily's energy. He seemed to be opening up small capillaries and inserting minuscule type needles in them to clear the capillaries out. As always, Scorpio worked very intently. When he finished he sealed Emily's energy field and slid it back into her physical body.

After the session was complete Emily felt exhausted, returning home and sleeping for the rest of the day. She came to see me the following week with great enthusiasm, saying that as of the day after the treatment she felt forty years younger and full of life. Emily's speech wasn't as slurred and she appeared revitalized.

I treated her once a week for the next six weeks, and on each operation that Scorpio performed, the blood clot appeared to be getting smaller and smaller. I didn't mention this to Emily at the time, since I didn't want to give her false hope. After each session she was quite worn out for a few days, but continued to return since she felt that she was becoming increasingly fitter.[3]

Emily was due for an appointment at Harefield Hospital after the sixth treatment, and I was curious to know how it went. Later that week an ecstatic Emily phoned to tell me her wonderful news. Her consultant had told her in amazement that her clot had completely disappeared. She told me he was absolutely speechless, but very happy for her. Emily had also had her usual blood and heart tests

---

[3] It is not uncommon for a patient to feel very tired after the gem treatment and /or an "etheric" operation. This is because of the patient's difficulty in relaxing or sleeping in their everyday life, which is often due to the body not working in alignment with its energy field. The gem treatment and "etheric" operation is working to realign the body to its energy field and the patient will feel tired and will have to rest until realignment of the physical body to the energy field is complete. The energy field is that aspect of us which, at times, can makes us jump sharply just before we drift off to sleep, something that has happened to most people at one time or another. Normally as your physical body relaxes, your energy field relaxes in synchronization with your physical body, and then you fall asleep. But if your energy field relaxes faster than your physical body you will experience a sudden jump as your energy field is "pulled" by your physical body.

that had (also to the surprise of the consultant) revealed Emily to be normal in health for somebody of her age. I asked Emily if she had told the consultant about the electronic gem treatment.

"I couldn't possibly tell him that," she said. "He would never have believed me!"

On that basis I didn't bother asking whether she had mentioned the "etheric" operations that she'd been having – I could guess what the answer would have been! At the same time, I did feel somewhat deflated that Emily didn't mention the gem machine to her consultant; simply because of the benefit to health it could have provided to many more patients. After all, it is a scientifically valid device – it's not a belief system. Unfortunately, I guess that conventional medicine will probably never be comfortable with such things. And as for Emily, her consultant slowly reduced her visits to the hospital from fortnightly to once every six months.

V   Harry and the Angel of Death

An unexpected consequence of my experiences with Emily was a further round of revelations and insights into the realms of Angels, again in the environment of the Gem Therapy sessions.

Introducing Harry

Emily was married to Harry, who was in his late sixties and – although prepared to support Emily fully in her quest for alternative therapies – had originally been very skeptical about the treatment she was having with me. He was astounded at her recovery, yet still remained somewhat cynical regarding the treatment.

Emily was concerned about Harry, who she felt was working really far too hard. Harry worried that the company he worked for would fail without him – it was a small family company and he felt loyal to them; he had been with them for many years and was part of the management team. By trying to maintain the same workload of his earlier years he was putting a lot of pressure on himself to keep up, and as a result of all this overwork had become very stressed and short-tempered.

Harry never complained about his health, but Emily could very clearly tell that things were not as they should be with him. She begged him to come and see me. Emily's recovery unblocked a door in Harry's skeptical nature – he succumbed to her pleas and arrived on my doorstep. I understood Harry's skepticism regarding the treatment, for I too still found it hard to believe that it worked so well! So I was not concerned that others might doubt its effectiveness. I told Harry about how dubious I had been during my own first encounter with the gem therapy; he enjoyed the story and began to relax. As I pointed out to him; "If all you get is a good night's sleep from your treatment, then it will still have achieved something!"

For his first treatment my aim was indeed simply to try and reduce his stress levels. As with Emily, he responded wonderfully to the treatment. He was very surprised at all the ailments and disorders I had picked up with him, and at the relief he gained by receiving the beautiful treatment from the beings and different energies that I worked with. Harry felt so good after the session that he decided he would like a treatment once every month.

Harry and Emily were devout Methodists and led a very active church life. However, some of the various beliefs and views held by Harry's church didn't sit comfortably with him, so at the end of a treatment session he would often ask me questions of a spiritual nature – something that was causing confusion in him. I would answer as best I could, based on the perception I had of life and the Universe. Harry would listen, and silently nod his head in understanding.

Achieving absolute openness

About a year after his first treatment, I received a telephone call late one night from a very distraught Emily. Through her tears of panic she explained: "Harry has had a slight heart attack and the doctors have told him they want to perform heart by-pass surgery. Harry won't let them until he has seen you. Can he come over?"

"Of course he can. I'll see Harry tomorrow." I gently reassured Emily as best I could. However, I felt uncomfortable – Harry would not make a decision whether to have surgery or not until he had seen me. A burden of responsibility had been placed on my shoulders, and I could not accept it. I asked for help from the Universe for Harry to realize that the strength to make the right decision lay in him, not in me.

Harry arrived the following day. We went straight into the room where I did my work. Harry sat down, told me what had happened and expressed a certain amount of confusion.

"I wonder why you hadn't picked up on a forthcoming heart attack, since you have been so accurate with picking up and treating all my other ailments?"

Well it wasn't me that picked those things up, it was Scorpio – I simply passed on what I observed during his "etheric" operations. But it was a touch difficult for Harry to appreciate that it came from Scorpio; an energy that he could not see. Harry therefore referred quite naturally to me as knowing what was unbalanced in his body.

Harry wasn't blaming me, or Scorpio, in any way for not forewarning him of this attack – he was just surprised and confused by it. I was also surprised about Harry's heart attack; it made me feel a little uncertain in my own ability and clearness in directing the universal healing energy. Once more I began to doubt myself. Yet at the same time I could clearly see that everything was as it was meant to be, in order to benefit Harry and his soul in the highest possible outcome. Reassured by the strong feeling of faith inside me, I let my doubts pass by. Then Harry asked me:

"Tonika, should I have the operation?"

With that question, I felt Harry had one hundred per cent faith in me and in all the light beings that worked through me (although the question Harry asked was directed solely at me, rather than the beings who had worked to help him throughout the past year. Which was fine because those beings work unconditionally). However, I remained uncomfortable with the idea that Harry had such faith in *me*, but not quite as much in himself! This was an important issue, and right now we were not equal on it. Harry's faith in me outweighed his own faith in himself. If I had taken the responsibility of answering this question, I would have taken away the responsibility and trust that Harry had in himself. I replied; "It seems to me Harry, you're a pretty good judge of things and you don't need me to tell you what to do. What do *you* think you should do?"

Harry sighed. "Emily and the doctors say I should have the by-pass, but I can't get it out of my mind that I don't really need it. I don't think I should have the operation."

"Harry, at the end of the day your gut feelings are the best guidance you or anyone is ever going to receive as to what you should or shouldn't do. So regardless of what I or the doctors or Emily may say, *you* have to make the decision."

In the year I had known him, I had found Harry to be a very open-minded person. And here he was now, open to his intuition – open enough to accept whatever consequences his decision led him to, be it life or death. Now that's pretty open! Only a year ago Harry had sat before me as a devout Methodist and very much a skeptic. Now, in front of me was a man truly expanded and ready to FLY!

The Angel of Death

Harry knew by now what to expect when he came for treatment. He was always sensitive enough to know and feel the areas of his body that Scorpio had operated on, and followed the advice I had passed on after observing Scorpio at work. This time, Harry was anxious to begin the treatment and relaxed himself very quickly. He took a deep breath and closed his eyes. After ascertaining my connection to Divine Will I waited to see who would come. An essence came through, but not one that had used my body before. This essence felt so very beautiful; very serene and focused. (These universal essences always have this wonderful sense of focus around them, whoever they are.) I asked who this was.

"I am the Angel of Death," was the answer.

I nearly pooped my pants I was so shocked. This was *not* what I was expecting to hear! My heart must have momentarily stopped – fear began to engulf me. Very carefully I opened one eye to look at Harry – fearing the worst! Yet he looked remarkably peaceful. Reassured by his restfulness, I gathered all my strength and composure, and asked once again for my bones and blood to respond to confirm that I was connected to Divine Will. There was always the chance that maybe my own desire in wanting Harry better could have caused me to draw an entity to myself which was impersonating a higher being. The response from my blood and bones was such that I was left in no doubt that my connection was truly Angelic. I went through a process of acceptance that if Harry were meant to die here and now, well that would be just fine – it would be as it was meant to be.

Fortunately, the Angel of Death was understanding of my fears and acknowledged me with so much love and compassion that my heart was filled. Tears ran down my face, and I felt an exhilarating sense of peace. The Angel then lifted my left hand forward, and in the hand was a list of names. She searched for Harry's name, found his name and then crossed it off her list. All this was done symbolically, for me to understand what was happening. I was left completely without thoughts and in absolute awe. The Angel then departed. As she left, I knew another being was ready to communicate with me. Remaining open as to who was relevant to this situation, I sat waiting.

My head came back, my body straightened, and the vibration of this being echoed through my body. It was a universal essence that offers help and advice regarding Karma. The *Karmic* essence told me that Harry was learning with such a depth that it touched his soul. A universal decision had been made for him to stay on this planet for a few more years. As the *Karmic* essence explained this to me, understanding enveloped my consciousness. Although we may believe that when our time is up, it's up – it seems that this is not always the case. I could see that a personality's learning is greatly magnified whilst still in the physical body and in so doing, one's individual soul becomes greater in power. (More on the soul in part VI.)

Harry had truly begun to open up and listen to the silent guidance that was around him. He listened to his own heart, and ignored what his mind was telling him – he allowed simple understanding to enter his being. He had begun to use his own discretion, without taking on the assumption of right or wrong. Using his own common sense in everyday living to make decisions, and being guided by that sense rather than by body, institution, organization, belief system or company (which on the surface may have seemed more well-informed than himself). I could see this spiritual growth in Harry that had occurred over the past year.

As the *Karmic* essence departed, I was left with a sense of expansion as I began truly to understand death or departure from this planet. The next essence to enter into my body was Scorpio and I relaxed in his familiarity – pleased as punch to feel him here.

Scorpio gently eased Harry's energy field towards him and began to open up the heart centre within the energy field. Intricately, he operated on Harry's diseased heart. He took it out and very carefully placed a new healthy heart in Harry's energy field. He secured the heart in place and then sealed Harry's energy field, before sliding it back into Harry. Scorpio then took a few moments to place his attention into me. He silently acknowledged the expansion and understanding I had just experienced, before departing from my body. Opening my eyes I looked at Harry, relaxed and peaceful as he rested in the crystals. Leaving the room, I left Harry to rest whilst I sat outside in the back garden.

Life is for learning

So, I thought – it seems that when your time is up, it's not necessarily the case. Harry received a life extension because of the depth of his learning. It is often said the Earth is very much like a school of learning, but I hadn't given much thought to this concept until now. If the Earth is a school, then for those of us who have lessons to learn, we should hopefully have learned them before we leave school, i.e. before we leave the Earth. If, therefore, a rare and unique opportunity arises whilst still on the Earth where a person is asked to look very deeply into himself, the answers to many questions the person had never asked before begin to surface. Their learning of life and life's mysteries take on such an excitement and enthusiasm, that to leave school (the Earth) as planned seems pretty nonsensical. The decision is made for the person to stay on at school and learn more. Harry stayed on this planet because his openness allowed him to stay on and begin to absorb new influences.

The more I began to dissolve my own fear and belief system, the more I began to understand life and its mysteries. I had never previously given much thought as to how one ended their time in this Earthly dimension – I certainly didn't know that an energy such as the Angel of Death would be involved. My understanding now is that there are many different "disincarnate" energies here to assist us in this process. I would not like to say for sure if the Angel of Death has this particular assignment, for I realize that she had come to me symbolically to erase Harry's name from the list.

The whole experience with Harry became an empowering and thought-provoking time in my life. On reflection, I was shocked by how my fear had tried to override my faith in myself – something which I suspect happens at times to many of us. I realized that my fear stemmed from information both consciously and subconsciously received throughout my life. We are always surrounded by the fear connected with dying. It is therefore perhaps not surprising that when the Angel of Death popped by, my response was largely conditioned by that fear. However, all the beauty and peace that poured out from her washed away my worries – for the very first time I felt that I had truly seen life, and within that vision I received so much clarity.

While Harry lay resting upstairs, I sat in the garden wrestling with my conscience. Should I tell him what had happened? Would he be able to comprehend the immensity of the experience? My experience with the Angel of Death and the *Karmic* essence was so profound that I felt he might not be able to grasp the complexity of it all. How wrong I was, for when I went back upstairs and sat in front of Harry, he gently opened his eyes and looked at me. Surrounded by a soft glow and with tears in his eyes he told me; "Now I know why I had to come along for the past year to see you. Although I always felt good after visiting you, I knew in my heart there was a greater reason for my being here."

He asked me what had occurred during the "operation". Trying not to give too much away, I replied; "You tell me what you felt first, Harry."

Harry described his experience. "I know this sounds silly and I don't know how else to describe the feeling, but I felt I had been given a new heart, and all across my heart a feeling that I can only describe as a deep, deep love and compassion filled me. I really cannot put this feeling into words. All I can say is from the bottom of my heart I thank you and all the Angels."

I could feel how deeply the Angel of Death had touched Harry, and that deepest of feelings really cannot be put into words. Having witnessed and felt Harry's openness, I now knew I could share with him all the details of our session. Harry was moved even more. We both felt an equal gratitude towards one another; we both felt honored and humbled to experience such an insight into death.

Harry returned to hospital only for the consultants to confirm with pleasure that, after various tests, Harry's heart was fit and healthy. To this day, some eleven years on, Harry still experiences good health.

VI   Angels and our Soul

I now wish to share with you some experiences that have helped me to understand another aspect of our human persona – the Soul. Originally I thought that this was just another word or term to describe our Angel, spirit or life force. However, as a result of an encounter with the Angel of a friend, I discovered that the Soul is not the same as Angelic energies – it is a completely different type of energy. But it took many more years and encounters to piece together my understanding and appreciation as to the true magnitude and power of the Soul...

The Keeper of Lost Souls

My first proper encounter with the Soul was thanks to Joanna – a friend who had emigrated to Australia. She'd been experiencing some turbulent times there, and after an encounter with her Angel I sent Joanna a message that had been passed on to me. This message clearly struck a powerful chord in Joanna's heart, to such an extent that she made the decision to return home to England.

As soon as Joanna arrived back in the UK she booked in for some balancing and cleansing work on her energy centers. Although she put on a brave face, she was in fact very tense – very vulnerable. The next step was to carry out a private sitting for Joanna, to see who came through into my body to communicate and help her further.

Joanna sat opposite me on the floor and as always I waited for confirmation from my blood and my bones that I was connected to Divine Will. Then my head was very gently eased back. My will stepped out, and in popped an essence very new to me. He announced himself as The Keeper of Lost Souls. It was explained to Joanna that during a past life she had sold her soul to some dark magician, of whom she had been very fearful. She had thought that by selling her soul she would not be harmed physically by him. (A bad plan indeed – words and intentions born from fear have a very destructive effect upon our soul's growth.)

The sorcerer had indeed gained more power over Joanna's earlier incarnation due to this act, but it was not her Soul that gave him more power (Although he thought it did). He gained simply from her vulnerability; as she became 'lesser' he became more powerful. This is what the Keeper of Lost Souls told Joanna. He then told her more of her previous life and took her on an inward journey so that she could see and touch the Light inside herself.

The Keeper of Lost Souls then leant forward and told her he was undoing the shackles around her feet and hands. Her vulnerability and lack of self-acknowledgement had somehow caused these symbolic shackles to develop around her limbs. Once he had released them he took a deep breath into my body, raised my arms and held open my hands. Very gently I could feel a soft and pure childlike energy being placed into them. The Keeper of Lost Souls then passed into Joanna her spiritual link back to her soul. He told Joanna that her spirit had learnt enough to know the soul was a wonderful gift from Creation, and can never be given or taken by anyone or anything.

Excited and energized by this experience, Joanna told me in amazement when the session was over that all the previous week she had been physically unbalanced. "It crossed my mind at the time that this is what it must be like to have your feet shackled together," she explained.

I was very happy for her, but somewhat confused. I had already communicated with Joanna's Angel, who appeared very strong and well connected to Joanna,[1] so clearly, the Angel and the Soul are not one and the same! There was obviously some further understanding to be gained here. I knew that the answer would come eventually, when I was ready to receive and absorb the information.

The journey to the Soul

Sure enough, a couple of years later I was inspired to host a workshop, in which people would be taken on an inner journey to meet their Soul. At the time I didn't have any prior insights as to what was going to happen during this journey, it just seemed the right thing to do. (Remember – trust your instincts!). Indeed, this workshop has now become one of the most powerful inner experiences that can guide a person.

It was a warm Sunday just before Easter. About ten people had come to experience the day's self-growth workshop. Two guided inner journeys had already taken place, in which the group had traveled into different dimensions in order to experience various aspects of themselves. The next journey of discovery was to meet their souls. Not having attempted this before, my expectations were that this journey was likely to be considerably less interesting and insightful compared to the previous two. How wrong I was!

---

[1] I had already observed that if an individual was pretty much on their life's path, the link from their Angel to me was always strong. Yet, if the individual was not on their life's path (due to social influence, belief systems, or mental illnesses) then the link from their Angel to me would be very weak, and sometimes slow and quite shaky!

Guided by my Angel, we went higher and deeper into and through many different dimensions, stopping for a while to observe the activities or energies within these dimensions. Everyone afterwards reported a sense of speed and expansion as they traveled through these many dimensions towards their Soul.

As we traveled, my Angel would immediately sense when someone was losing his or her focus. Her voice would become firmer as she pulled their energy back on track. She never needed to say which specific individual was going off track, but the person knew instinctively her words were for them and automatically pulled themselves back towards her guidance.[2]

We had got to a point on our journey that felt incredibly high and so infinitely removed from our human dimension. My Angel, having control over my body was by now barely breathing. It was as though she was calming her breath so as not to intrude on the stillness and sense of focus that every cell in my body seemed to be experiencing at that point. She guided everyone to individual doorways that they were to pass through, to see and touch their soul.

This was all taking quite a lot of time; so much so that I was starting to hope the rest of the journey would not take too long since I was getting really hungry (all this inter-dimensional traveling was really building up an appetite in me!). However, my Angel took absolutely no notice of my physical hunger and my hopes that we wouldn't take too long. These thoughts never touched her, which I found odd.

My Angel then slowly encouraged everyone to walk to their door. And every step she took towards my doorway – which as I now

_____

[2] One or two people have after my workshops expressed their frustration towards my Angel pulling them back. They would tell me, "I was really losing myself and enjoying that sensation, but then your Angel's voice became firmer and jolted me out of my dreams." I would remind them that the Universe and all its dimensions are vast beyond comprehension. When you're navigating through such infinite and unknown territories, you stay with the guide!

appreciate was hers also – was of complete awe for what was about to happen. Stunned by my own Angel's reaction, I realized that this was an incredibly sacred place in Creation – one which was rarely visited. Furthermore, it was a place that Angels do not have free access to, which also surprised me greatly. This journey was just as sacred and special for my Angel as it was for us all! My impatience subsided; I hadn't until that point realized the sacredness of what we were about to do – my Angel most certainly was going to take as much time as was required to fully absorb the atmosphere of this purest of pure dimensions. She guided everyone to open their doors to their individual soul. As they did so she encouraged them to be aware of the colors that emanated from their soul. She told them to spend a few minutes absorbing the beauty of the colors and the way they moved. Moments later she gently reached my hand out, and guided everyone to do the same. As we all did this, my Angel's sense of awe was absolute. (As I now appreciate, this was possibly a first for her as well!). She touched my soul and very gently brought a tiny piece back and placed it tight into my heart centre. She encouraged everyone to do the same.

Shortly thereafter we stepped back and the doors closed slightly. My Angel then brought us back through all the dimensions that we had previously passed through. In just a matter of minutes she took us right back to this Earth dimension, which was a very fast journey indeed – so much so that when everyone opened their eyes at the end of it we all felt quite dizzy and disorientated, myself included.[3]

After we had all returned safely to our physical dimension my Angel departed. A sense of empowerment and understanding filled

---

[3] I have repeated this journey with people on many occasions since, and every time we all come back really fast. The significance of this I now realize is to enable us to "ground" the tiny piece of our soul that we are taking back to our Earthly existence. We travel back to our earthly dimension fast to prevent our soul energy dissipating into the other dimensions. A simple analogy would be taking a trip into town to buy a tub of ice cream, to take home and   *Continued*

me beyond words – my impatience and hunger seemed a million miles away. There is nothing I can share with you to compare with this feeling. I did not want to speak and neither did anyone else; it was as though we were still in that dimension of complete pureness and wonderment. I felt humbled with a renewed appreciation for the Earth, her people, Creation and infinity. This was the most empowering journey I could ever offer anyone.

What is the Soul?

My observation of my Angel's reaction to this experience demonstrated to me how sacred the Soul was. Yet, still I wondered quietly to myself – what *is* the soul? Further insight on that question was given to me a few months later, when I was giving a series of monthly seminars at a Spiritual Sanctuary near London. I began to feel sleepy, which was quite common when I'd been searching my mind for answers. So off I would go and take a quick nap in the armchair in my bedroom. I would usually wake with a lot more clarity. On this particular occasion I felt a Universal Essence by my side who telepathically showed me I was going to be taken up to meet the power of my soul. Following the being's instructions, I found myself facing an immense power. It felt like the Concorde aeroplane coming towards me at its most powerful (yet three times stronger!). Shocked to my core by this power, I was advised to take a deep breath and breathe in some of that power, which I did. After this my consciousness was slowly brought back to a waking state. At that point I don't think I have ever felt so powerful, so strong and so focused; the three feelings together created

eat later whilst watching a film. But there are also some other things you need to do whilst in town. Common sense dictates that you buy the ice cream last and hurry back, otherwise it would melt by the time you get home. It's the same with the soul; the journey back to this dimension is fast so the soul fragment you are bringing back won't disappear along the way!

an immovable sense of understanding in me. I thought to myself that people go on about possessing their own power, and yet faced with such a force, most could not either cope with it or know what to do with it. I know that I certainly couldn't!

What this experience made me realize is that our soul is our individual power store that increases. It grows from every life experience we have learned from. Every pain and suffering, every hardship, enables our soul to grow for our power to expand. This was a fantastic insight to gain. The soul does not touch either this dimension or the Astral Realms, yet we all have an "etheric" link to our individual soul. The magnificence of our soul is beyond comparison with anything else within the Universe.

Seeing and experiencing my soul energy, along with the insights which followed, have given me a greater understanding of humanity, and why we are here and where we are going. Only a limited answer I'm afraid, because our human brains would not be able to fully comprehend the whole picture. The journey of self-discovery is endless, and no one has all the answers. We are all unique, and yet we all have one thing in common – we are searching for expansion in an ever-growing Universe.

VII   Why are we here, and why some people are so disconnected from divine will

The journey of discovery and understanding outlined in these chapters has allowed me to see very clearly what the purpose of our time on this planet is. However, I still didn't really understand why we are here. Nor could I fathom why – if everybody has an Angel filled with love and compassion trying to look after them – some people are so desperately disconnected from Divine Will. The answers to these questions eventually arrived, each in the most unlikely circumstances. Together they give great further insight to the big picture...

Why are we here?

This revelation came to me like a bolt out of the blue. I had been watching a science program about new stars forming; stars exploding and sending a wave of energy to the edges of our Universe. As I was watching it, my brain suddenly began to pick up images and explanations as to why we are here. I will do my best to translate this into words.

When I first began working closely with Angels and universal beings and energies, I would constantly be told that I was from the stars; I (and near enough everybody else) did not come from Earth but from somewhere very distant. For years this didn't mean much to me – I did not understand it so I paid little attention to it. It was only when I mentioned it to my astrophysicist friend Bill that I was able to get a satisfactory explanation. Bill told me how carbon, calcium and all the other essential minerals and elements which make up our body originated from the immense thermonuclear fusion factories at the heart of huge stars – in simplest terms, our Earthly bodies stem from stardust. This helped me to understand what I had been told by the Angels. But despite our physical body stemming from the stars, it still didn't explain the origins of our Angels, our spirit and our essence.

Then, whilst watching this science program, I was telepathically shown stars bursting through into this dimension (the stars being symbolic of our individual essences). These stars were fragments of our whole energy. To use a metaphor, it's as if our whole energy is the "mother ship", and she sent out a small craft to act as a scout to ascertain what the atmosphere was like. It was shown to me how we have the role of these individual scouts, searching and figuring out this dimension. Our essence – our Angelic Self – sends out a fragment of their wholeness to inhabit a physical body, so that we can learn and overcome the obstacles native to this dimension, and pass safely through this Universe and into the next. I could see how our whole essence had expanded through the Universes, but was now restricted to move through this one until it had become familiar with it. We are here for just a short time, merely passing through. I could see why people become lost, uncertain, lonely, without direction and searching for home – they had lost their connection to their whole essence (their mother ship). The solidness of this human dimension had blocked their receivers to their essence, or Angelic Self.

The vibration on which our whole Angelic Self resonates is far too overpowering for the solidity that is the human dimension, which is why only a fragment of our Angelic Self is sent out to inhabit a human body. If our whole essence were to fully inhabit a human body there would be a shattering effect within this human dimension; as when an opera singer sings a very high note and the frequency of that note shatters a glass.

Why are some people so disconnected from divine will?

So what of the discordant people around us who seem to ignore the laws of this dimension and the Earth – why have they become so disconnected from their essence? The answer to this question came to me whilst I was cuddled up on the settee with my little girl Atlanta-Rose watching a video of the Disney film *Mulan*. This is about a girl who saves China from the evil Hun leader Shan-Yu, whose ruthless aim was to take over the country. There is a scene where Shan-Yu and his warriors had just been presented with a small doll, stolen and dropped into his master's hand by Shan-Yu's wicked falcon. Shan-Yu smelled the doll and knew the Imperial Army (the good guys) were in the settlement where the doll came from. He could smell gunpowder ashes on the doll. Sinister pleasure rode over his face as he told his men that they must pay the settlement a visit and return the doll to its owner – his intention being to surprise and wipe out the Imperial Army. The next scene is of a devastated and burned out settlement – Shan-Yu and his men had been there and murdered everyone and burned the settlement to ashes. The little doll lay frazzled on the ground.

Watching this, I couldn't help but angrily think that some people are really yuck! Once during a channeling session someone asked the being in my body a question along the lines of morality. The answer came back, "If you cannot see Light in your fellow man – then where is yours?" I have always tried to remember this answer. But sometimes people can be so unbalanced in humanity that it can be really tough to appreciate the wisdom in that answer.

Watching this scene in the *Mulan* video was one of those moments. I despaired at myself for feeling so much distaste towards this Shan-Yu. Whilst in despair, another image filtered telepathically into my brain. I could see stars being blasted dramatically from their whole essence. But these were stars shot off too fast, (not for any specific reason but simply because imbalances and irregularities will sometimes naturally occur.). They were denser in form than the stars I had seen in my first explanation of our existence and purpose. They were out of balance in light and dark – there was only five to ten per cent of light within the star, leaving ninety to ninety-five per cent, a dark mass, too weighted down to have a conscience. They were out of control, and anything that got in their way got damaged. It wasn't that they meant to cause destruction deliberately; they were simply shooting off too fast, out of balance with the rest of this Universe. This image explained the motives of the evil Shan-Yu!

Using a metaphor; if you have a catapult and you want to knock an apple off the tree in the distance, you stick a stone into your catapult, aim and fire it. On the stone's journey towards the apple it may hit a fly or gnat, but the stone doesn't stop and say "after you" to the fly or "excuse me" to the gnat; its target is the apple, and if anything gets in its way – well that's tough! That is exactly how I saw these power-hungry individuals that we share our planet with.

VIII   Archangels and God

I will finish this chapter by sharing some insights on Archangels (which are not the same as our own Angels) and how I have come to understand the Ultimate Creative Energy – God.

Understanding Archangels

As I now understand it, Archangels are messengers that come direct from creation, God or whatever one chooses to call this Ultimate Creative Energy. Archangels are the consciousness, the strengths, the qualities that make up this Ultimate Creative Energy. Just as the human body requires many different organs to function to optimum capacity; heart, lungs, liver, kidneys, brain etc, the God energy has Archangels and various other godlike figures[1] for its organs. They each have their individual roles to play, and they all retain their own unique personalities.

God as an individual is not a separate energy unto itself. If we compare the God energy to the human body, we could say our outer core, our skin, is like the Universe, and God is our DNA within the Universe. However, in order for our body to function, we have envoys – the lungs, muscles, heart, etc. all doing a brilliant job, each complementing the other. That is how I've come to understand God. God is the life that is breathed into all of these envoys – the Light beings that exist in and around, endlessly, infinitely with God's energy.

The best way I can explain our place within the Universe and our closeness to this God energy is by relating some extraordinary experiences and revelations that occurred during a "Sweat Lodge",

---

[1] It's difficult to find the right term for these other qualities that make up this ultimate creative energy. However, it is my understanding that they are special godlike energies or frequencies that have been worshipped in various forms throughout the ages; figures such as Aphrodite, Zeus, Neptune and the like.

some seven years ago, in the Malvern Hills. A Sweat Lodge is an ancient Native American Indian ceremony, carried out with a "bender" and an external log fire, shaped in the image of the sea turtle. The bender (representing the body of the Sea Turtle) is made from hazel sticks bent over each other and secured in the ground to produce a small dome-like structure. Skins are placed over the top of the hazel sticks to keep in the heat from the rocks, which are previously heated within the log fire until they are almost white hot, and then placed in a shallow hole dug into the centre of the floor under the dome. The entrance to the dome has a large skin covering it, which can be easily lifted to enter the dome. The fire where the rocks were heated would burn a few feet from the entrance (representing the head of the sea turtle). One person would have the honor of keeping the fire going and then feeding the heated rocks into the 'belly' of the dome. They did not enter the dome during the ceremony. The participants of the Sweat Lodge entered into the dome and sat in a circle around the central hole filled with the hot rocks.

The Native American people believe that every person born onto the planet enters through the energy of the Sea Turtle. They believed that by entering this man-made image of the Turtle they would receive new life, new insights and new understandings of their path in life.

The Sweat Lodge ceremony, when performed with understanding and focus, is a very powerful process indeed. During the ceremony, hot rocks are passed into the bender on four separate occasions. Each occasion represents one of the four directions and elements (North and the Earth, South and the Fire, East and the Air, West and the Water). Everyone present would be asked to honor and acknowledge the four directions and the four elements (all of which we need to live and gain nourishment from on this planet). When the Sweat had finished, each person leaves the bender reborn with greater vision, clarity and understanding. It's called "Sweat" because that's exactly what you do whilst you are in there; more so than in a sauna, and the more water that is thrown on to the hot rocks the hotter it gets. By the time the ceremony gets to honoring the South and the Fire element an awful lot of water gets thrown on those rocks, and it becomes intensely hot – almost unbearable. Yet it has to be like that so the people present can draw out dormant strengths and disciplines within themselves, to freely experience their rebirth and greater understanding.

I had been invited to take part in a Sweat Lodge in the Malvern Hills planned for late September 1992. Andrew, the person who was to lead the "Sweat"' was someone who had spent a number of years with a practicing spiritual Native American Indian. He had gained much knowledge and understanding of the Earth, the elements and the cycle of life. My invite came because of my ability to "lend my body" to all in creation (which includes all the elements). Andrew hoped that perhaps the elements of Air, Water, Fire and Earth would use my body to share with us their roles and their understanding in the Universe.

Malvern was about four and a half-hour's drive away from my home so Adrian and myself faced a long journey. However, it felt right for us to go. I have learned to trust my intuition with these things. If at any time I had felt it became wrong to be there I would have returned home, regardless of the distance. Sometimes the journey itself is the learning, rather than the destination!

Sitting restfully in the passenger seat, as Adrian drove us on to the motorway, I gazed up at the sky, then began to doze. As my mind calmed I began to wonder why I can communicate with the Sun, the Moon, the stars, the trees, with Angels, unborn children, animals, deities and all the different kingdoms in creation. A clear answer came into my thoughts, telepathically from the Universe; "Because you *are* the Sun, the Moon, the Earth, the stars. You have no separation, you are whole, you are complete."

My wondering was gently replaced with a sense of peace that expanded within each of my cells.

We eventually arrived at the location for the Sweat Lodge; a beautiful large stone home set in twelve or so acres of garden, and secluded in its position. Views of the Malvern Hills could be seen from every angle of the house; a brilliant setting for it, I thought. We rambled down to the small woods south of the big house and met up with Andrew, who was very pleased to see us, and likewise we were happy to be in his company.

A vision of Truth

Four others were to join in the Sweat, which made a total of seven people including Adrian and myself. Eager to get to work and assist in the building of the Sweat, Adrian and I began to get busy. It wasn't long before I began to sense that many of the people around me were unfocused – I hoped it would pass and they would soon become more focused on the task ahead. However, it seemed that these people were actually becoming *less* focused, and more impartial to the task. A Sweat should be built with honor and respect to the Earth and the Universe, and with the intent of unification of all people. Hopefully, this Sweat was also to have the added sacredness of everyone being able to communicate consciously with all the elements. What could happen here had the potential to be very powerful indeed. I expressed my concerns to Adrian – I couldn't stay under these conditions. Adrian suggested I chat with Andrew, and tell him how I felt.

With quiet respect I explained to Andrew my concerns. If the energy surrounding the building of the Sweat didn't change and become focused and open, then I would have to leave, since I would feel uncomfortable to be there.

Andrew agreed that the energy was scattered, and he would talk with the others and do the best he could. I said I would see what happens, then make my decision. Adrian and I returned to the building of the Sweat, deep with intent but playful and light in our approach.

Andrew spoke with the others but they still were not as focused with honor for the Sweat as I would have liked. Slowly I was steering my mind towards a decision to leave. As I contemplated my actions carefully, one of the girls came to me and asked me my view on something that had confused her, during the short time she had spent in a Buddhist monastery. The conversation was quite deep and lengthy – I shared with her my observation of the situation that she had described, and suggested that in order to calm her confusion, she should try to look at it from a different viewpoint so that she may get her answer. During this time, rain started to fall gently from the clouds that patterned the blue sky and sunshine.

Edward (one of the people helping to prepare the Sweat) came running up from the north side of the woods, where he had been gathering more hazel branches.

"That's amazing," he said, "Just as you were talking a rainbow appeared and its end was the spot that you stood on!"

Edward was quite breathless in his excitement. I didn't really know what to say, so I stayed quiet, my eyes widening as I shook my head slightly in wonderment, whilst my body posture projected a sense of "wow" to Edward, who was really buzzing over what he had just seen. Minutes later Andrew came running to me from the west wide of the woods, hazel branches in his arms.

"Do you know a rainbow appeared as you were talking and you were inside the rainbow at its end position – it must be a sign!" he said happily.

So that's what is at the end of the rainbow, I thought – Truth. I decided to stay – I most certainly could not leave now. After the rainbow appeared everyone began to get excited and they all became more focused.

The bender was near to completion. Adrian had been assigned by Andrew to be "keeper of the rocks", which he was a bit disappointed about since it meant he would not join us inside the Sweat. His role would be to make sure the rocks were well heated and pass them safely into the bender as each direction and element was individually honored by us all inside the dome, who were sharing the experience.

Inside the bender it was very dark indeed – so dark that you couldn't see your fellow participants. You could of course see the glowing rocks but total blackness surrounded all those participating. Since the idea of entering and experiencing the Sweat was to free yourself or confront yourself, whichever was necessary, the complete darkness assisted in the process of shifting consciousness. It was important for each individual to share any relevant insights or experiences they had during this sacred time. A person would first ask for permission to speak; this would be addressed to Andrew, the leader of the Sweat. A participant would not say their name, but simply say, "this one would like to speak." Then, when the person got the okay from Andrew, they could then share what they had to say.

Every time I felt a being or energy approach close to me, I would ask to speak and inform the group that I was about to step aside from my body so the energy would step into my physical essence. This always prepared everyone in the Sweat for whatever was going to occur next.

We had already gone through two directions and elements, the north and the Earth, the east and the air. On both occasions the group spoke its thanks to the new rocks that came into the bender with each new direction. The new burning rocks heralded the start of honoring – focusing on the relevant direction.

As we were about to enter into the element of fire and the direction of south, a being appeared close to me, impressing upon me a feeling of urgency. So I informed the group of the presence around me. The being entered my body – it was the spirit of an ancient American Indian, who told us he was known as 'White Flight'. I felt comfortable as I had met with this Spirit twice before.

White Flight was very old and wise. I had enjoyed his wisdom and gentleness on previous occasions. He asked if he may offer some words to the group, who eagerly replied in the affirmative. While listening to White Flight the group could feel his strong energy; an energy that was filled with peace and connection to all living things.

A'ho ma' ta qe' um! (to all my relatives!)

The Native Americans knew they were not separate from anything; they knew they *were* the sky, the trees, the rocks, the animals, the Earth. They honored and acknowledged everything as equal and supportive to them. White Flight spoke.

"When you next acknowledge the rocks that enter into the heart of this vision, [i.e. the Sweat bender] do not acknowledge them as being separate from you. They are *part* of you; they symbolize the strength of the rock within you. There is no separation between yourselves and the rocks, you are equal."

The group silently absorbed those words then thanked White Flight, and off he went.

The next set of rocks entered the bender, representing the south and the element of fire. We all thanked the rocks, and took the space and breath to remember their connection to us. Moments after our thanks were given, I looked at the large hot rocks, and – I know this sounds daft – but it really looked as if they were breathing. They appeared to have softened, like sponges – very gently they breathed, in and out, in and out. I looked and looked, my eyes growing wider as they continued to breathe in and out. I thought that the heat in the Sweat might have been getting to me! I spoke, "This one would like to talk" and got the okay from Andrew.

"I don't know if it's me seeing things," I told the group. "But those rocks look as if they're breathing; shrinking and growing as they breathe."

I half expected everyone to say, yes you are seeing things – it must be the heat. On the contrary, one by one they all began to share their individual amazement of what the rocks were doing. We all could see them breathe, in and out, in and out, expanding and contracting each time – it really was quite fantastic.

White Flight's words had touched everyone and we had all responded to them on a deep level. We all felt the rocks acknowledge the rock strength within us. We responded to them as if they were our own brothers and sisters, the bond was there. Now I don't think for one minute that the rocks *were* actually breathing – what I think occurred was that all our eyesights and brain patterns went through some type of momentary shift so that we could see the life in the rocks. That we could not only feel, but *see* the equality they have to us. No one really wanted to say anything after that. In the silence of the Sweat they wanted to absorb what had just happened.

Encountering the Great White Spirit

I began to think. Native Americans give God (creation, the source) the name Great White Spirit. It is just a name – different cultures use a different name to acknowledge this Great Universal Energy; whatever epithet is complimentary to their culture. So I thought, if when these different beings, essences, spirits, planets, stars, Angels, animals, talk through me, projecting their different personalities and vibrations (which is beautiful and always incredible) then I wondered what would it be like if the voice of the Great White Spirit spoke through me? It would surely be absolutely awesome; so much energy, so full, so strong – I couldn't imagine how powerful it could be. Quietening my thoughts, I concluded that it just wouldn't be possible. Then I felt that another Essence was around me, and informed the group of this. My will again stepped aside so that this Essence could enter. Calmly and precisely the energy began to speak, "I am known as the energy you call Great White Spirit."

The energy bowed, in equality to us all. 'Wow', I thought. And for the life of me I cannot remember what was said; I was too absorbed in observing this energy. I do remember though that Great White Spirit shared with us words and insights and answered questions from the group. I wish I *could* remember what was said! Normally I would have a tape recorder nearby, as I believe it's important to record what has been said by these energies to prevent any misunderstanding or exaggeration of their communications. Unfortunately, it was not possible to record in the Sweat due to the extreme temperatures.

My observations were of confusion, rather than wonder at this most encompassing of energies. This energy, the source of creation, the energy within absolutely everything was certainly pretty powerful, but – although I really didn't want to admit it to myself – it was not as I expected. Great Spirit appeared not nearly as powerful, for want of a better word, as White Flight or the different Angels, Archangels and the many different beings and spirits that have communicated through me. I was a touch confused. However, I knew that it was important to recognize this confusion, so that in my recognition I may gain some clarity, and accept this energy as it existed and not as I had understood it. I intuitively knew that clarity would eventually come; maybe in a few days, weeks, months or years. There was no time limit, but it would come unforced. Actually, it was only a week or so later that my confusion began to lift.

When Angels or Archangels, spirit animals, unborn children and many other universal Energies had spoken through me, they projected their full Essence.[2] Their whole energy was at that moment complete and within my physical body. However, the voice of Great White Spirit was only an aspect of the great and powerful energy of creation. It was the aspect of creation within me, a tiny, tiny aspect of God, creation, or whatever one wishes to call this

---

[2] When I lend my body over to a light being or Archangel, it is their *whole* essence at that moment which enters my body. Whereas when I communicate with someone's Angel, it is the major Angelic part of that person which enters my body (as a fragment of the Angel is already residing within that person on Earth).

glorious energy. This minuscule aspect of creation, the spark that gave me life, was now talking through me; it was not the whole energy, just a fragment. Now I could see and feel clearly; creation, God, White Spirit is in absolutely everything, no end, no beginning. It is there in us, as it is there in the rocks – we are one and the same. Understanding and accepting this helped me to appreciate the roles that these many different energies (essences of creation) play as envoys, messengers, job-doers, whatever. It showed me how we all have a part to play in supporting this wonderful universal energy which so many call God.

In the body we have our organs and the body can function productively. And God, creation, has the many different beings that I have written about, and of course a whole lot more. But, just as the physical body can become restricted by our thought forms, bad diet, stress etc, so can creation. If we do fail to realize that we are part of creation, if we do not accept our uniqueness and spark, if we carry on being egotistical, aiming to control and dictate in any way or form – we then become 'toxic' to Creation. Our individual Angels cannot help us, they cannot exist at their full potential if we feed our thoughts and body with impurities.

3

The Astral Realms

Is there life after death? Where did we come from?
Is there a heaven – is there a hell? These fundamental
questions have perplexed mankind since the dawn
of civilization. The answers to them all lie within
the Astral Realms, as I was to find out in the next
phase of my journey of discovery. In this chapter I
shall recount the experiences of my first two "guided
tours" through these non-earthly dimensions,
and share with you the insights gained about the
place that so many people think of as heaven.

What are the Astral Realms?

My interest in these dimensions began after being invited to speak to a local and very open-minded spiritual group about the Astral Realms. Although I agreed to do the talk, at the time I actually had very little experience or understanding of this part of the universe. I had previously communicated with Guides (spirit helpers) who co-exist with disincarnate spirits within the Astral Realms, but I had never been able to experience the environment within which they resided.

To be honest, at that time I still held certain reluctance towards the idea of becoming more intimate with the Astral Realms. These realms are commonly thought of a heaven; the place we go to after we die – a place where we will have peace and security. Many people here on Earth hold rigid belief systems about this place, heaven, professing to know and understand a great deal about it and the treats in store for them there. Indeed, for many people tightly bound within a rigid religious belief system, their view of heaven is a central focus of their life – yet if their life on this planet is totally devoted to that next stage in their existence, the true essence of life itself is lost. I have met and observed people living their lives according to what they had read or what their belief system had taught them about those heavenly realms, but as a result seemed disconnected from the beauty and life that our current existence has to offer them. There is a certain hopelessness projected by such a viewpoint towards life on earth!

I observed people being spiritual; following their chosen belief system (convinced of course that it was the right one!) and by so doing, assuming that their place in heaven was assured. I witnessed people being good on the basis that goodness took you to heaven; people trying to change the lives of seemingly misdirected others, and thus earning their place in the better afterlife. Something so intangible as this idea of the heavenly afterlife seems to hold great power over the minds of many.[1]

So all in all, I was skeptical about whether these heaven-like astral realms even existed at all – and if they did, I was pretty sure they wouldn't be anything like the heaven so many people believed them

---

[1] I say *minds*, as I have never encountered anyone truly speaking from their *heart* when they offer reasoning for their belief systems and their thoughts as to what happens when our physical body dies. Yet when people operate from their heart there is openness to the cycle of life and death, there is trust in Creation and there is no longer the need to create a false sense of security within themselves. An inner knowing that unconditional love unites us all and there is no need to make judgments regarding other people.

to be! But as I had accepted the invitation to talk about the Astral Realms, I decided that I had better let go of any final reluctance that I may still have towards those realms, and with angelic assistance take a journey of my own through the Astral dimensions to see if they really did exist, and what they contained.

The first journey

Sunday morning, mid April. The energy of new life, new beginnings filled the air, a sprinkling of clouds created softness in an otherwise clear blue sky. Whilst absorbing the sparkling energy this new day had to offer, I wondered what would be discovered on my journey into the Astral Realms. I made myself comfortable, surrounding myself with my favorite cushions. Breathing in the scent of the incense stick I had lit earlier, appreciating its delicate perfume, my gaze drifted slowly to two candles flickering gently. Then I closed my eyes and began completely surrendering myself to Divine Will.

With angelic assistance I was taken telepathically through a relaxation process, letting myself go, easing myself from this world. Being a natural skeptic, I was certainly not expecting to see fluffy clouds or cherubs when entering the Astral Realms, as are often depicted by Renaissance painters. Yet as my release from this world was completed and my awareness of the Astral Realms came into focus, I was amazed to see clouds everywhere – large soft clouds.[2] Then I was introduced to an energy who I shall refer to as Pierre; an immensely light and ancient being who was to be my guide in

---

[2] I still don't really understand why the clouds were there. For sure, the scenes I witnessed during my two tours of the Astral Realms were clearly created very much for my benefit and understanding, and thus were often very metaphorical in the way they were presented to me. However, everything else I saw seemed to make perfect sense. Whereas to this day I cannot fathom why the clouds were there, or what they were meant to signify!

assisting my consciousness to explore and experience the Astral levels. Pierre came from a dimension within our universe where he and many other energies are responsible (and continue to remain responsible) for the creation of mankind.

He asked me to watch, as the clouds parted and a passageway was created. Slowly a male figure appeared, dressed in long white robes with shoulder length hair and a beard of about a year in length. He walked towards me. "You know this person well from many lifetimes past, and he knows you well," explained Pierre.

I have to confess that actually I didn't recognize the figure at all, though I did feel completely safe with him. He didn't appear to be aware of my non-recognition of him, and held his hand out to take mine. As my hand fell into his, great warmth rushed through me; immediately I recognized this person with a feeling so strong in my heart, although my logic still held no recognition of him at all. As our hands touched, instantaneously I found myself in what appeared to be a huge library, containing numerous bookshelves about forty feet high, and stretching away into the distance.

The library was vast and very spacious; light and airy, its size was exaggerated because it had no roof. There appeared to be no beginning or entrance, nor ending or exit. Within the library I was aware of three or four spirits close by, busily choosing books from the shelves. My helper pulled out a book that had a peachy-moleskin type covering to it. On the front of the book was a spoke-wheel shaped diagram that contained lots of compartments and segments, similar to an astrological chart only far more complex. Pierre explained that this book held information that was relevant to a future life I was to have on Earth. The information did not concern the next life, but the life after that. My helper opened the book a third of the way through and explained (using some kind of telepathic communication) that I was allowed to read those pages from the book. This I did, but the information somehow bypassed my conscious mind and went deep into my subconscious. So I haven't a clue as to what it was all about!

(The information had entered directly into my spirit memory, which is separate and distinct from our mental memory). Neither then nor now have I ever been able to recall this information. It is enough for me to know that the information remains within my being and I will become aware of its contents when the time is right. The book was placed back into position.

Moses' acknowledgement

My enthusiasm and wonder began to wane slightly, but then I suddenly found myself traveling into a surreal landscape with gentle hills, vibrant trees, and intense green grass filled with small wild flowers. My helper was not with me now, though I remained aware of Pierre's continued guidance. In the centre of this magnificent landscape was a large rock, covered in soft plump moss, which looked damp but was actually very lush indeed. I decided to take advantage of this well-cushioned "seat", to relax in comfort and gaze at the beautiful dusk-like sky. I marveled at the different shades and intensities of pinks and mauves, each color containing its own vibration, its own sound, which appeared capable of blending harmoniously together and yet at the same time managing to retain its own uniqueness. As I breathed and gently exhaled I could sense the absolute peace and vitality surrounding me.

A spirit person then approached me, wearing a neutral brownish long gown and carrying a rod that was slightly higher than his tall frame. This time I instantly knew who I was encountering – it was Moses. He appeared alive and well but seemed out of place in this lush landscape, since there did not appear to be any connection between him and the terrain – although I was so astonished at his arrival that it would have seemed pretty strange in any environment!

However, as I then found out, it was all for a reason. A few months previously I'd had one of my time-travel experiences, in which I had been inspired to experience Moses' life as he truly lived it (see chapter

7). During this experience I had become aware that his Spirit and light had grown very weak; almost no life appeared left in him. The truth about Moses' life had been obscured due to some aspects of his life being greatly exaggerated and hugely dramatized, and because of all this rubbish that has been spoken and written about him; his true light was beginning to diminish. Our light – our inner core – grows and is nurtured by truth, and this growth (or lack of) continues after we pass on. Untruths grow in layers upon layers through generation after generation. If you place a glass over a candle's flame it will suffocate; there is no air and so it dies. In similar fashion, if many untruths are spoken and believed over and over again, the light that is created from truth begins to suffocate. Layers of untruths about a person and his life become placed over the person's true light. The spiritual essence of that person becomes isolated and unheard and their true existence is increasingly smothered by the weight of these untruths, until we can no longer see the person's true light, and this is what was happening to Moses' Spirit.

Moses had come to be with me now in order to acknowledge the part I had played in my time-traveling journey to release the truth of his life; for the power of this truth enabled his light to grow and for Moses once again to walk and glow in abundance. He sat down beside me and we communicated as friends, though I felt more restrained in speaking than he due to my utter surprise at meeting with him! He explained that he had arranged this meeting while I was traveling in the Astral Realms, so our spirits and consciousness could connect equally, without any interference and presupposition being made by mankind.

Bathing in the freedom and joy

Moses departed with as much ease as he had arrived – one moment there and sharing his thoughts, and the next moment gone! My mind was now as empty as the space on the moss-covered rock that had been occupied by Moses. I was then asked: "Would you like to hold something?"

It seemed an odd question and quite out of context to my surroundings, but I still found myself saying yes, as I warmly thought of holding a tiny baby. Immediately I found myself in what appeared to be a hospital ward, only there was no hospital, just a bright white airy peaceful ward. This peaceful, calm and reassuring place was filled with a great sense of joy. There were lots and lots of newly born babies sleeping peacefully in their tiny cots, cared for by nurses dressed in traditional European nurses" uniform. The nurses shimmered in white as they moved around the ward, checking and caring for all these newborn babes. These babies I intuitively understood to have been miscarried or stillborn on Earth.[3] It was so rewarding to experience the absolute love and care they received from those nurses. A baby, swaddled and cozy in its blankets, was placed in my arms – a feeling of love and joy filled my being.

As I discovered during this journey, the feeling of peace and joy found in these wards was echoed throughout the rest of the Astral Realms. It was within the very air that swept through the Astral planes. They were, for the most part, a beautiful and comforting place to be.

---

[3] It seems that babies who miscarry or are stillborn are all part of the universe's grand plan – they were never actually meant to experience life on this planet. Putting it symbolically, the fetus was there simply as a vehicle for carrying the spirit from A to C, but not ever stopping off at B (being the Earth). However, this is not the case for aborted babies. Abortions are not the universe's way of doing things, even if it may seem the right thing to do for the child. So what happens to the spirit of babies that are aborted? They were meant to experience life in a family structure, so they will usually get assigned to an earthly family. They aren't visible to the adults, but the youngsters in the family will pick up on their presence, and they will become those invisible friends that many children have. However, the family will not necessarily be in any way related to the spirit of the aborted baby – it will simply be the right family to meet the child's requirements, according to universal flow.

How spirits connect with mediums

In the next scene (each scene occurring spontaneously, but with perfect timing), I found myself in a warm summer's day in the country, fresh green open landscape, with gently sloping hillsides and a scattering of wild flowers. Suddenly I was surrounded by young children happily playing games with each other, without a care in the world. These children hadn't known each other on the Earth plane, but had formed their friendships whilst in the Astral Realms. They seemed comfortable and free to be themselves, in the company of children of similar ages. There was a feeling of absolute freedom around these young free spirits. In the distance I saw a lady dressed in white walking towards me, although she did not appear to be aware of my presence. As she walked closer towards the children I saw darkness and blackness around her right breast and the top half of her right arm. I knew I was being shown this to be aware of how she had died (although I was not told directly, I understood that she had died from breast cancer). My guide Pierre informed me that the lady was drawing close to the Earth in order to be near to her son. A service was soon to start on the Earth, where a "Medium" would connect and communicate with spirits that have passed into the Astral Realms, and relay messages to those on the Earth. These messages were of "proof" to bereaved family and friends that the spirit and personality of their dear loved ones continues to live, even though the physical body is dead and lifeless. The spirit simply vacates its physical vehicle and rests and reflects on the life they had and, in general, replenishes itself whilst in the Astral Realms.

"Would you like to observe from this side [the Astral Realms] how spirits are able – through using a Medium – to make their presence felt?" asked Pierre.

Yes, I thought this was a very good idea, an opportunity not to be missed! I immediately became excited and curious – what was I going to witness?

My "consciousness" was then escorted to what I can only describe as the boundary, or interface between the Astral planes and physical world[4]. As I drew closer to the physical world I observed many spirits doing likewise, attracted by the energy (almost an electrical pulsation) being sent out into the ether by the Medium. I became aware of the environment on the earth plane where this Medium was located; it was something like a hall or church, with a central aisle and seated rows of people – families and friends who were gathering for this service.

As the spirits moved closer to the hall and the Medium (who was on the stage area) they began to become more dense and solid in appearance. It was almost a chameleon effect; the spirits changed in appearance to match their new earthly environment and took on a more solid and condensed form. Whereas the spirit's appearance in the Astral Realms had been similar to white gossamer (not unlike the traditional "ghostly" image), the Earth plane's vibration seemed to cause this condensing of the spirit form.

The main sensation most of the spirits at this point were experiencing was a sense of celebration, as if they were going to a big party. This made me realize as to why, when giving messages of proof, spirits will often recall memorable dates such as birthdays and anniversaries. These were happy memories and good reasons to celebrate. The spirits definitely seemed most comfortable with this sensation and were attracted to such a frequency.

Having been to a few earthly meetings of a spiritualist nature, where the Mediums connect with the "dearly departed" (a term so often used to describe spirits in the Astral Realms) I must digress to share an observation.

I have observed the lightness of heart, of optimism and excitement

---

[4] I refer to my consciousness, since my physical body remained on Earth, acting as an anchor to help my return to this earthly reality, throughout the entire Astral journey.

that many people bring with them to these meetings, which are all great and positive emotions that the spirits sense, enjoy and feel strengthened by. However, particularly in Spiritualist churches, hymns are sung, and they're often awful! The hymns are so dreary that the lightness of heart experienced before the service is often destroyed and replaced by a sense of uncertainty. The church organ is often out of tune and only a few present allow themselves to sing freely. Most of the hymns are not familiar to the people and so only a few feel they want to stand out with their singing in case they miss a note and make a fool of themselves.

These oppressive hymns create a restricting, unloving and dare I say almost cold and an unwelcoming atmosphere, at a time when many are attending the meeting in the hope of receiving a message. Sadly, those attending are usually unwilling to challenge the rules and governing committees of such churches by requesting the hymns change to something uplifting, something one would enjoy singing. It could be anything – even "Happy Birthday" would be better than the mundane, archaic songs in the hymn books! I wonder if people actually take note of the words they are trying to sing? I bet that most of the congregation look up at the board displaying the hymn numbers due to be sung at the service and either hope it is something they know or if not, that the hymn is short.

The reason I feel strongly about this is because I witnessed those spirits arriving at the "church" meeting, bringing with them their earthly memories of celebration and feeling excited about those memories – and yet when they have entered the Earth's vibration, it's often not quite as they seemed to remember. It is not surprising that spirits talk much about the beauty within the Astral planes, if when they draw close to an Earthly service – instead of them entering an atmosphere of celebration, joy and happiness – they are met with people appearing as cold and as flat as a week-old pancake!

Anyway, quite a crowd of spirits were gathering, having sensed this seemingly electrical current coming from the Medium – they seemed to home in on this frequency. It was through this current that they seemed able to make their connection. Most did not appear to acknowledge the Medium as a person; it was purely the current that attracted them to him (I say him, as the Medium at this service was male).

The spirits were initially drawn by the sense of celebration and excitement, and this atmosphere of celebration would grow as different individuals made their decisions to attend the planned meeting. As an individual on the Earth plane began focusing on this service, a spirit connected to that particular person would begin to feel their loved one's focus. Hence, through the sense of celebration and expectancy, a reuniting of spirit to their earthly family / friend would occur. It was only as they drew nearer to the focus or intent sent out by their loved ones, that they began to feel this electrical current from the Medium. To the spirits, the Medium was simply like a telephone. How many of us acknowledge a telephone? I certainly don't; I simply pick it up and make a call – and that's what the spirits do also. The impersonal nature of the relationship between the spirit and the Medium is because no emotional bond existed between them – a connection of love did not exist.

As the Medium begun to tune in to the spirit world I noticed his aura growing rapidly.[5] As I was observing this, a large burly male spirit appeared to forcefully push himself in front of the other spirits and very firmly gave the Medium a kick up the backside. The Medium jumped forward in response to the burly spirit's forceful message and then described to the attentive audience what had

---

[5] This observation revealed that it is neither necessary nor wise to place one's focus into any particular energy centre (or *chakra*, as the East refers to them) in order to communicate with the Astral Realms. All one needed to do was to take one's awareness away from themselves. The Medium has simply to step away from their ego and allow their trust in Divine Will to flow through them – it's as simple as that.

just happened. The Medium's attention was directed to someone in the audience who it seemed needed shaking up to get on and do whatever they were hesitant about doing. This was apparently one way the spirits ensured getting their message across to the Medium – albeit somewhat painfully!

Whilst noting that this message had created a renewed excitement and energy from the audience, my attention was then drawn to the lady spirit who I had previously noticed whilst with the children playing in the Astral Realms (the one who had died from breast cancer). She had been drawn to this meeting, but appeared unaware of the Medium and the other gathering Spirits. Her form was as it had been when I witnessed her earlier – still wearing only a long white gown, unlike the other spirits whose images had become stronger, more solid and were now in earthly garments. Her awareness focused on a young boy of nine or ten years of age, who sat next to a lady in the audience. I wasn't certain of her relationship to the boy; I simply knew that they were together. The Spirit lady moved towards the boy who, behind his fashionable streetwise appearance, seemed lost in his pain and sadness. As the lady placed her arms around the lad, I became aware that he was her son and all the love in her heart poured into him – she bathed him in her light and held him gently to her. Watching this wonderful act of love, I could sense there was no pain caused in the lady by being physically parted from her son. Her feeling was a sense of freedom; free from everything she had found restricting during her life on Earth. Whether that was body or time restrictions, the need to fulfill a day's work, accomplish goals in life, deal with all the stresses she or others put her through (all of these so often stifling the flow of pure unconditional love) – she was now free from all this. So great was her love for her son that in her mind she was not separated from him; she was in fact now more close to him than she had ever felt whilst on the Earth.

It was truly an honor to witness this reuniting of love, and it helped me to understand how love can grow stronger when we pass over; so much so that it would be difficult to contain such a feeling whilst in the earthly body!

The young boy's sadness lifted, although I could see that in his mind there was still a sense of disappointment that he had not received a message from his mum via the Medium. If the boy had *not* traveled to the meeting with the expectation of receiving a specific message from his mother (which admittedly would be a tough thing to do, since this is the fundamental point of these meetings!), but had instead simply entered the hall with absolute openness to whatever may happen, then his spirit would have truly experienced the outpouring of love from his mother. In the boy's mind there would have been no doubt that his mother's spirit still existed and they could still reach each other.

Once again, it seems that the mind can over-ride the openness of the spirit. But when a person totally steps beyond any expectations of what may be or not be, the spirit can rise like a Phoenix and completely overcome the restrictions of the mind. The outcome is freedom of knowing in the spirit, whilst the mind becomes balanced and humble in the path of truth.

The young boy's disappointment saddened me slightly because I knew the outpouring of immense love from his mother was far greater and more powerful than any message of words received and communicated by the Medium could ever have been. Too many people trust words, which are of course very limiting, rather than the feelings of love, which are infinite. Why do we wish for our trust to be confirmed? Perhaps because we're scared of being wrong. Yet it is the fear of being wrong which restricts our feelings, sensitivity and receptivity.

The Lower Astral Realms

As my awareness drew back to the edge of the Astral world, I was asked, "Would I like to observe the Lower Astral Realms?"

A small part of me had wondered if these realms – where evil and all that is negative and disharmonious allegedly resides – actually existed. Now I was to receive my answer. My guide Pierre directed me to a place of height, from which we could both look down and observe the Lower Realms. Gazing down from this lofty viewpoint reminded me of the scene in the film *Jason and the Argonauts*, where the Greek God Zeus and the Goddess Hera were looking down from the heavens watching what went on, and at times guiding Jason on his travels to find the *Golden Fleece*, which held the secret to eternal life. It was quite a surreal experience for me to have this feeling of "looking down", like those ancient gods and goddesses of Greece.

As I looked down, observing closely with both my heart and vision, pain – deep soul pain – from the tortured spirits I was about to observe engulfed me. So many spirits living in darkness, limbs tangled amongst each other, terrible heart-wrenching sights – this was restriction at its greatest; no place to move, no place to escape, no freedom. Suffering more than is imaginable; cries of anguish, cries of desperation. My heart bled for these souls, tears ran down my cheeks. So great was their pain – there was no evil here; there was no room for it. It was just pain, pain, and more pain. Getting a grip on my senses, I asked Pierre if anything could be done to help them?

In answer I was shown Angels walking in these realms, but the suffering spirits were not aware of them. This could not occur until they had "burned themselves out"; until the judgment and restrictions they had placed on themselves could tie them no longer to this place. Only then would they become aware of an Angel and be escorted, by the Angelic presence, into peace and light.

After my observations of the Lower Astral realms, freshness and understanding crept through my veins. Although I wanted those pained spirits to be free from their suffering, I understood the flow that existed in those lower realms and in us, and I saw that divine beings walked amongst them, ready to assist. By observing this, I could see that no one was ever "lost" – the help is always there for us if only we can accept it. Even in the darkest of times, much hope truly exists for all of humanity.

How spirits create their own reality

Very gently I was taken from my observation post, and I found myself back in the peaceful realms once more. A corridor appeared in the clouds, and on either side of this passageway were many doors. It was telepathically explained to me that I could enter through any door I chose. I decided that I might as well go through the first door, seeing as it was nearest!

On opening the door I found myself in the living room of my Grandma's flat in Plzen in Czechoslovakia. My Grandma, who I used to call Babi (Czech for Grandma), was in her small kitchen. Her sleeves were rolled up to her elbows and she was busy baking small cakes. As I entered my Baby's living room I wondered why the light was considerably dimmer than in the other parts of the Astral Realms I had visited. (Everywhere else I had seen had been bathed in light, apart from the lower realms where the only light came from the divine beings that walked amongst the pained spirits.) Realization slowly came to me. Sitting at the dining table was my grandfather, who had died thirty years before my Babi finally departed this earth, some ten years prior to this experience I was currently undergoing. I looked at him, and knew his spiritual essence wasn't really there. This was all very confusing! I walked over to my Babi, who was still busying herself with her cake making. She looked up and seemed very pleased to see me. However, her first action was to take hold of my left hand and begin to gently smack it two or three times. I wondered what I had done to upset her. But then (without words), she told me not to leave it so long visiting her next time. Looking at her with even more confusion, I said in my mind to her "Babi, what are you doing?"

My Babi wasn't aware of my confusion or thoughts – she seemed very happy. What Babi had done, I realized, was create her own comfortable reality in the Astral Realms. The little flat in Plzen had been her home for quite a number of years whilst she was alive. I had only been able to visit Babi there twice, and on each occasion I was greeted with much love, and numerous cakes and coffee (two of the most enjoyed things in Czechoslovakia).

Babi had recreated her flat almost exactly within the Astral Realms. Her kitchen was identical to the one in Plzen. The window in front of the kitchen table was half open, and she had just taken some small cakes from the oven and placed them on a rack on the table, the fresh air from the window helping to cool them. She seemed to be having a lot of fun. My guess was that Babi was expecting visitors, because Czech ladies make an awful lot of cakes and everyone who visits a Czech home is always offered a sumptuous array of homemade baking! To make her environment as comfortable as possible, Babi had recreated my grandfather's image and "installed" him sitting reading a paper at the table in the living area. But my awareness told me that he was not really there – I was viewing the scene objectively and thus my perception was almost like X-ray vision. My grandfather wasn't moving and his form appeared much darker than Babi who was light, bright and full of happiness and fun. My grandfather on the other hand, appeared almost like a cardboard cutout.

Babi had created her own reality. She didn't appear to be aware of her actions, because she was so enveloped by her own absolute contentment and happiness. Babi and I hugged, and as I departed I was aware that Babi, as she carried on busying herself with cake making, seemed unconcerned as to when I would visit again.

Although a Spirit has the ability to create their own reality, this doesn't mean they have not accepted that their physical body has died and they have passed over into another realm. What seems to happen is they have a surge of remembrance back to times in their life where they were most happy. This joyful remembrance then becomes a reality for them; their memory becomes alive around them and they gain energy and strength from these memories. When they are fulfilled from that memory, and their spirit is overflowing with joy, they are then ready to expand automatically and begin to understand more of existence and the part they play in Creation and the Universes.

At this point of expansion provided by these life memories, they are then ready to learn or assist others unconditionally and for the highest good. They will automatically find themselves in Halls of Learning or becoming assistants to others in the Astral Realms, and on some occasions assisting us here in the physical world. If or when they become somewhat weakened in spirit they will rest or recreate another memory. Like Babi, these spirits are not aware that they are experiencing a "re-creation"; for it is indeed a very real situation they find themselves in.

*   *   *

Babi's flat then faded from my awareness, and I found myself in another place, where I became aware of a dog and a rabbit wandering past me. I then saw a figure accompanied by a donkey coming towards me. It was a gentleman in his sixties, who I recognized as my other grandfather – from my mother's side of the family. I had never met him whilst he was on the Earth but I had seen photos of him when he was young, although there was no similarity between those photographs and his image now, which appeared much older. It must have been by sheer instinct that I knew who he was. With great enthusiasm and pleasure he threw his arms around me, clearly very excited to see me. This left me feeling slightly puzzled since we had never met on the Earth, yet his actions were as if he had known me all his life!

My grandfather had lived in Czechoslovakia with my grandmother (my mother's parents) and his immediate family. Unfortunately, because of the communist regime that Czechoslovakia was under, my father (a refugee) and I, who were both living in England, were never able to meet or even have contact with them (my mother having died in England when I was six months old). As I grew in life and matured into adulthood, I realized how much pain this separation from their family must have caused them.

Since I really did not know him, I was taken aback by my grandfather's joy and enthusiasm of meeting with me in the Astral planes. However, he seemed unaffected by my lack of response to his enthusiastic greeting – he did not appear to acknowledge that we had no prior physical contact and continued communicating with me as if we were great friends. I enjoyed my grandfather's vibrant personality and energy immensely. My heart warmed to him, triggered by his unconditional joyous behavior. My grandfather explained to me that he had brought me the donkey.

"When things get too much, and you begin to tire, just sit on this donkey and it will carry you." he said.

I looked at the little donkey and thought to myself "there's no way I can sit upon its back, I'm too heavy!" Although donkeys are meant to be strong creatures, their feeble looks don't necessarily fill you with confidence!

Nevertheless, my grandfather was clearly happy that he could be of help to me, and seemed unaware of my concerns for the donkey's health. I thanked him telepathically, and enquired as to what he was up to in the Astral Realms. He told me he was studying ecological architecture, which was to be his occupation in his next life – he explained that he would design and construct ecologically friendly business and commercial buildings. He was aware, yet unconcerned, that there would be only a limited income involved from this line of work and that he would experience a reluctance from big businesses to accept his ideas. But, he knew there was a great need on the Earth for this work, which was what inspired him to learn about it.

It was time for me to leave the Astral Realms. As I observed my grandfather gradually diminish into the distant ethereal horizon, my spirit body began to return gently back to my physical body. I began to feel more solid, more alive, as I slowly returned to my physical body. Taking in one or two deep breaths, I opened my eyes. My garden was the first scene I saw, just as it had been the last I had seen before my journey started. It was still bathed in spring sunshine, but now seemed to possess more vibrancy and solidity – a different world to what had previously been there only an hour ago. It appeared to be more magical; a reminder as to what a gift it is to be here in such a physical/solid dimension. It was a wonderful feeling yet very difficult to describe. My experience within the Astral planes made me realize that I hadn't fully appreciated the beauty the Earth offers.

As I began to recount my journey into the astral worlds to my husband Adrian, a feeling of emptiness enveloped me. I could not get over the immense joy and peace that emanated throughout the Astral Realms. As beautiful and as wondrous as the Earth is, she has different qualities to offer us. Now, through my inter-dimensional experiences, I had become acutely sensitive to the different feelings and sensations that are unique to each dimension – the Earth is solid, colorful and alive, in contrast to the peace, joy and flow of energy in the Astral worlds that I had recently visited.

The second journey

Entering a finely tuned dimension

A few weeks later I had another journey into the Astral Realms. As grey clouds crowded out the blue sky and rain beckoned here on Earth, I sat quietly in my back room, responding to the intense build-up of etheric energy passing through me, ready to travel once again into the Astral Realms. Initially I sense this gradual build up of energy as a subtle inspiration, which expands and grows within and around me until I reach a point of needing to respond. It is this energy that enables me to go on my journeys, to enter into and travel to many different dimensions within the universes.

Stilling my mind and thoughts, I waited until the sensation in my blood and bones confirmed that I was connected to Divine Will. My consciousness was then allowed to enter the Astral Realms. However, this time I was not aware of a higher energy there to assist me.[6] Instead I found myself hurtling past the different levels and dimensions to a place that seemed very hallowed and lofty. It was as if I had traveled through what I can only describe as a porthole, which allowed my energy to travel to an area high above the Astral Realms. I felt as near to the centre of Creation as one could possibly perceive.

*   *   *

Entering this uppermost area, I became aware of light beings; different from Angels insofar that Angels are more compressed in their energy. Whereas these light beings held within their energy the highest sense of knowing that I have ever come across within Creation. They resonated on a pure frequency, whereas the Angels" frequencies are closer to our own.

Whilst I observed the Astral realms in fullness from this position of great height, these beings explained to me that energy must always be kept flowing in the Astral Realms. If a block in the flow of energy within these realms were to arise, an angelic presence that helps and

---

[6] "Higher" being an expression of their oneness with the god force, the clarity and wisdom they hold and not to be understood as physically higher level within Creation, or any other view of better than or greater than mankind. These energies have no ego and all is created in perfection and are as one in the universe.

assists spirits in the astral realms would receive instructions (in the form of inspiration) from these "higher" sources as to how to prevent the block from occurring. The Astral Realms, the spirits and angelic essences within them, do not contain matter – they are energy, and because of this everything has to be kept moving and flowing.

It was explained that disruption in the flow of energy within the Astral planes was the consequence of one or more spirits becoming restricted, stubborn and unresponsive in disposition. Just because we leave our physical body behind when we die doesn't necessarily mean that we leave behind those personal traits, beliefs and differences of opinion that make us who we were in that particular lifetime! These traits and differences are contained within our spirit body, and thus get carried over with us into the Astral dimensions. We are still the same as we were on Earth. One may have within the Astral planes a greater picture of the events that molded our lives and perhaps a greater understanding – but that is all.

Observing the activities of these "higher" beings reminded me of a scene from a Second World War film showing the Air Force headquarters during the Battle of Britain, and the coordinating of the entire air battle over the country. Positioned on a giant table in the middle of the room was a map of the UK, with model R.A.F and German aircraft placed strategically upon it. Senior military officers looked down upon this map and used the information received from coastal observers of incoming German planes, to decide where they should send their fighter squadrons in order to intercept the German aircraft. As the senior officers made their attack decisions, the model planes were moved accordingly on the map and instructions sent to the British fighter pilots.

The "higher" beings appeared to be working like those senior military officers, using their combined wisdom and knowledge in order to sense where blocks were beginning to occur within the Astral Realms, and then inspiring direction and flow to the Angelic beings below. These Angels could then travel to the area of stagnation that required clearing, and sort things out so that the energy could continue to flow.

A dimension of absolute purity

My body took a deep breath and I found myself moved to another part of the Universe, a locality that was not connected to the Astral Realms. It was explained to me that this was a "sterile unit"; an area that was kept almost isolated. It appeared like a huge brilliant white bubble of light. You were only able to enter this area if you were free of any attitudes, rigid belief systems etc., which still required "breaking down" and learning from. This was a very pure area indeed.

As I entered into this dimension I immediately felt an overwhelming sense of peace and serenity; for this was the place to which people who had died traumatic and untimely deaths were taken. These were people who had died from malicious attacks, from earthquakes, hurricanes, floods, other natural disasters, and people who were so traumatized that they had taken their own lives. This was a place of absolute comfort and healing, where each spirit had a one-to-one relationship with a superior energy to assist their recovery. These energies came from many different parts of creation, and were not merely the energies we on Earth have come to know as Angels. They were enlightened beings that had actually assisted in the original creation of the physical body. They had much knowledge and were able to help correct the pain in the spirit, which remained in shock since leaving its physical incarnation.

Other energies present to assist in these realms were pure sparks of remembrance of a spirit's origins. These energies appeared especially to those spirits who had taken their own lives. It appeared that the spirits who had committed suicide felt so lost that they truly didn't want to exist any more, and so these "sparks", these energies of remembrance, were able to reawaken the spirit to its perfection, its true essence, and thus help reconnect the spirit's soul to creation.

The power of love and homecoming in this isolated unit was immense; it was truly a wondrous place. The traumatized spirits were receiving so much care and encouragement. I observed that as one spirit recovered they were able to assist other weak spirits in their recovery – this gave the assisting spirits a sense of purpose. When they were ready and the spirit had fully recovered from its trauma, they were able to leave and visit the Astral Realms in order to reflect and learn from their previous life experiences.

Debating rooms in the spirit world

I breathed in deeply again, and found myself traveling away from this wonderful sterile bubble. I was now back within the Astral Realms, and once again at the passageway formed from clouds with numerous doors running down either side of it. As with my last visit, I was told telepathically that I could choose to enter through any door. "Mmmm," I thought. "I'll go through this one," opting for the third door on my left.

I opened the door and found myself in a room about twelve feet wide by fifteen feet long. There were two more doors in the room, one in the middle of the wall on my right, and the other directly opposite me.

The light in the room appeared to be dull, when compared to the rest of the Astral light dimensions. It was similar in level to that inside the flat that Babi had recreated. However, I was made aware that this room was unlike Babi's flat since it was *not* a recreation of someone's earthly memory, which at the time baffled me! In the centre of the room was a large oak rectangular table, with seven chairs randomly placed around it. There were four spirits in the room; three spirits were male and clear in appearance, whilst the fourth one seemed a somewhat vague, indistinct image. One of the three spirits stood to the right of the table, and was attempting to convince another spirit that his viewpoint and strong opinions were correct. Meanwhile, the other spirit listened contemptuously as the details of this spirit's particular viewpoint were explained to him. The third spirit was simply observing.

I realized that this was a debating room, specifically designed for the purpose of formal discussion of beliefs and opinions of an earthly nature. The spirit who was leading the debate had in front of him a small book laid open on the table, which appeared to be a Bible. As he expressed his views he suddenly became very angry, violently bashing his hand on to the table in frustration. His opinions were clearly not being accepted by the other spirit, who continually dismissed his beliefs whilst slouched on a chair on the other side of the table. Eventually the argumentative spirit became so angry and frustrated that he walked out of the room through the door to my right. Immediately, he found himself in the corridor of bright light, a welcome contrast to the dimness of the debating room. He was met by an Angelic being, who tried to encourage him to go back and carry on with his debating. It seemed in order for this spirit to learn he needed to experience continuous frustration caused by others not listening to his beliefs. When he eventually became completely worn down by his frustration of others not accepting his opinions, he would then finally realize that he did not *need* the acceptance of others.

It was explained to me from higher sources that during his life on Earth this spirit had been, for most part, uncertain of his direction in life. This caused him to look to impose his views on others, and by others agreeing with his every word he gained a false sense of security from their passiveness. Although appearing to be self-assured, he was in truth uncertain and unstable in himself as to what he believed to be true, and as a result he needed that confirmation from others.

What he hadn't realized was that truth has many facets and many forms. But what truth *doesn't* have is control, or a need to control, or a need to be part of a religion or organization. Truth is freedom and freedom is truth – truth holds no boundaries.

The Angelic being was unable to encourage the spirit back into the debating room. The dogmatic spirit was very stubborn indeed! Now, as has already been explained, continuous flow within these Astral Realms must always occur, so he was immediately transferred to somewhere else in these realms that was more comfortable for him – a different (yet comparable) environment which would assist the spirit to further resolve his many internal struggles.

Curiosity took me back into the debating room, and the door directly in front of me there. I asked, "What's through that door?" The door opened and I walked through to enter a beautiful bright conservatory, where many unusual lush plants were bathed in wonderful light. Two spirits, apparently oblivious to my presence, were relaxing – soaking in the calming atmosphere.

"Why are they here?" I asked.

"Because they know the answer," came back the reply.

"The answer to what?"

"The answer to their debates."

"What's that?" I asked, feeling quite ignorant.

"That there is no right or wrong – this is what they have understood. Debates come from a need for an individual to understand a situation and project their 'rightness' onto others. Discussions on the other hand, come from a readiness to expand one's understanding of others' lives and existences."

The formation of life before birth

Understanding this answer, my body took another deep breath that moved me to the next location. This was a place of great stillness. As I looked in to this place I was startled to see a fetus of around three to four months in development. It was in the womb and surrounded by the amniotic fluid. Flabbergasted by this unexpected sight I asked; "What's with the fetus?" My amazement then became greater still, as suddenly the fetus appeared to be in possession of a violin! But this explained what I was seeing. The child was destined to be a violinist, and for this to happen the fetus's growth had to adapt to be able to play the violin, the cells beginning to assume an ability to play it, the fingers forming around the instrument. I realized that when fully formed and born into earthly life the child would have a great desire and need to play this classical instrument. They would instinctively be at ease with the violin, because its influence had surrounded their cells during their forming as a fetus.

Another fetus then appeared, this one busy tapping away at a computer keyboard, its fingers very quick and nimble. So, this child would be interested in computers and may pursue this ability, being formed at its fetal stage, into a career.

Yet another fetus appeared – this one, even though only four months developed, had a huge smile on its face. My first thought was that this fetus was learning how to smile and be happy; maybe it had been too serious in a previous life? However, my thoughts were completely wrong. As I continued to watch with amazement, three gold coins were thrown to the left side of the fetus and three to the right. This fetus was going to have what we would call a charmed life – a life of material riches and status. I wondered if this was a future king or queen, or an honored ruler? Seeing this made me realize that vast wealth is a matter of destiny, something that your inner self will have an innate sense of. It is not something the person will have to strive for; the wealth and status a person is born with or achieves later in life is with them even while they are developing as a fetus.

The society that we have become dictates a class system, where everybody is measured in "greater than" or "lesser than" terms. However, from my observations in the Astral Realms it seems that we all have gifts or talents, which our cells were formed around whilst in the womb. But instead of looking to find what this talent is; this gift that fulfils us the most (no matter how insignificant society may say it appears to be), we constantly look at other people's lives, other people's "goodie bag" – and think they've got the better deal!

So many of us want our lives to have a purpose, people want to be a success; they want to feel special – in terms of how society grades success and special to be. We want to make the most of what and who we are and not just be a number, yet many of us, in our struggle to achieve these ends, strive to be what we are not. We did not have this struggle in the womb; we were not swayed off our life's path by impossible goals.

Disharmony begins to occur when either person thinks the other has achieved more. I'm a great believer in drive and ambition and one most certainly requires these qualities at times in life in order to develop the gifts that were first formed around the fetus. What there does not need to be is stress, panic and greed to enable a person to live their life to the full. The gardener who grows beautiful plants and flora can feel as fulfilled as the wealthiest ruler in the world.

Finally, one more fetus appeared – again of about four months development – only this fetus was forming without a right leg. The energy required to create that leg was instead being directed up to the head, in particular to the right side of the brain, which was growing rapidly and developing with great speed. I understood that this child was going to be very creative and would possess an intelligence that was to be beyond normal human level. In order to achieve this very high degree of creativity and intelligence, the child would be born deformed (deformed that is in the eyes of humans, not of course in the eyes of creation, God or whatever one wishes to call that omnipotent power.) What was very clear was the child's deformity was not due to some past karma, as some on Earth have suggested. The deformity was because so much of the fetus's energy needed to be used to produce the highly developed intelligence and creativity. This is not to say that every genius has to be otherwise physically deformed in some way! It's not always as simple as sacrificing a leg to be a brain box, but often some aspect of a person's character will be less well defined as a result of their being gifted in other areas. It's well known that many recognized geniuses have been prone to some sort of instability – they often become alcoholics, or manic. Or simply a bit spaced out and not able to deal with reality.

* * *

My spirit retained silent wonderment at the images I had just observed, but the journey was not over yet. My body took in another deep but gentle breath. I became aware of a blue sky and sunlit landscape. Underfoot, lush green grass was scattered with flowers that appeared quite magical – almost unreal, as if they were there, but not there. It was as if these flowers were present in this landscape to create a magical scene, but were actually placed there from an entirely different dimension. There was a tree to my right – it was silver in structure and its leaves were gold. The tree wasn't very dense or very full, but with enough gold leaves on it for me to be able to appreciate its beauty. The leaves were about the size and shape of the leaves on a Rhododendron bush. To my left was a beautiful spruce tree, with the same structure as it has in this earthly reality.

Whilst I was looking from one tree to another, a young girl aged around seven years old bunny-hopped past me. She seemed to come out of nowhere. Just as I was beginning to wonder where she came from and why she was bunny hopping, a young man appeared, holding a javelin. He was preparing to throw it, as if he was competing in a sporting event. As he passed me by, a lady also walked past me typing away on a computer keyboard, which somehow remained suspended in mid air and maintained the same distance and position from her regardless of the direction that she took.

At this point I realized what I was seeing. This was where spirits practice the skills they were to have in their next earthly incarnation. Coinciding with this realization came many other spirits, some with books, some in doctor's uniforms; some were builders, some in national costume, some singing in microphones, some as nursery assistants. They all came by me so fast that I was unable at the time to fully appreciate what was happening. (Even to this day, I remain a touch confused as to the little girl bunny-hopping!).

Déjà vu

Just as I was starting to feel somewhat overpowered by this scene, I suddenly found myself in another porthole or level within these realms. Again, another sun-filled day greeted me, this time with a Hawaiian feel about it.

Throughout my visits to these many different aspects within the Astral Realms, I found that almost immediately I could make sense of what it was I was observing when faced by a new scene. My feelings and senses grow stronger, my mind and thoughts become dormant, as my energy quickly adapts to the energy of what I am seeing. And upon arriving at this "Hawaiian" scene I immediately understood that I was watching a scene of the future. Yet rather confusingly, my senses also informed me that this "future" had already occurred many hundreds of years *past* on the Earth! Fortunately, this cloud of confusion lifted as I became aware that important past life existences are played back in real terms to spirits that have "lost" themselves. These scenes are played back to remind them of who they have been; to encourage them to break free of the many physical restrictions and doubts they put on themselves during their most recent earthly life. (Past life scenes can also be played to a physical being, whilst they are actively living their life on the Earth. The person will receive the scene as a sudden "I've been here before", type memory flashing into their conscious mind. It appears to come out of nowhere and for no apparent reason – what we refer to as déjà vu. It can be played to us either to encourage us that we are on our life's path.)

The Hawaiian scene that I observed was a crowning ceremony,

involving about twenty people. The person was being decorated with laurel leaves; many garlands were placed upon him and the top of his crown was full of exotic looking flowers. The scene created a pure type of ambience; a sense of purpose and nostalgia that would make up the déjà vu experience.

Flying back to the human dimension

My body took a deep breath and I found myself standing on a barren rock surface. Behind me, a distance away and in slight darkness, was a town scene with lots of buildings. The ground between the town and me was similar in texture to the Arizona desert (amber in color, rocky and barren). I was standing at the edge of a deep and endlessly wide canyon. The being that previously had escorted me to the Great Halls of Learning (the big library) was close at hand. He told me quite simply: "You can fly."

At which my arms opened, and like an eagle I began to soar high above and across the rocky canyon. Feeling freedom and exhilaration in every cell, my heart warmed to my new friend in response for helping me discover these realms. My friend was rejoicing in my freedom and understanding – and I just flew and flew.

Gradually I began to travel back into this dimension. Every cell in my body was tingling with what I had just witnessed and experienced. Opening my eyes, I looked outside to the garden, which was still looking somewhat grey and dismal but despite the grayness now didn't appear restricted – it seemed to be resting. My journey had created in me a refined sensitivity of the subtle atmospheric conditions created by changes in weather.

I walked to the kitchen, eager for a cappuccino. Adrian looked at me in anticipation; he always loves hearing about my journeys, but his excitement turned to slight concern, "You look really pale!" he exclaimed.

I looked into the mirror hanging on the kitchen wall and was shocked at what I saw. Even with my make-up on I looked very pale indeed.

"I guess that's because I bypassed the Astral Realms and went straight to an area where these beings were watching to make sure no blocks were created within the Astral Realms..." Adrian looked confused.

"I'll get my cappuccino and put extra chocolate on top, that should bring my color back! And then I'll start at the beginning..."

In conclusion

With all these insights, I was very well prepared for my talk with the Spiritual Group! They were fascinated to hear of my experiences, and I have spoken about them at other gatherings and seminars many times since. However, inevitably some of the insights I have gained do not go down well with those holding deep religious beliefs, as they contradict traditional views and teachings. It seems that it's not just a simple case of heaven for the good people and hell for the bad ones! A person's future is certainly determined by their actions while here on this planet, but a happy ending is not guaranteed by following any fear-based rewards system. Indeed, it is ironic that trying to live this life by following some rigid dogma actually creates a blockage in the pure truth and energy flow of the universe, and in many ways reduces one's likelihood of a smooth passage to that much-anticipated heaven.

Personally, I'm glad that heaven is not simply sitting around on fluffy clouds playing harps – that always sounded pretty boring to me! Our times in the Astral Realms can indeed be filled with wondrous love and contentment, but ultimately they are based on and determined by our earthly experiences. Which brings me nicely to the final great insight from my journeys. It is now even clearer to me that it's a tragic waste of one's life to spend one's entire time on this earth worrying about what happens next. It is up to us to make the most of this earthly existence. Our world is a wonderful place – take the time to experience that wonder. Learn how to live – in harmony with yourself and with the universe.

4

Spirit Guides

As my journey of discovery through the many
aspects of the universe progressed, I gained
more understanding of phenomena such as
Spirit Guides and ghosts. In these next two
chapters I will attempt to explain what I have
learned, and how it all fits into the big picture.

Many readers will be familiar with the idea of Spirit Guides – a
discarnate being who has had a life in this human dimension, and is
now perceived to be guiding a person through their current life. These
Spirit Guides are Spirits who have attained a level of understanding
of how as individuals we can work within the Universal Flow of life
and creation, realizing that struggles and suffering occur when we
are not in harmony with the Earth and Divine Will (God, creation,
Universal Flow or whatever one wishes to call this omnipotent
power). These Spirits have mainly achieved this understanding by
learning from their previous Earthly experiences.

Guides commonly present themselves as Native American Indians,
nuns, monks, philosophers or priests, although this is not always the
case. Guides are simply any Spirit that has attained a certain level of

understanding of the natural flow of the universe. These guides are sometimes seen by the person or communicated with via a Medium, or the person just feels their guiding presence around them. Many people place a great deal of trust in these Spirit Guides, and lead their lives according to what they feel they are being told to do, thus placing a great deal of responsibility on the guide!

However, as I was to find out – the relationship between Spirit Guides and their human counterpart isn't as simple as it may seem. In actual fact it is not a one-way relationship. The Spirit Guides are also often here to learn from us. And the wisdom that these guides are entrusted in having is sometimes questionable – there is no guarantee that the Spirit is there to tell the truth, nor does it necessarily have your best interests at heart…

The Trance Medium

Before describing my own experiences with Spirit Guides, I'd like to recount an observation of someone else's experience, as it quite nicely sets the scene for what I want to talk about in this chapter. I had come across an advert in the local paper entitled: *Demonstration of Trance Mediumship – a Psychic Phenomenon*. This sounded intriguing – I wondered if it was something similar to what I do. I've not ever had any physical training or guidance in what I do, so it would be really interesting to see how someone else experienced an energy other than their own entering into and borrowing their body.

The demonstration was in a local community hall, and about forty people had come along to watch the performance. We were initially addressed by another lady, who was also a Medium, and was acting as an assistant to the Medium who was to perform the demonstration. She welcomed us all and informed us that we were about to witness a very rare psychic phenomenon. She explained the trance Medium's guide would enter into the Medium and would share wisdoms and insights into our human lives on this planet.

The guide would welcome questions from the audience and would indicate when the audience could do so. The assistant asked us all to send our love and energy to the performing Medium, as she was about to enter into her trance-like state. "Your love and energy helps the Medium and the connection to her Spirit guide will be stronger," she explained.

Oh yes? This was the first of many points through the evening when I was taken aback or confused by what was being said. Why would any Medium require all the love from the audience to be projected to them in order to assist their connecting to a Spirit Guide or similar entity? Surely I thought, if they were coming from Divine Will / Universal Flow there would be endless love and clear energy flowing into them from the universe. So why would they need any extra love and energy from the audience?

Pushing this confusion to one side, I sat and observed as the Medium entered into her trance state. Breathing and exhaling – a grunt here and there, the head jerking slightly… And then finally her guide, who had apparently lived in India in his previous life, began speaking. He told us how happy he was to be with us, then proceeded to lecture us; advising us to love the world and everyone else, telling us that this was the only way forward and how our actions have cause and effect – hardly any revelatory insights! He spoke for a good twenty minutes or so about nothing that we didn't already know. I for one was waiting for those unheard before words of wisdom. Unfortunately, they didn't arrive.

This Indian guide told us he took a while to get used to "his vehicle's body" (as he called the Medium). "It took me a while," he explained, "because in my last life I had been paralyzed and so in my movement and voice I was very restricted." Immediately I realized why the guide liked talking so much; he couldn't express himself in his previous life! I wouldn't be surprised, I thought, to find out that a lot of guides who work through Mediums had lived lives with certain restrictions, either monks or nuns etc. who took vows of silence. It must be a great relief to find out one doesn't need to do this to evolve Spiritually!

My attention was pulled back in when the assistant said we could now ask the guide some questions. I looked round but no one else was putting their hand up. Well I had a question, so bravely (and I say bravely since I knew everyone would look at me and I didn't fancy their glares as I asked what they would probably think were stupid questions!). The assistant came over to me, indicating it was OK for me to speak.

"My question is that you have come to share with us your wisdom and your insights, so we are learning from you." (I felt myself cringe inside as I said this, feeling a bit of a hypocrite because there certainly hadn't been any fantastic insights and knowledge shared by the guide – he'd actually spoken a lot of rubbish and was really boring! But it seemed clear to me he enjoyed having what he would perceive as a higher status than everyone else in the room, and for a great part was feeling self important. I also felt he rather enjoyed being back in the physical body and being heard, since I was aware that he felt a bit of a nonentity in his last life and now he was enjoying the attention.) My question continued...

"I was wondering, as everything is a two-way flow within the universe, there must be something you are learning from us. Do you know what that is?"

The guide took a deep breath and spoke another load of rubbish for the next five minutes, with absolutely no reference to my question.

"What am I doing here? This is a circus!" I thought.

A couple of people did ask questions to the guide who replied to them but again failed to answer their questions. The guide then began talking about the difference between his energy and the energy of his Medium.

"I have to lower my energy dramatically to enter into my vehicle body. At the same time her energy heightens to meet my lowered energy and this is how I can talk to you through her," he explained.

The guide then explained that while his vibration was controlling her body we were not to touch her, as she would burn. He used different analogies of burning scenarios that would happen to her.

This did not sound right at all. I have heard of people saying that you must never touch a Medium in trance because the shock of the touch could kill the Medium. Other stories were of Mediums humanly combusting with such energy. But I just couldn't see how the burning scenario could occur if the Medium was simply channeling. Even though her guide had tried to explain how this could happen, I knew that I had to immediately ask the guide for some more information on this. I had by this time lent my own body to over four hundred different universal energies – gods, goddesses, angels, archangels, archetype Spirit animals, planets, stars, elements and so on – and sometimes if relevant, a universal energy would offer those physically present "etheric" gifts to place in their aura to give them strength with regards to a life situation they were in at that particular moment. The recipient is encouraged to take the gift from my hands, which the universal essence is holding out to them. So of course there is physical contact by the recipient as they take the gift from my hands. As they do this, the only feelings experienced either by the recipient or myself are of love, honor and gratitude. As yet I have never once burst into flames!

So this was something I had often wondered about. How can a Medium combust if they are channeling guides, whose vibration is in synchronization with the Astral planes and therefore not too far off our own earthly vibrations anyway? And now I had a great opportunity to have my contradiction answered. The Medium's assistant had not indicated for there to be any more questions and so looked a bit put out when I endeavored to butt in, but I did not wait for her to acknowledge me, as my hand went up. I clearly and firmly said:

"Excuse me, but I am really confused – I do not understand what you mean?"

The Medium assistant guided the trance Medium towards my direction.

"I know I'm really ignorant," I continued, "But I really would like to understand!"

"What is it you don't understand?" replied the guide.

"I don't understand why we can't touch your vehicle while you are in her [the Medium]. I hear your explanation, but I still don't understand?"

The guide explained in more confusing detail. Listening to every word caused me more confusion.

"So are you saying, if I was to get out my seat right now and give your vehicle a poke, she would combust and burn?" I queried. (I was actually really tempted to give it a try, as I was sure that the guide was talking nonsense – but out of respect to the Medium, I refrained!) The guide replied:

"Yes, that's right, she would combust and burn."

"I'm sorry," I said; "I know I'm ignorant and I really want to understand, but I'm just not getting it." I really could not see this happening! The guide said, "I will help you understand. I will sit down and remove some of my energy from my vehicle so that you may touch her and feel the warm energy."

"Thank you," I said, feeling somewhat embarrassed because I really didn't want to have to stand up in front of everyone!

The Medium sat down, took in a few breaths and again exhaled deeply. I was then called over by her guide.

"Now take my hands," he said. I stood up, walked over to the Medium and held her hands.

"What do you feel?" enquired the guide.

"Er…" came the uncertain reply from me.

"Do you feel the warmth, the love, the energy?" the guide asked.

Everyone was staring at me waiting for me to be converted into one of the people who admired the king's new clothes, not daring to say that he's really naked. I felt very alone at this point, but decided that rather than upset the applecart I would just agree. I was going to agree for the sake of the situation. So thoughtfully, I said to the guide:

"Well, I was cold earlier on, but now I am warm." (I didn't let on it was my nervous energy and embarrassment that had warmed me up.)

As he listened I gently said; "What is it you can feel?" inquisitive as to his response to our hands holding. The guide appeared to not hear my answer and then began telling me about a man who had died of cancer and who was now in the Spirit world. The guide described a man in detail, apparently someone close to me and helping me in my life. The guide asked if I knew the man – I hadn't a clue who he could have been talking about, but felt that I had to say "yes" to the Medium, just so that I could return to my seat. I decided that I'd been a pain to this guide for long enough. For I had received my answers into how Mediums channel, and had witnessed the supposed amazing phenomena.

I have no doubt the guide inhabiting the Medium's body was genuine. But it was pretty obvious that this was no great psychic phenomena – simply because this guide was actually no wiser than any other person in the room! I don't know if anyone else could see this – it was easy for those present to be caught up in the mysticism and magic of it all; to be impressed by any communication with an entity from another realm, and thus not actually really concentrate on the waffle of information being expressed by that guide.

After I returned to my seat the assistant concluded the session. She told us that the guide would now be leaving the Medium's body and when the Medium returned to consciousness she would be very exhausted. On no account were we to approach her; she would need a great deal of rest.

As the Medium opened her eyes everyone applauded her, she nodded in thanks. The assistant went over to her to help support her in walking. I looked at the Medium with shock. She was absolutely exhausted and seemed to have aged ten years. I was really stunned! I thought to myself, this cannot be in balance with Universal Flow or Divine Will to look so exhausted after performing a channeling session. My impression was that the Mediums believed that they were doing this type of trance channeling for the highest good. But the sheer exhaustion on the face of the Medium, who was unable to walk unaided after the event, was a big contradiction to what they believed. My own experiences after any channeling session that I have had (where I lend my body over to a universal being, Angel etc), have certainly never included exhaustion. In fact, the reverse happens – I have *tons* of energy. I feel totally rejuvenated, as though I could run a marathon!

Filled with concern for the Medium, I left the hall thinking to myself that this did not seem right at all. This type of trance channeling should carry a health warning in CAPITAL LETTERS!

An untruthful Guide

My first personal experience that Spirit Guides (Spirit Helpers) were not as clear, good willed and as holy as many assume them to be was when a friend asked me to explain (with the help and assistance of the Angels) more about her pictures of Spirit Guides. Valerie had visited a few psychic artists, who between them had produced a dozen or so pictures of the different Spirit Guides that were supposedly around her. Although pleased to have received the drawings, Valerie had been left feeling pretty much as if she had been given a key but was uncertain which door it would unlock. What did it all mean? She had kept the pictures for a few years, and after a number of private sittings with me regarding other matters she felt comfortable enough to show me the psychic drawings. Valerie asked if the Angels could provide some insights as to why these Spirit Guides were around her, and why they were assisting her.

Well, one never knows what is going to happen during a private sitting. In fact, everything I do on a Spiritual level is open to change; I have learnt that one must always be open to the unexpected. By *not* restricting oneself to expecting certain outcomes or results enables Divine Will to flow freely in and around the sitting, and the relevant help and assistance for that person or persons will come from the highest and purest source in creation.

So, Valerie and I sat down and made ourselves comfy – the pictures of the Guides lay in front of us. My Angel poured her essence into my body and began examining the pictures, explaining to Valerie who these people had 'been' when they lived here on Earth. All was going very smoothly, until my Angel began considering one particular picture, which depicted a lady of around twenty-eight years of age. At this point there was a very definite change in energy in my Angel, who up until now had been expressing fondness and love, playfulness and joy to my friend as she passed on the information and remembrances regarding the painted Guides. However, this picture changed that energy. My Angel sat upright and very firmly explained that this Guide did not have my friend's best interests at heart. In fact, this one was determined to cause as much disruption as she could to my friend! This supposed Guide of Valerie was actually doing its best to influence her to take a wrong path, make a wrong decision, or simply confuse her as much as she could. This Guide had a big grievance that she blamed my friend for, and as a result was determined to get her revenge on Valerie.

My Angel explained that Valerie had lived a previous life in Egypt many thousands of years ago, in a green and lush area of the country – I guess somewhere on the Nile valley or delta. She was one of two daughters of a farmer. However, Val was having an affair with her sister's husband – the two were very much in love. This eventually caused great disharmony to occur between the two sisters, for obvious reasons! Valerie's sister ended her days in that life with great hatred in her heart towards Valerie, and this sister was the lady Spirit Guide now around Valerie, still focusing all her power towards disorientating Valerie in this life. Indeed, by the sound of it this Guide had also managed to cause a certain amount of disruption to Valerie in past lives.[1]

My Angel became stronger and direct, uncovering the ill-placed intentions of this guide. Certain *Karmic* energies were called to assist in the removal of this Guide away from Valerie, so that she could feel free once more.

After the sitting Valerie confirmed that she had indeed occasionally felt guided to do certain things, make certain choices, which turned out to be unproductive; a waste of time and money.[2]

Valerie felt extremely relieved to be rid of that Guide! However, I suspect that in order to create harmony once more in that area of Universal Flow, the two will need to meet once again, so as to understand the position and emotions of each other. Such a meeting would need to occur back on the Earth, since the blockage they had created occurred whilst on the Earth. This does not mean they have to be family or close friends[3] – they only need to meet once and

---

[1] I cannot say for sure exactly where these Spirit Guides actually reside. They may be in the astral realms, and communicating via vortexes, they may exist primarily in some other dimension. It isn't clear where they come from, as they are just *there*. But I do not feel them around me in the same way that I can feel the presence of an Angelic Being or a ghost as described in previous chapters. The classic conception of Spirit Guides is that they are there all the time. But the way I see it is that they pop in and out of our dimension, maybe homing in on the energy flow from our thoughts or whatever. Where they are at other times, I don't know.

[2] Sometimes we all act impulsively, at a cost to us (financial or otherwise). Fortunately, this does not necessarily mean that we are under the influence of a disruptive Guide! I find the best way to determine as to whether or not a spontaneous thought is a productive one, is to make sure your heart rate does not suddenly increase. Deceptive spontaneity starts in the head to the point where it blots out everything else, then the heart beats faster and excitement follows. You cannot think clearly, and as a result do not have focus and direction. It is therefore important to clear your head, in order to be able to discern spontaneity

momentarily, on an equal basis and in an equal situation, for this restriction between them to be cleared. By meeting equally, neither one is more or less powerful than the other. Their individual Spirit then recognizes the other's light and equality to theirs, and in that moment's recognition, the blockage will be released. This Spirit Guide was not a bad person, she was simply angry with Valerie.

"Hmmm!" I thought to myself, as I realized what all this meant. Guides are clearly very similar to us. In fact, the only difference between Guides and ourselves is that we are the ones who breathe air, have life, and have a body...

A departed husband who would not say what his widow wanted to hear

My understanding of Guides continued to grow. I had met and come to know a Medium whose third husband had recently died. She dearly loved her husband and was devastated at losing him. One day, during a sitting that I was holding for the Medium, she said to me; "I have often seen my dead husband's back, but he will never show his face to me, which is very confusing. He knows I would dearly love to see him!"

My Angel told her, "Your husband loved you so much and he still does, but he will not deceive you as other Spirits do. Other Spirits tell you what you want to hear, but they do not mean to deceive you, they know how to lift your emotions and will say what your heart wants to hear."

This was a direct reference to the fact that this Medium was

(which comes from "etheric" guidance) and impulse that comes from conscious and subconscious desires of the head.

[3] It is important not to confuse Spirit Guides with the energy of departed relatives, family etc, who may also come to help you in difficult times. This is very different to being a Spirit guide.

always hoping to either win or somehow come into a lot of money. One of her Guides, a Native American Indian of the Blackfoot tribe, would often give her indications that she would soon get her wish and receive her fortune. This always lifted the Medium's emotions, providing her with a renewed focus in life that took her away from her material struggle.

The Medium, needless to say, was very upset to hear what my Angel had to say. She had always assumed the Spirits who came to her spoke the truth. Well they did – they spoke *her* truth! The thought of winning a lot of money was an uplifting thought to the Medium. The Spirits' intentions were not bad; they were simply pacifying the Medium. Plus which, I actually suspected that it was being done to keep the Medium from going off the rails. She'd had a hard life and was prone to excessive alcohol intake; so the Spirit Guides, by keeping her hopes high, were simply looking out for her in the short term.

One must not confuse sincerity and real truth, with convenient truth that stems from desire. The hope, joy and uplifting which can be experienced by a grieving person when given proof that the human Spirit does live on after death is indeed real truth. The grieving person is fulfilled and has their hope restored by finding that the Spirit of their loved one continues to exist. Unfortunately, the Medium can also misinterpret the information they are receiving from the Spirit world, and this is where the sitter has to discern the difference between a good and not so good Medium. It is up to each individual to discern what's what.

As we learn from guides – they also learn from us

The common assumption is that those who have passed over become endowed with infinite wisdom, along with endless love and holiness. However, that doesn't actually appear to be the case. For sure, once a person passes over they are able to see the bigger picture; they can see other's viewpoints, see where they could have responded differently to an unharmonious situation, see how they affected outcomes either positively or negatively. They can understand how they could have appreciated life more, and they can see how unconditional acts of selflessness have helped so many still here on the Earth. Yet for many inhabitants of the Spirit worlds, there are still lessons to be learned, and the best place to learn those lessons is from us humans. Spirits in the Astral Realms cannot learn while remaining in those dimensions. They can understand, and they can let go of beliefs, but they cannot *learn*.

So our Guides are not only there to help us on our way – they are also there (in many cases) to learn from us. Angels – knowing what's best for each individual's growth – will advise departed Spirits as to which humans they can learn from, and which humans they can be guides to. To explain this more fully, here are a few examples of the two-way learning we can all experience, from us to Guides and from Guides to us.

I had invited a number of people to my home in the hope and intent that we would all have a greater understanding as to what the Astral Realms were, and the true role we have between our individual selves and our Guides. My guests settled themselves and after making certain they were all comfortable, I began my process of making sure I was in touch with Divine Will and not my ego. A rush of clear energy entered my body as I felt my will departing. A beautiful being entered my body; an Archangel, who I have encountered before and have found to be a great communicator between our world and the Astral Realms. The Archangel explained that the Astral Realms were created *after* the human race. We were originally created in perfection, but because of the way we were adapting to life on Earth, creating difficulties in our lives – it was decided a place of reflection was needed; and so the Astral realms were born. As explained in the previous chapter, we go to the Astral planes to reflect on the lessons learned during the life we have departed. However, we retain our individual personalities when we pass over, so if we were arrogant on Earth we will still be arrogant in the Astral Realms. If we were rather proud or stubborn, then we will remain proud and stubborn. However, what does expand as we arrive in the Astral planes are our *better* qualities. Those are the qualities that have often touched and helped people unconditionally.

The Archangel told us he would step aside to allow one of our guides to talk. The Archangel left my body, and then a very elderly Spirit stepped in. This was a lady who had died when she was very old.

My hands began to curl and become stiff with age, my shoulders rounded, I felt myself age dramatically. The Spirit felt weak and my body began to tremble very gently. She spent a moment or two getting used to being in a physical body once more. Breathing gently but deeply in helped her to become settled, ready to communicate. She placed her gaze around the room, and even though my eyes were shut, she used her senses to contact each individual present in the room. This took her only a minute or two to do. Slowly, and with all the strength she could muster, she brought her senses and focus to rest on Adrian, who at this time was sitting on the floor to my right. She directed her energy to lift her left hand and uncurled my first finger as she pointed to him.

Adrian welcomed her, as he did so she appeared to be conferring with some of her advisors (Angels). The old lady was enquiring as to what words she was and was not allowed to use. (Certain words can hold an element of judgment in them, and so the Spirit was enquiring as to which words would best describe what she needed to share).

Very slowly and quite meticulously, she told Adrian; "Many lifetimes before, you were my husband." She counted on her hand that it was fourteen lifetimes ago for Adrian. She continued to hold back her energy, in restraint.

"I feel I can now say what I feel, but the terms I wish to use are not quite acceptable from where you are sitting." Wow, this lady was really annoyed with Adrian – she was only just containing her emotions, hence the trembling within **my** body.

"I served you well," She explained. "But you were extremely unresponsive and as a result I lost a great deal of self worth."

It turned out that Adrian had been a philanderer and had paid very little attention to his wife. The lifetime they had shared was in China, around the time of the Ming Dynasty. Women were suppressed and men were free to womanize here and there, which is exactly what Adrian had done. She continued;

"I have not yet returned to this planet. I have not seen a side of you that I particularly like until this lifetime [that you are currently in], and I must say I would have liked to have seen this side when we were together. I have not had much trust in men and this is why I have been put with you now, and I know your Soul is pained. I know this because I feel it also, but through your pain I have become free."

At this point her tears of relief ran down my face, as she was filled with awe and honor for the Angels, who had advised her to walk with Adrian in this present day lifetime. Her heart now filled with love and great respect for Adrian, at which point his heart also filled with love and regret of his philandering ways. Tears fell from Adrian's eyes also. She explained:

"The freedom I now hold in my heart tells me I was also very stubborn."

I could sense that although the Angels had advised her to walk with Adrian in this lifetime of his, she had felt it wasn't the wisest of advice. But now, she was humbled by the great wisdom that she realized the Angels' possessed. She could see how her stubbornness could have worked against her, hence the great relief her whole essence experienced.

"I now know I do not have to walk with you any more. I see you in the light you are. But before I go I wish to say with all my Soul, I honor you."

She reached out her hand. Adrian took it gently, and she bowed low before him, tears continuing to pour from my eyes. This was a truly beautiful experience for me to see pain transformed into an incredibly pure and deep love, filled with honor and gratitude. Adrian bowed to her also and said, "Thank you and I honor you."

Later that evening, Adrian told us all that he knew immediately this lady was oriental (something which I knew also, but had not been shared with the group). He could feel and intuitively remembered how he would go off with many other women, showing little or no respect to his wife. He felt he had continued in his philandering ways in quite a few of his lives subsequent to that one.

The oriental guide was advised to walk with him so that she could see how much he had grown as a man, changing from a relatively raw male, to one who, I have to say, is the most perfectly balanced man I have ever met. Adrian is balanced equally in his male and female aspects, and can talk with anyone – regardless of class or culture. So it was for me a surprise to hear of a life he had lived that was so different to his life now.

We both felt that this lady, now free of her lack of self worth, was shining in love and ready to reincarnate. We sensed that her task for this next reincarnation would very likely see her campaigning for womanhood. Not necessarily for women's rights, but a campaign away from girl power towards encouraging the natural femininity of women and for women to be respected as much as men – for their own unique innate feminine qualities.

This lady had been stubborn to the point that she found it difficult to take the advice of the Angels. So, it seems life repeats itself in the Astral Realms! How often do we choose to ignore the well-meaning advice, given freely and with love and concern, from our friends or family? – Advice to help us on our journey through life. Many of us, by ignoring help and assistance, then take the long and hard route in life.

The oriental lady took a long time to be free of her sense of worthlessness. Freedom is bliss at any time, but it's especially potent when one reaches freedom after traveling a long hard journey.[4]

Adrian had now been opened to the idea that Guides learn from us as much as we learn from them. Eagerly, he asked if he could have a private session with me in the hope that a few more of his guides would communicate to him, so he could understand more of them.

The Roman officer assigned to Adrian

Saturday afternoon, we were sitting in my special room; candles and incense lit and the tape ready to record whichever of Adrian's Spirit Guides decided to come and talk.

The first guide that came to communicate was also learning from Adrian, so in fact it was more the case that Adrian was *his* Guide! He found it quite difficult to use my voice, so I knew he had been in the Astral Realms a very long time. This man had been a very high-ranking soldier in Caesar's Army – someone very close to the top. He came through wearing his uniform. I was only aware of the top part of his uniform, deep red in color edged with gold. He was a rather large chap, bearded and stocky. We had to be very patient with

---

[4] "Who is to say, a child's long journey may bring them the deepest red rose, that others miss in their rush?" an Angel once asked somebody, during a personal sitting. It reminded me of someone I knew, who was always going to do something with their life but did nothing. I could never understand why they convincingly told me of their detailed plans, but never did instigate those plans.

The same person told me, "If you put your mind to it you can achieve anything."

In my frustration I replied, "Yes but the mind cannot do it alone, the body has to make an effort." I wondered if this person was ever going to find that rose. Interestingly, it is the view of the Angels that if you only take one step forward in life – then that's just fine.

him since he was really struggling to communicate. Immediately, I sensed his heart was closed down; a very tight feeling in my chest which was projected from him. This restriction was not helping in his efforts to communicate.

After the Roman soldier had finally relaxed and felt more comfortable being back in the human body, he began to communicate. The following is the conversation between Adrian and the soldier:

ADRIAN: Welcome.

ROMAN OFFICER: I am the one who walks at times with you.

ADRIAN: Can you explain why you walk with me?

ROMAN OFFICER: I walk so I can begin to heal wounds in my heart. When my being last walked on Earth I was immensely powerful. I was one of the ruler's advisors. I gave much advice and the advice at times would be to destroy other peoples. I was within the Roman armies. My heart is so frozen. I walked on your Earth knowing only power and strength, and I have now been encouraged to walk at times around you. But I do not place any of my restrictions upon you.

ADRIAN: Are we connected from a life in the past?

ROMAN OFFICER: I knew you when you were a weak child; you were the son of a woman who was rather...

At this point the officer hesitates, not wanting to use a particular word that would be judgmental to the woman. The Spirit confers with an advisor as to how to best give an appropriate and fair description of the woman of whom he spoke, with as much respect as was possible. It would appear that the woman of whom he spoke was the local prostitute. The officer finally describes her as "loose". He continued.

I hesitate because that on my part is judgment, but I have been told it was necessary to use this word so you can feel the connection."

ADRIAN: I understand.

ROMAN OFFICER: I used this woman as did many, but now I know this wasn't the way. My task at times now is to observe. I watch the strength from your heart and I like what I observe, and this strength encourages my heart to unfreeze.

ADRIAN: Will you be re-born onto Earth?

ROMAN OFFICER: I shall, but I shall not until my heart has unfrozen. I am allowed to choose whether to come back or stay here, but such was my power and strength that advice I gave [when I was last on Earth] was not from my heart. I do not wish to make the same error."

ADRIAN: I understand. How else do you hope to unfreeze your heart?

ROMAN OFFICER: At times I go to the Great Halls and I also assist in bringing over many people who are hurt – but I do not lead the way, I only assist. And when I assist I feel the pain from them, and these are beings who have been destroyed by wars and man's ill deeds."

ADRIAN: Are you aware of the Angelic Realms and the Angels?

ROMAN OFFICER: I am aware of wondrous Beings who walk all around, and when these beings are around there is so much oneness and joy. They appear when I myself feel I am struggling – and then all is well. And where I am now is a wondrous place.

ADRIAN: I know deep inside that you are a good man and I pray your heart will truly shine freely.

ROMAN OFFICER: I am honored to share my essence with you in these moments.

ADRIAN: I am grateful for you to come here. Thank you.

The Roman Officer had been Adrian's father, but because the child was a sickly son of a prostitute, he had nothing to do with him. So now the Officer walked with Adrian, observing the true strength that emanated from his heart. Adrian is strong physically, and yet, is open enough to work with his heart. The Roman Officer was observing how to have strength in the heart and to understand and see that there is no weakness in using your heart. He was a Spirit who had suffered very much in his own judgment of himself. The spiritual progress he seemed to have made was in being an assistant and helping people pass over whose lives had been ended in wars and such. As he took on their grief tenfold, his heart would slowly become free. He was very uncomfortable about the idea of returning to Earth, and would only do so when his heart was unfrozen, and he was able to live a life using all his senses.

High spirited Elsie

The Roman Officer departed, and another Guide came to communicate. She introduced herself as Elsie.

ADRIAN: Welcome Elsie.

ELSIE: I passed [over] when I was a child – I was only nine years of life. I passed very quickly and without much pain. I passed when the bombs landed on my home. I lived in South London, and there was the terrifying sky above, but my passing was quick. I am around you because I often had great imagination. I played with thin air, and I see at times your mind becomes like a dead weight. So, I have been asked at times to dance around you and play with you. I do this, and sometimes I blow on your face, sometimes I switch your mind. [*She whispers:*] Although we are not supposed to play with one's mind, [which appears to be a universal law] sometimes I do. But I mean you no harm and I watch how you become confused, and I find this wonderful because it stops your mind becoming a lead weight.

ADRIAN: Thank you Elsie, I understand.

That was it from Elsie. She spoke very clearly and with great ease, and this was because she had only been in Spirit form for around fifty years or so, whereas the Roman Officer had not experienced life for hundreds of years. Speech is not used in the Astral Realms, so the longer a Spirit is there, the harder it becomes to re-use a "lender's" voice, should the opportunity ever arise for them.

Elsie was guiding Adrian very well. Adrian said he would be focusing on thought forms that were unproductive to him, and all of a sudden he would forget what he was thinking about and lighten up a bit. Adrian was very grateful to Elsie, who by the way had no relationship to him. She could simply help someone who needed help, and was happy to do so. Elsie was a very light Spirit, full of fun and with an air of playfulness. Great for Adrian, who sometimes needed help to release his congested mind. As Elsie departed, one more Guide entered.

Sheba – killed by loose words

"I am known as Sheba," explained the Guide.

ADRIAN: Welcome Sheba.

SHEBA: We shared a life so long ago, I loved you so, but the love I felt was not returned. You had many women."

[*I was amused that poor* ADRIAN *was having to take on all these home truths about his rather colorful and at times less than pleasant past activities. But I knew he could handle this information – after all, he was the one who wanted to know about his other Guides!*].
Sheba continued:

You were a tyrant! Your post was quite high, but you felt you were higher. Now I walk close by you, and often I would like to make your voice become still. I find words you speak at times empty and when those moments occur then I take the meaning from those words and discard them. I do this to help you understand words can destroy and words can create. Words are so powerful. Your words, when we shared a life, caused my death.

My death was unpleasant – and yet you had no remorse. I have
incarnated since, but because I have the strength to discard your
empty words. I choose to walk with you now.

ADRIAN: I am so sorry for all the pain I may have caused you. I
apologize and I wish I had allowed my heart to have enjoyed our
time together. I can sense you are a very kind and loving person,
and my love goes with you and I thank you for all your help.

SHEBA: I walk because I always could sense the better side of you."

ADRIAN: Thank you for seeing that.

Sheba walked with Adrian, encouraging him to discard loose words;
words that are from someone else, and words that are only spoken
but not felt. It was his meaningless words that caused her very
painful death (I didn't get the full details, but it was something very
bloody and horrible) and because of this Sheba chose to influence
him in this life, to help Adrian to choose and use his words more
wisely.

I could see them living together in a Bedouin environment. Sheba
was proud and refused to let her husband's arrogant ways destroy
her personality. She was a very strong lady. Sheba told Adrian she
had since incarnated to another lifetime, which was also now passed.
But it seems that it is possible for Guides/Spirits to revert back to a
past life when there is a necessity to clear away old blockages, old
patterns of behavior, belief systems or mental patterns of thinking.
So a guide may appear to us in the life that they experienced with
us, even though they may have had others since.

Conversation with Archangel Michael on Spirit Guides

My understanding of Spirit Guides and their relationship to us was
soon to take on a massive expansion. I had been inspired to hold a
lend-my-body-to-the-universe session, whereupon, if appropriate
to Divine Will, we could learn more of our relationship to the Spirit

Guides. I made a provisional date for a number of healers and psychics to attend. As always I remained open to the outcome of the evening and if nothing happened then plan B would come into play – plan B being coffee, chocolate biscuits and a good chat!

As it was, on that particular evening Divine Will did flow, and in abundance. An Archangel came to communicate and answer questions from the group – it was my friend Archangel Michael, who we encountered in Chapter One. The following is the direct transcript of that evening, with all questions from participants indicated Question. Note that the Archangel refers to all peoples on the Earth as children, regardless of their physical age. He also uses the word "so" as an assent – to mean, "yes" or "correct".

ARCHANGEL MICHAEL: I am known to all as Michael. (pronounced Mikha-el) I come to bring forth many answers, if you so wish, as to other worlds.

ALL: Thank you.

QUESTION: Can I ask a question about energies that are called Spirit Guides? How clear are Spirit Guides?

ARCHANGEL MICHAEL: The Guides that you refer to as Spirit Guides are only as clear as yourselves.

QUESTION: Do they have a purpose?

ARCHANGEL MICHAEL: Often many people on your planet are guided by their words, and so this in many ways has created a need for such Spirits to assist the physical dimension. Also what is happening is that many of these guides are becoming astral-bound: they cannot move on, because constantly they feel a need to justify their existence by being as you label a Spirit Guide.

In true essence, if one works to Divine Will, then why should one require the assistance of another? Divine Will flows as freely through the worlds of Spirit as it does upon your planet; and yet by creating physical and Spiritual worlds there becomes a void [in between]. Often Spirit Guides have to cross this void and in this void only energies that aim to cause disruption upon your planet exist. And yet by having a need to call upon such guides, almost a demand comes from the being; this may be so subconscious, nevertheless it is there, for reliance comes from the physical aspect in the hope that the Spiritual information is so.

QUESTION: Do Spirit Guides always tell the truth?

ARCHANGEL MICHAEL: Now, I say to your heart and your Soul: the words you speak, are they always of truth?

The questioner pauses, a little embarrassed to admit that he at times speaks untruths!

QUESTION: No, not always.

Everybody laughs, recognizing that at times it is so easy to exaggerate and stretch the truth!

ARCHANGEL MICHAEL: There is no difference, the only difference between the physical plane and the Astral planes is: man [on the physical plane] has a body for now. This is the only difference, and yet many feel that when one passes into the next world, suddenly they are enlightened. They can see more clearly so they do have a deeper understanding, but they cannot learn as you learn here and this is why they choose to incarnate once more.

The Astral planes exist only so far, one cannot move freely beyond unless one has learnt freedom, and one can only learn freedom within the physical body. At times, a Spirit Guide will attempt to use a child's body to remember the feeling upon the Earth. They know there is much learning to be learnt here, and so they will use a child's body; but this is often without asking, and this causes much distress to many children.

Most people within their daily lives will at some point or another have had a number of these experiences, and often you will say; 'This person is strange, this person is not quite him or herself.' And how such Spirits can enter the body is because a weakness exists within the child; a weakness of unworthiness, or a weakness of better than, and also of all attitudes, and all these are stepping stones to allow Spirits to enter.

QUESTION: There are many Spirit Guides who in previous incarnations were doctors, and they now come and work through people who are known as healers. Is that a role in which the Spirit guide is learning? Is that a positive role?

ARCHANGEL MICHAEL: At times helpers, such as you talk of, will be asking if they can assist the physical; and in a normal situation this is so. [*i.e. this is O.K!*] But what often occurs on your planet is the physical child performing such deeds begins to feel somewhat gifted, or somewhat superior. When this occurs, the physical child will prevent the Spiritual doctor from growing. Often such Spirits will only need to be around a child for maybe one moment in time; but it is the desire of the physical child to hold onto that Spirit, or repeat the experience, that prevents also the Spirit from growing."

QUESTION: When you say Spirit Guides are only as clear as the person [Medium] concerned, does that mean we are not able to channel or receive guides from higher realms at times?

ARCHANGEL MICHAEL: More often the guidance that many children experience will come from their Angelic self. This is the most potent form of guidance. But, if one begins to say "higher" or "lower" or such, then one cannot already grasp what is around them. Often when children are not searching and not asking, this is the times when they are most connected to higher guidance, and yet it moves silently, it moves without thought. Often you may say, "This is a fine thought, I must have been guided by Spirit," and yet it was your own openness to receive such clear guidance that gave you the inspiration. It was your own light and not the light of others."

QUESTION: How would you explain visions, or clairvoyance? People say they come from Spirit Guides?

ARCHANGEL MICHAEL: Many energies will take on a form that is already within your aura. When you are reborn, so all your lives and memories come forth within your aura, every one of these memories; and many entities can see such, and many energies can take on many forms.

QUESTION: Are you saying they mimic those images within the aura?

ARCHANGEL MICHAEL: Most of the time these images are not what they appear to be. If consciously you ask that you are purely guided by Divine Will and not by the needs of any being around you or any Spirit Guide, often you will find the path you take somewhat different.

QUESTION: Would you then agree that, from the Spirit world, there are impersonators and assimilators?

ARCHANGEL MICHAEL: There are many, but the ones who pass into Spirit from, shall we say, from the family structure, often those beings will stay close to their children until the children are settled; and this is not to be confused with Spirit Guides, do you understand my words?

QUESTION: Yes.

ARCHANGEL MICHAEL: Many of you will have experienced a dear one that has passed; and always the love that flows when they are around is unconditional, and this you will feel.

QUESTION: There are many books detailing the thoughts of Spirit Guides who have passed their information on through various Mediums: these Spirit Guides seem to have much knowledge and wisdom; would you agree with this?

ARCHANGEL MICHAEL: Only to the point of saying that they have already seen what is in the minds of man. Many words are brought forth in a certain amount of truth, but more are brought forth for mystique. Man always, within his aura, gives out a thirst for more knowledge, and so this need is often picked up by these guides that you speak of; but these guides are restricted to the Astral level [*and are thus by definition not all-wise or all-knowing!*].

QUESTION: Would you accept that in our seeking for knowledge, when we want the masters from higher realms to come, that we can only receive the knowledge that we are capable of understanding?
ARCHANGEL MICHAEL: So.
A short answer, but that was all that was needed!

QUESTION: Could I ask another question about Spirit Guides? There was an instance once with a lady who had a Spirit Guide, and this Spirit Guide had to be taken away from her by the forces of light, because she seemed to be influencing this person on the Earth in a negative way. Can this really happen?
ARCHANGEL MICHAEL: Many times Spirit Guides have took unto themselves the laws of *Karma*, and often they will lead a child to the wrong path; this is so.

QUESTION: Are they then not working to Divine Will?
ARCHANGEL MICHAEL: There is no greater or lesser. [*Intimating the Spirit world is no greater or lesser than the physical world.*] Only on the physical plane does man have a body. How often does man work to Divine Will? But of course at times they shall.

QUESTION: How can we learn to work to Divine Will?
A long silence...
ARCHANGEL MICHAEL: My hesitancy is quite simply because you

do not acknowledge your light. If all children acknowledged each other's light and their perfection, then at all times you would be working to Divine Will – yet this simple answer holds very little understanding.

QUESTION: Would it be true to say; if your motivations are from your highest thought, your highest ideal, then you are working to Divine Will?

ARCHANGEL MICHAEL: A fine example would be if your motivation, as you say, or your intent was purely for the highest good of all; I would say: "Would you give your life?" and if you answer so, with all consequence to go back to your being, then you have Divine Will touching every part of you. Never, ever feel of service to anyone; the moment this occurs you have humbled yourself or raised yourself: either way there is no balance. [MICHAEL *uses his hands to demonstrate this part of the answer*].

Look always to see what joy from the heart, work or deeds, or just living, brings. If there is heaviness, or if there is a need that is there, then it is not Divine Will flowing. And although many begin to heal, one must always be aware negative energy can flow also through the healer's body and create seemingly positive results; many will receive such healing, but negative energy will heal at a price to either man's Soul or the Soul of the Earth. Only healing flowing from Divine Will knows unconditional love.

QUESTION: Would you say that Divine Will is very difficult to operate on this planet, bearing in mind that across the planet we are constantly abusing our lesser brothers; our four-legged friends and our feathered friends?

ARCHANGEL MICHAEL: But, this is a judgment; immediately one has a judgment then one is not with Divine Will.

QUESTION: But surely the animal kingdom is as important as a human being?

ARCHANGEL MICHAEL: The kingdom of animals is at this moment more profound than the kingdom of humans; there is more insight and freedom in those kingdoms and yet it is man's constant need to control that moves him away from Divine Will. But do not judge the action of others, adhere always to your truth and your light and all will flow. But man can only take responsibility for his own individual self, and to allow others to grow at their own pace. Yes, talk of your views, this is how growth is shared. But often man is silent, and that is when great learning occurs.

QUESTION: You cannot be truthful with yourself if you ignore what is going on around you. I am particularly concerned about our four-legged friends, the way they are abused in science for experimentation?

ARCHANGEL MICHAEL: And yet the Spirit of those creatures has survived, they have harmed none, but as man begins to understand the harm he is creating, that burden will eventually hold his Spirit from growing. And so we say here: "Who truly is free, is it man or the kingdom of animals?"

QUESTION: Would you say our Angels, our higher self, could they be a guide for us?

ARCHANGEL MICHAEL: Your Angels, all your life, are the greatest guidance you can receive here on the planet.

QUESTION: Some people say that meditation can bring them closer to their Angels; what does bring you closer to your Angel?

ARCHANGEL MICHAEL: What brings you closest to your Angel is non-judgment. Now I shall depart, if you are all free.

ALL: Yes, thank you.

5

Ghosts

Everyone is familiar with the idea of ghosts – spirits trapped in this human dimension. Since starting on my journey of discovery, I have encountered many such spirits, all of whom had their own tale to tell. The discovery of these ghosts – and in many cases the techniques used to clear the thought forms that have restricted these spirits from moving on – offer some fascinating insights into the ways of the universe...

Annie – St Martin's Tearooms

The somewhat unlikely setting of St. Martin's tearooms in the Sussex town of Chichester, was the location for my first conversation with a ghost. My family and I had recently moved from our home in Surrey to West Sussex, and Chichester was a ten-minute drive from my new home. Chichester is steeped in history, Roman in origin, and still possessing many buildings dating back to the 16th century. It has a beautiful Cathedral that boasts the most wonderful acoustics.[1]

---

[1] If you are lucky enough to get hold of a ticket for the Christmas Carol concert, you are guaranteed an uplifting experience from the pure and wondrous melodies of the male and boys' choir.

Only the frontage of the shops in Chichester have changed in appearance, the buildings that house them remain true to their original architecture.

St Martin's tearooms are delightfully antiquated in atmosphere. The carpeted floor is uneven, log fires blaze. Oak tables, quiet corners, tiny windows where you would not expect a window to be, and a wealth of original oak beams overhead. The stairs to the upper levels are so steep that warnings hang from the walls asking that you go up and down them slowly in case you slip and fall, landing on the occupants sitting at the table directly by them. Every table has fresh cut wild flowers and foliage on it. St Martin's is a real step back in time!

I was sitting there one day enjoying my tea and teacake, and started to wonder. Surely there must be some ghosts in residence in such an ancient place? I decided to "tune in" and find out. Making sure I was connected to Divine Will, I waited for my bones and blood to respond – then I knew it was okay to begin.

Very quickly I felt a presence. An old lady came through, she was called Annie. She told me she plays with the light switches in the tearoom. She touches the switches causing the lights to flicker. I asked her why she was doing this, and she explained that in her time (which I guess to be somewhere around the 17th century) this building had been a drinking house. I then saw an image of many men in this alehouse, very drunk and very loud. I could feel the atmosphere of the time. It was certainly not a pleasant environment at all; it certainly wasn't a place I would wish to go to. It was brash, loud and very raw – very different to today's mellow ambience!

One of the reasons that Annie was a ghost in this tearoom was that at in her time many young boys would be kidnapped and brought here. They were being press-ganged for the Navy.[2] I could

---

[2] It was apparently fairly common practice at this time for children to be taken from the streets or children's orphanages and made to work on the ship as "powder monkeys". The powder monkeys helped to load the cannons with gunpowder during a battle.

see those nine or ten-year-old boys, very frightened and trying to hide themselves away. The feeling of terror and fear from these boys was immensely strong. How Annie knew the boys had been brought here I do not know. Maybe she worked at the drinking house – but that is only conjecture.

So Annie was now in the tearooms acting as a type of guardian, to oversee the activities in this building and ensure that this would never happen again. Annie told me that she had been killed outside the drinking house by a fast-moving carriage, which had knocked her down. She said it would not have happened if the area had been well lit; and so this is why she now played with the lights – I guess this was to ensure they were working. The owners confirmed that they had problems with flickering lights; I didn't feel it was appropriate to tell them about Annie – their friendly ghost.

Annie knew she was "dead", but she was in what I call a time-lock – where a spirit stays in their own time, and they are not aware that time has moved on. However, although Annie was not aware of the present time, she was still capable of playing with the electrical lighting, which obviously did not exist in her lifetime! This is indeed curious – I don't really understand how she was capable of doing so. Maybe her sheer intent of playing with the lights was enough to make them flicker.

Annie sensed me as a voice, a voice that became a quiet thought in her energy. She felt a strong sense of responsibility to the young boys who were kidnapped and so for some reason she chose to stay in the building. She felt fulfilled in her need to prevent any more children having to suffer as those young boys did. She will not be able to move on or want to move on, until the great pain that she felt from the boys has diminished. The pain she felt for them had clouded her freedom. She did not trust that all would be well if she moved on – so it was her choice to stay within this dimension. Annie felt there was something she could have done to prevent the boys from being kidnapped. In actual fact, there was of course nothing she could have done. Yet she believed if she had not been killed by the carriage, she could have saved them. Her pain and her beliefs kept her in the time warp.

Annie also told me of a body that was hidden in the cellars at the time of her life in that building, the body was that of the "Robin Red" man. It was later explained to me that this was the name used for the postman in those times. Why he had been murdered I do not know.

Mary – Bosham Church

My next encounter with a ghost was on a wet and blustery day in late October. The location was the crypt of Bosham church – one of the oldest crypts in England and steeped in history. Bosham lies in an inlet of Chichester Harbor in Sussex, and is a focal point for many tourists to the West Sussex area.[3]

Adrian and I had visited the church the day after the local harvest festival. The ladies responsible for decorating the church had once again created a marvelous display. An abundance of flowers, fruit, vegetables and bread had been artistically placed all around the church and in the crypt.

The crypt is situated just below the main church. There are tiny stone steps down to its entrance. We walked down the steep steps into the crypt to view the harvest arrangements. As soon as we entered, I felt a strong presence fill my senses, so I told Adrian what I was feeling. He eagerly offered to keep a watch out and ensure no one was coming, while I checked to see what (or who) was around. I sat down on one of the few chairs that the small crypt

---

[3] The high tides in Bosham are notorious for catching out unsuspecting tourists, who disregard the signs warning visitors not to park beside the road on an incoming tide. The road runs parallel to the village pub, tearooms and houses, and leads up to the sailing club. The tide rises very fast, and before most people realize, the road disappears and parked cars are submerged by the incoming sea. Bosham church is unaffected by the high tides, as it stands on higher ground.

could accommodate and "tuned in". A lady of around fifty years in age entered my senses. She looked quite weathered in appearance. Her sleeves rolled up to her elbows, I sensed she appeared to have been baking bread.

"What's your name?" I enquired.

"Mary," she replied.

I asked her what she was doing here, and she told me she was waiting for her husband to return home from sea. She spoke in an Olde-English type of way. It appeared that, like Annie, Mary was also in a time lock; Annie knew she had died, but Mary seemed unaware that she was no longer in her physical body – that she had died. I then communicated with my Angel, who explained to me that Mary was not aware that her husband had died at sea, since she died shortly after him. Unfortunately, Mary thought that he was still alive as a sailor and yet to return home. Her thought to greet him on his arrival had become her main focus and intention in life, and this was enough to prevent her from passing into the Astral Realms – she was trapped in a time lock, created by the intensity of her thoughts. It wasn't an uncomfortable place to be. Mary had died in the mid 1600s, but because of her tireless intent, it could have been only yesterday that she had vacated her physical body.

I was confused. Mary, as a ghost – an Earth-bound spirit – didn't seem concerned at all by the situation that she was now in. She was not a bother to anyone, she was just waiting. I was uncertain what to do next and so I asked my Angel (my Angelic essence) for assistance.[4] It was explained to me that because of Mary's intention

---

[4] Trying to communicate with my Angel while also maintaining communication with the ghost is quite a challenge – I have not developed my skills sufficiently to be able to maintain simultaneous multiple communications channels as yet! It's as if I have to put the ghost "on hold" while I go off to get some back up. However, this is a very delicate operation, as the last thing I want to do is instill in the ghost any feeling of being abandoned. As described in the case of Sarah Martha Collingshaw, many of these ghosts have a deep-seated sense of unworthiness, which is why they are in their present situation.

to greet her husband and welcome him home was so strong, there was no Universal Essence or spirit that could convince her that her husband had died, without shocking her spirit slightly. The easiest and most uneventful way to assist her to pass over would be for Mary to be met by her husband's spirit whilst she was still in her time lock. He (her husband) could then help her to accept his death and in doing this she would also accept her own demise. Mary had never accepted her physical death, as her intent to wait for her husband had overridden her acceptance of death.

However, there was a slight hiccup in the proceedings. Mary's husband, I was informed by my Angel, had incarnated three more times since his life he shared with Mary. In fact, he was incarnated at this present time as a wealthy West Country farmer! Psychically, I could see him as a well-rounded farmer of livestock. Well, I knew she would never recognize him like that! But then my angel explained to me that when he next slept, his spirit would leave his body and take on the memory of who he had once been; he would enter into Mary's 'time lock' as her husband, and then reassure her and encourage her to let go of her strong intentions, and allow herself to pass over. This entire scenario was shown to me while I remained inside the crypt. I knew this scenario would occur within a day or two. It was also shown to me that Mary would accept her husband's visit, and I was made aware of the freedom and expansion that her spirit would then feel.

As we left the crypt I felt brilliant and clear, filled with yet another understanding of how this incredible Universe operates. I was in awe of how the Universe works to retrieve people/spirits that are lost or stuck – creating an effortless way around what appears to be a seemingly immovable situation.[5]

---

[5] You may wonder why the universe cannot simply track down and sort out the problems of these spirits stuck in our dimensions – after all; the higher essences and Angelic beings I have been describing in previous chapters have immense

Sara Martha Collingshaw

One summer's day during my children's school holidays we had all decided to go for breakfast in Chichester. After breakfast my children wanted to go into the Cathedral to light some candles.

Whilst I was waiting for the children to light their candles, Adrian suggested I find out if any ghosts were around and see if they wanted to talk with me. The children would take a good ten to fifteen minutes to light all their candles. So, leaving the children with Adrian to continue lighting candles and conjuring up endless dedications for their candles.[6] I went off to sit down in a quite part of the Cathedral to see if I could make a connection with a ghost.

Sitting in the Cathedral's chapel, a place for quiet prayer, I begun to centre myself. There were five other people in the chapel; some sat quietly enjoying the peace, and others in quiet prayer. I took in the scene as my body relaxed and breathed in deeply. I began to sense the presence of an old lady. I was taken aback by her image as she looked like the old wicked witch in the film *Snow White and the Seven Dwarfs*. The lady I was psychically seeing looked evil, just like the cartoon witch, except that she was covered in what appeared

power and work tirelessly to maintain the flow of energy in the universe. So why was it necessary for me to take a hand in freeing trapped spirits such as Mary, and Sara Martha Collingshaw? It seems that, as was clearly illustrated in the case of Horatio Nelson, when blockages or problems occur as a result of actions within our human dimension, it requires an interaction from within our dimension to shift the blockages. I am in a sense simply working as a three-way connector in these situations, giving grounding to the human dimension to let the energy flow and Angelic help to arrive.

[6] We always made sure we had enough money on us so that we could pay for all the candles they would light. Every candle they lit would be dedicated to someone or something. If they had run out of people or situations that they felt could be helped with the light of a candle, they would make things up. Toby I recall once lit a candle to the chocolate croissant he had just eaten!

to be a shabby dark cloak. Her posture was hunched over and she looked extremely frail and quite elderly. Seeing this image of this old lady was a bit of a shock to me!

I asked this old lady what she was doing in the Cathedral. She was aware that she had died, but the Cathedral was the only place to which she felt she could go. She felt that she would not be wanted anywhere else. She carried this strong belief with her because, for most of her earthly life, she had been shunned by society. I was dismayed to hear this because I immediately realized that I too had instinctively put labels on her because of her appearance; creating similarities between herself and Snow White's wicked stepmother. I was grateful for the opportunity to face this weakness in myself. I made a mental note to work it.

Sara showed me how she had lived mainly on the streets, without money or a home as such. She had been physically crippled and she dragged her right leg behind her. It was like a dead leg and it was because of her disability that she had become an outcast.

Towards the later part of her life she was taken into the Cathedral by a person whom she called a priest. He took this lady in and gave her food and a roof over her head. She felt she could not go anywhere else because she would have been shunned all the time and so towards the end of her life she stayed at the Cathedral. It was here and only here, that she experienced warmth and care – she felt safe in the Cathedral.

Her name was Sara Martha Collingshaw, from which I guess that her parents must have been involved in the lace trade. (If you take the name Collingshaw and divide it up, you get collar and shawl, so perhaps her parents were lace or clothes makers.) The reason that she remained in the Cathedral after her death was because she felt she did not have anywhere else to go. She could not have 'passed over', because she either did not feel worthy enough, or she felt she may have been shunned. Sara needed to learn and know how to pass over. Despite encouragement from me, she did not want to go. The only person she seemed to trust was this priest, so he was brought back to meet with her. She trusted the priest and with this trust, she found strength to free herself from feeling she may be rejected. As the priest approached her, familiarity and pleasure filled Sara, and she allowed herself to 'let go' and pass over into the light.[7]

What I have learnt from Sara Martha Collingshaw is that, within the "etheric" structure of the Cathedral and other similar places of worship, light and peace exist; creating a vortex of energy that one can travel through safely into the Astral Realms. However, if a spirit is carrying with it a sense of rejection and unworthiness, they will feel they do not have the right credentials – the appropriate passport if you like – to allow the pull of the vortex to ease them gently into the after-life. It wasn't that Sara was sad not to be worthy enough to enter the Vortex. She was simply caught up in a time bubble; a bubble that she felt safe in. It allowed her to remain in the Cathedral unseen and unheard, not causing any bother and just minding her own business.

Whether Sara was aware of the physical changes that had occurred throughout the centuries, I cannot say. I did not actually ever have any actual conversation with her – I 'communicated' with her by tapping into her thoughts and sensing her feelings. Some ghosts do talk to me, but in Sara's case I was simply tapping into her memory banks – she was unaware of me as a person or as a physical form.

---

[7] As with the ghost of Mary, I was telepathically shown that this is what would happen at some suitable time in the future. Interestingly, the priest had already passed over and more than likely had reincarnated since Sara's time. In fact, he may well be incarnated at this present time! If the priest has a physical incarnation now, then he would have been to a large extent unaware of the good deed he had just done; although on waking from his dream state or sleep state (or whatever he was doing in his physical incarnation at the time), he would have felt very good within himself – due to the deed he had just carried out.

Horatio Nelson

My family and I had decided to visit HMS *Victory*, at its current home on display at the naval base in Portsmouth. It was my five-year-old son's love and fascination with pirates that first inspired our visit. The *Victory* was everything Toby imagined a pirate ship to be; full of excitement and adventure. For the rest of us it was the ship that held the memories of England's most famous Admiral, and our trip was one of discovery into a great moment in English History. The *Victory* was now in dry-dock, with the *Mary Rose* and the HMS *Warrior* as its neighbors. It had undergone much refurbishment over the years, and is now breathtaking in its splendor and magnitude. Looking at it, you cannot fail to be taken back to the time when England's navy ruled the waves. The ship seemed very much alive with a personality of its own, retaining its air of freedom and confidence to take on the might of the seas. It was indeed a very strong and proud ship.

Just before we boarded *Victory* I felt a man standing next to me. No one could see the man as physically he wasn't there. However, I could feel his presence very clearly – and what's more, I knew who it was. This was the great man himself! I had seen pictures of Nelson before and the facial description I was seeing fitted these pictures, although the one thing that did confuse me was that he seemed quite short – not much more than five feet in height. I had always thought of him as at least reasonably tall – he seems big in his portraits, and the monument of Nelson in London, which I have often driven past, also depicts him as quite a big man. In my mind, he was tall and yet, standing next to me, he appeared smaller. I realized that this confusion was clouding the reality of the moment.

Our guide welcomed us aboard the *Victory*. As Nelson's presence became stronger I felt I had to ask the guide how tall he had been. "Around 5 feet 3 inches," was the reply from the guide, who then went on to elaborate more about Nelson's physique. Ah hah! I thought. My confusion cleared, and I sat back to enjoy both the words from our guide and the spiritual presence of the great Admiral.

Our trip around the ship lasted around forty-five minutes, and included a visit to Nelson's living quarters. We were told of Nelson's amazing strategic plan with which the English Fleet won the Battle of Trafalgar, and how his other officers were initially apprehensive about going with this form of attack. It was an unusual battle plan, involving immense risk, but which could succeed with great timing and accuracy. The energy surrounding this plan was both silent and strong. Nelson's belief in it gave strength to the officers to carry it out – and as history points out, it was indeed a brilliant plan.

As we left Nelson's quarters, I felt Nelson leave my side. After we left the ship, I told my family of the experience. My husband asked, "Has he reincarnated yet – what is he doing now?" My husband was as always eager for answers, yet I had none. I had no insights into what the spirit of Nelson was doing or becoming. Nevertheless, I had enjoyed feeling him around, and I enjoyed our trip to HMS *Victory*.

Nearly a year to the day passed, then, out of the blue, I had a strong urge to visit the *Victory* again. No reason in particular; just a strong feeling that I really ought to make another visit there. We decided to go on the very next Saturday, which was the last weekend of the children's summer break. It was the same Saturday as the previous year when we had first visited the ship.

A few minutes before we were due to leave, I sensed an energy around me that was impressing upon me the need to communicate. Logically, the timing of the communication seemed extremely inappropriate; the children were already sitting in the car, excited about the journey ahead. Three children and an energetic toddler should not be kept waiting whilst I responded to an "etheric" call to communicate! Nevertheless, off I went to do just that. Adrian explained to the children what was happening and that I would not be very long. The children (used to this type of occurrence!) accepted Adrian's explanation and played happily in the car while they waited.

After checking I was connected to Divine Will, I felt an energy of great precision enter my body, which then identified itself:

"I am the Angel of the being you call Horatio Nelson. Many admire my child and yet his heart has bled for so long. He did truly perform his task for his country well. Accolade has been projected towards him. This accolade has prevented him from moving forward. He stays in limbo."

Telepathically I asked, "Is he a ghost?" – realizing at this point that Nelson had not incarnated since the battle of Trafalgar.

His Angel answered; "Not so, his Spirit is not held within these spheres of existences."

I felt this to mean he was not Earth or Astral bound, he could move quite freely, but only so far.

His Angel explained further: "He cannot progress, as he feels he must inform the world that the plan that was talked of was actually remembered to him in a dream state."

At this point I could see – from what must have been a memory from Nelson being projected toward me – that he had originally become aware of this plan when he was a mere boy, whilst in conversation with two men who were discussing an unusual maneuver used during another naval battle, albeit on a much smaller scale than that of Trafalgar. The ships involved were foreign vessels. The men were discussing the maneuver with surprise and almost disbelief at its success. Nelson was around twelve years' old at the time when he overheard this conversation. The words Nelson heard had touched him on a very deep level; deep enough not to cause analysis or breakdown of these words – he simply stored up the memory and words in their entirety.

His Angel continued:

"He knew he gained much influence."

The influence he gained, as I understood, came to him during his dream state. During that time he was being influenced to re-create the plan he had overheard years previous, and to bring it to life on a much larger scale. The Angel then went on to explain that it was not Nelson's nature to impulsively, and that the plan was actually very much out of character with the normal Nelson.

"He was more gentle in his approach. He feels he has gained undue credit."

So much pain and compassion was felt in my heart; the pain that Nelson was now carrying, and the compassion that I felt from his Angel. People may think Nelson should not be concerned with receiving so much accolade even if the idea for the battle plan wasn't totally his own; after all he brought pride and honor back to the English nation. Why should Nelson ever feel restricted by the immense remembrance we shall always feel towards him? It seems that in actual fact he felt the credit was too much, and it had begun to weigh him down. The myth about his apparent brilliance and maverick-style risk was being repeated daily right there in his own ship, yet it wasn't actually the way it happened. The plan was a shared responsibility. What Nelson had was the courage to say in his soul "yes!" to the battle plan, and to project his conviction to his officers and men.

Anyway, some ten minutes or so later the children cheered as I got into the car, and we began our journey to Portsmouth. We headed straight to the ship, and waited for the allotted time of our tour. I knew I would sense Nelson near me once more as we approached, but this time I felt it was okay for Nelson's spirit to invade my body and share it for awhile with me.

I had some trepidation about what was to follow – never before had I shared my body with a spirit that had incarnated more than once on this planet. I had previously simply communicated with ghosts; they had not entered or used my body. Usually it is either beings who have had only one incarnation on the Earth, or otherwise energies or beings who have never incarnated, which enter and borrow my body to communicate. Nelson had incarnated more than once – I do not know how many times – so this connection was going to be something new. With this in mind, and really not knowing what to expect, I certainly did not relish the prospect of my head being eased back allowing my will to step out so that a connection could be made, amidst the throng of so many tourists milling around! I saw a sign for the ladies' toilet, and so I raced there straight away to accept the connection in privacy.

Going into the toilet, I noticed that the paper roll had accidentally been knocked down the toilet and was soaked. Seeing this, I telepathically apologized to Nelsons' spirit for the state of the surroundings. Entering into the toilet Tonika Rinar, I came out as half Tonika and half Nelson! It brought to mind the image of Clark Kent entering the telephone box so that he could discreetly transform into Superman…

During a half-and-half state, I can consciously switch from my personality to that of the Spirit that is in my body. In order for me to stay fully connected, it is not possible for me to answer the children or to be distracted – otherwise I would lose the connection. As I returned to the family, Adrian explained to the children that I would not talk to them during our trip onto *Victory* as I needed to remain focused on Nelson's feelings and his persona. It was not long before I realized Nelson was neither aware that he was in my body, nor aware of the modern time period he was now in.

As we entered HMS *Victory*, Nelson became confused – this entrance was unfamiliar to him. I guessed by this reaction that the officers' entrance was separate from this one (which the tour guide later explained was actually the entrance for cargo and for the sailors). Nelson was unaware of any other presence on the ship, either physical or non-physical. He was like a ghost on his own ship.

The tour guide led us all to Nelson's quarters. I calmed the small part of my personality that remained within my body in order to hear Nelson's spirit more clearly. He looked around the quarters; nothing stirred his emotions. But then he looked over to the picture of Lady Hamilton, which remained hanging on the wall in his quarters. This certainly did register – he did not want to part his gaze from her image.

Later, as he scanned the room again, he smiled at the watercolor painting of a child hanging on the opposite wall. The guide later explained the child Horatia was the daughter Nelson and Lady Hamilton had together. I was surprised I hadn't heard about this before, but it was nice to feel the only warmth that Nelson's Spirit showed was towards this child. His gaze went back to Lady Hamilton's picture and stayed there until we moved on.

All through the tour I could sense that Nelson seemed more physically fragile than the portraits depicted of him. He also had difficulty in turning his neck to the right, and because of this he would tend to turn his whole body to the right in order to compensate for this neck restriction. His posture was slouched; his normal posture was for his head and shoulders not to appear upright. Nelson seemed very serious – a personality with little humor. My energy searched to feel a memory of his that may have been fun, but I felt only continued seriousness.

At times when I concentrated intently upon Nelson's persona, my body began to sway, moving as if I were at sea. Gradually, I began feeling the physical changes within my body that Nelson experienced whilst at sea. My legs became weak and I began to feel nauseous. I knew these were not my sensations, they were Nelson's, and was surprised to discover that our greatest Admiral suffered from seasickness! So strong was the nausea that I telepathically requested that Nelson step aside from me so that I could momentarily gain relief. My request was granted and I immediately felt relief. A few moments later, I allowed Nelson's presence to "step back" inside my body. As he did so I remained strong in my breath, keeping the nausea at a distance.

We soon left this part of the ship to go further down into the belly of the Victory. As we walked down the steep wooden steps, I realized we were below the waterline. I began to feel an increased pressure all around me; my ears were blocked. I realized we were below the waterline. I found myself swallowing and stretching my ears to encourage the release of pressure that I was experiencing. I took this to be some symbolic indication of extra pressure outside the hull, as would be the case if we were at sea. This made me wonder – was Nelson's persona reliving the memory of the ship while at sea, or did the *Victory* herself hold memories of how she responded whilst in her favored state – out there ruling the waves?

As we continued our tour inside the ship, the tour guide took us to the place where Nelson died in the arms of Hardy, his first officer. Nelson was reputed to have said as his last breath was about to leave his body, "Kiss me, Hardy". Whether this was true, I cannot say, since I did not sense this from Nelson. It was at Nelson's place of death where I consciously acknowledged all aspects of the courageous plan that sealed the victory of Trafalgar. In doing so, Nelson's spirit was released from the prison that had been created by the immense accolade from the public. As the original situation causing the blockage had occurred here in this dimension, the process of release also had to occur on the Earth.

Why should it be myself required to perform the release? Well, if someone is in prison it only needs one person to turn the key – I just happened to be available, nothing more than that. There needed to be a balance of understanding of the energy involved in the success of the battle, to 'water down' the undue praise and adulation which the public have projected towards Nelson and his image. This understanding had to occur in our physical dimension. In so doing, Nelson's spirit was set free.

This is yet another example of how we are all connected in humanity's consciousness, of how a simple thought or understanding can either strengthen or weaken our mass consciousness. If we choose to believe stories from history that have been exaggerated and taken out of context, then we weaken our link to Divine Will and Universal Flow.[8]

In summary, Nelson's spirit and soul growth was becoming burdened with the immense accolade being directed towards him. Such a misdirected understanding caused an imbalance and as a result Nelson's soul could not grow. Nelson's Angel was able to inform me of this imbalance, and it seems Nelson's spirit needed to remind us, lest we forget, that the success of the final battle plan at Trafalgar was due to the heroic efforts of many. One man may lead a fleet, but many hundreds all have their individual part to play.

At the end of the tour I asked our guide what had he heard of Nelson as a person. The guide, being a member of the Nelson appreciation society, enjoyed relaying his knowledge of Nelson. He told us that Nelson was a very serious person, quite sullen, without humor and that he suffered constant seasickness, especially in the early days of a voyage. This was exactly what I had sensed and experienced from Nelson. Elaborating more on Nelson's life, the tour guide explained how a soothsayer had told Nelson that he would die as his greatest victory triumphed. He had even told London to have his coffin waiting for him when he returned[9]. It seems Nelson had an understanding that is rarely seen these days!

Christian Thomas

One warm and sunny Sunday afternoon, my family and I took a drive through the beautiful countryside in West Sussex to the small city of Arundel, nestling amongst a hilly landscape immediately south of the South Downs. The highlight of this charming and

---

[8] This demonstrates how time-traveling between various historical events will bring about truth and clarity, and in so doing, strengthen man's consciousness. More on this in the time-travel chapter!

[9] It is possible that "Kizmet" (Destiny) and 'Kiss me" was the dying statement uttered by Nelson to Hardy, in light of what the soothsayer had revealed to Nelson.

picturesque town is the magnificent Arundel Castle, home to the Duke and Duchess of Norfolk, and open to visitors during the summer months.

Our plan on this day was to wander through the town and stop off for tea in one of the many old-style tearooms dotted around the town. These tearooms have a plentiful supply of fruit scones and tea, which replenish the weary tourists in need of a 'pick me up' after walking up and down the many hills in Arundel.

We had started our walk on this occasion at the lower end of Arundel and had decided to walk round the outer streets of the town, before heading to the town centre. Our journey took us to Arundel Cathedral. We had never visited the Cathedral before, so Adrian suggested we may as well look inside.

The Cathedral isn't as grand in structure as Chichester Cathedral, and its appearance for me was unexciting and unappealing. However, Adrian loves Cathedrals immensely – the lack of grandeur doesn't seem to bother him in the slightest. He looks at a Cathedral in the same way as a child may look at Santa Claus – with excitement and wonder[10].

We entered the Cathedral. The children asked to light some candles and Adrian suggested that I see if anyone (i.e. a ghost or spirit) was around who wanted to talk.

---

[10] Adrian's diverse personality has always intrigued me. He once, along with his rugby companions, "kidnapped" the Carnival Queen – who was sitting on her throne on the first carnival float (the one that headed the Carnival parade as it went through the town raising money for charity). The rugby float carrying the players was quite brash and noisy and had consequently been designated a position at the back of the parade. Hence, the rugby lads were not collecting as much money as those floats leading the parade.

In a mischievous moment, and to the delight and enjoyment of the locals who lined the streets, the rugby boys – led by Adrian – ran up to the Queen's float, "kidnapped" the Carnival Queen, installing her on their own float. Their antics were immensely appreciated by the locals, who filled the buckets on the

As I sat down on one of the Cathedral pews, glad of the rest after walking up Arundel's steep hills, I almost immediately felt the presence of a brown dog around me. The dog telepathically showed me that he was with his master. The dog's master then appeared. He wore a large floppy beret – a bit like the type of traditional berets worn by artists, although much larger.

The ghost told me his name was Christian Thomas. He had been a very wealthy landowner and farmer. He explained to me that the bastard king who reigned at this time was very fierce. Christian Thomas hated this king, hence his less than respectful name for him! This king was sending armies to burn all the farms and capture all the land owned by the wealthy landowners. They took all of Christian Thomas's land and burnt his farm and killed his wife and children. Their bodies were mutilated and burnt. Christian Thomas was captured and made to join the king's army – he had no choice.

I asked Christian Thomas what this had to do with him being in the Cathedral. He explained that he was waiting to avenge his wife and children's deaths. He explained that the reason why he was in the Cathedral was because it was a place of light. As he said this, I could see a vortex of peace and serenity, a passageway that opened up to the Astral Realms – to the afterlife. It was the heartfelt energy created from pure prayer, held within the walls of this Cathedral, that gave birth to this vortex of light.

Christian Thomas explained to me that many spirits pass by to enter into the after life. He was waiting within this vortex so that he would confront the spirit of the murderer who carried out the

rugby float with all their spare cash. Everyone was happy – except the carnival organizers. The rugby club was banned from subsequent Carnivals.

As we were entering the Cathedral I couldn't help but wonder, would Adrian's fellow team members have the same enthusiasm as Adrian had, going into the Cathedral? The same enthusiasm that filled Adrian was no different in intensity to the enthusiasm that inspired him and his members to steal the Carnival Queen.

king's orders and killed his wife and children, and then take revenge on him one way or another. By doing this he felt his family's spirits would be set free from the terror they had endured.

Although this is what Christian Thomas thought to be the way to salvation, it was in fact an assumption that he had created in his own spirit; a way to get his revenge. He appeared a solitary figure within this vortex. I realized he did not fully appreciate the power of this vortex of light, which actually held within it "stop off" points. A spirit could only transcend to the highest point of the vortex if they had no *karma* or excess baggage to weigh them down – the more baggage they had, the less high they could ascend. Spirits were getting off at different "stop points". I could see one spirit whose glow shone brighter than another's, and thus transcended higher up the vortex. The one whose spirit was denser or indistinct, got off the vortex at a level that resonated harmoniously with their vibration. I became aware that the particular spirit that Christian Thomas was after, had got off the vortex at a level that was lower than where Christian Thomas was waiting. Christian Thomas was at a higher level, not because he chose to be, but because it was the most comfortable level for his spirit to resonate with. He wasn't aware that there were many, many levels within the vortex. So that is why he remained waiting at this level, because in his mind he assumed *all* spirits entered into the after life at this point – and so he waited and waited and waited.

There was nothing either I or anyone else could do to free Christian Thomas of his desire for revenge. Telepathically I was shown a situation that would eventually occur, whereby having waited for so long in that vortex, he would eventually forget what it was he was waiting for. It would be at this point that he would leave the vortex and go into the Astral level where his spirit was most comfortable. It was as simple as that.

As I came out of Arundel Cathedral, I left with a greater understanding of the power of prayer. It reminded me of an answer once given to a person who had come to me for a private session. A beautiful Universal Essence had for the session used my body to answer the person's questions. The person, who had a strong faith in the Catholic religion, said to the Essence:

"I often pray to you, do you hear my prayers?"

The answer, spoken softly, with great compassion and love direct from the heart of this most wonderful divine essence using my body was:

"It is never your words we hear. But when you pray direct from your heart, where feelings of love and oneness are alive, it is then and only then do we hear."

Remembering this answer helped me to see how this vortex in the Cathedral was created. So many people must have gone to this Cathedral, and to others like it, to pray from their hearts. Many people have gone to churches and other holy buildings and prayed for someone they had 'lost' (who had died). Each time people pray at a low point in their life for help and guidance, each time they pray unconditionally for others who were suffering and in pain, each time someone prays from their hearts rather than from instruction or duty or religion, each time a person opens their hearts unknowingly to the flow of Creation – these vortices expand and grow, nurtured and fed by the collective passion of heartfelt prayer.

The fundamental point is that prayer, true prayer is incredibly powerful. It is something never ever to doubt. I am truly in awe of the power prayer creates. If anyone saw the vortex as I saw in the Cathedral – the vortex created from the love of ordinary people – then they too would be in awe of the power of prayer.

＊   ＊   ＊

All the ghost encounters described in this chapter were of a very gentle nature. With the exception of Annie in St Martin's Tearooms who liked to flick the light-switch occasionally, none were manifesting themselves in any way, or would have been any bother to the current human inhabitants of that location. These ghosts are a far cry from the evil spirits and woo-woo ghosts of popular human imagination! In fact, I haven't actually come across any evil ghosts as yet. As described in chapter two, the idea of evil is misleading anyway; malignancy is usually simply created by pockets of unproductive thought-forms.

There is no need to have any fear of ghosts. They bear us no malice. Fear of ghosts is actually usually just fear of the unknown. Turn the lights out, get the imagination running, and you can make anywhere feel spooky! But all you are feeling is your own fear.

6

Past Lives

As the experiences described in the preceding
chapters unfolded, my awakening to and awareness
of the wonderful energies that exist in all dimensions
expanded ever more rapidly. My 'journey home'
was gathering pace! I was like a child surrounded
by many beautifully wrapped presents, energized
and excited by each new discovery that led me to
new worlds and experiences. It was not long before I
realized I could also see into people's past lives…

One evening, driving along the M25 (the motorway encircling
London and the suburbs) in the rush hour traffic, I started to think
about a powerful and popular American speaker, whose subject
was past lives and Native American Indian traditions. A few years
ago I had attended a couple of lectures and workshops held by
this speaker, who was very clear and sincere in manner – I had
thoroughly enjoyed the lectures and workshops.

I had just heard from a friend that this speaker[1] had arrived in

---

[1] For reasons that will soon become apparent, I do not intend to give any clues
as to the identity of this person!

London (from the US) a few days earlier. There was a large festival taking place, lasting for a week or so, and the speaker was one of the main contributors of lectures and workshops. It was advisable to buy tickets early to attend one of the lectures since they were always sold out.

Anyway, there I was driving home, music playing in my car, busy watching out for any drivers not keeping to the rules of motorway driving. After the initial memory of the speaker, my thoughts drifted to wondering how they were getting on in life. Suddenly, like a light switch being turned on, I started to become aware of a past life connected to this person. The images and feelings I was experiencing were almost overwhelming, to the extent that I had to focus even harder on my driving. The images and feelings began to form a story.

In this past life, the speaker was a physically strong male, living in Peru at the time of the Incas. This male had great insight and strength. He had married the tribal princess – she was pure and innocent in her ways, and had given herself totally to him. He on the other hand had the ability to bring much power in a positive form to the tribe – but he began to misuse this power. He felt that his strength and insights were not acknowledged by his tribe. A neighboring tribe, who were not too pure in their ways, began to revere him and see him as a link to the gods that they worshipped at that time. This man began to enjoy the attention and sense of power that came with being revered by this other tribe. His ego became over- inflated at the thought of being special. This caused his home tribe to feel he was betraying them and therefore endangering their existence. They turned against him – and buried him alive.

The ego of this man had required recognition and acceptance for whatever powerful vision or insight he offered to the tribe. However, the tribal Elders would not respond to the man's need for recognition. They knew that the only way insights of a true spiritual nature could be delivered to the tribe – insights which would strengthen their existence and work in harmony with nature and creation – was if they came in purity, and if the person bringing them had quietened his/her own ego. This caused him to become frustrated with the way his tribe viewed him. But the Elders saw him as equal to every other person within the tribe – they just wouldn't acknowledge his oversized ego. Unfortunately, the man was not aware of the imbalance to his ego and his spirit, and so when the neighboring tribe respected him over their own people, the man's ego was elevated and his betrayal of his tribe began.

Despite his death, his wife remained true to his spirit and memory. She could see the purity in his heart, she knew his power and she knew his intentions had been judged harshly by her Elders. She knew that his power was not directed positively, but she did not believe that it was his fault – the people wanted a bit of his power and were manipulating him accordingly; falsely feeding his ego so he would be drawn more away from his own tribe to theirs. The other tribe just wanted to take from him. So strong was her love that she vowed at his graveside that she would always be with him when needed.

As this image subsided, another image just as strong as the last entered my head. Still concentrating hard on my driving, I became aware of this popular speaker alone in a very small prison cell. Yet hundreds of people were the other side of the cell's bars, trying desperately to reach the speaker. The people were trying to touch, pull, grab – they wanted and demanded more and more from the speaker. Looking bewildered, the speaker felt the only way out of the cell was to deliver what the public wanted. A sense of manipulation entered this scene – a feeling from the speaker of needing to deliver spiritual insights and experiences. "Keep feeding the people with these insights, then I'll be free from this cell, and they'll leave me alone," was the thought.

During this vision, a message came across for the speaker from the speaker's own Angel: "You are repeating the life of the Inca tribesman. Although you are born into mankind, you are not of mankind, and yet you are trying to be as mankind. You have created your prison within mankind; you have let yourself be influenced by mankind's ways. You are here to deliver universal truths to mankind – and yet you let yourself be manufactured. This has caused you to separate yourself from Great Spirit; you are imprisoned by man's needs. Remember the freedom that soared within your soul – do not compromise your freedom into acceptance of mankind. Step out of that prison and be who you are, not who you think you are."

I continued to concentrate hard on my driving, as the images and words from the Angel faded. The experience left me with an overwhelming need to relay what I had witnessed to the speaker – I knew I had to pass on the Angel's message. This need grew stronger and stronger as I continued my homewards journey in the car.

I arrived home, trying to organize the evening ahead in my mind – cook the family's dinner, listen to the children read, make sure they do their homework, who's going to want their bath first…? How I would give my time and attention to them individually so they could each tell me how school was that day. Make sure they have clean school clothes for the following day… And before all this – a much-needed cup of tea! But I couldn't concentrate at all on family life until I had spoken with the speaker.

I telephoned the festival's offices. They informed me that the speaker was to arrive there in the next half-hour and they agreed to pass on my request for the speaker to telephone me. However, the speaker had to catch a plane that evening, so they weren't sure whether there would be time for a call. So I wasn't really expecting the speaker to call back, but felt that I had made an effort by telephoning the offices. To my surprise though, twenty minutes later the telephone did indeed ring. I briefly (shortened version!) told the speaker of the past life experience connected to them, and with very carefully chosen words shared the message that was from their Angel. The telephone line fell silent, then very gently the speaker confirmed the past life and their connection and interest with that time span in Peru. The speaker knew there was something in the past that was causing a block in their life now. With calm and centered honor, the speaker acknowledged their Angel's words. "You speak with great courage," the person said. "Yes," I thought, "having to relay such sensitive information to someone so well known and respected wasn't easy!' To tell the truth I was a bag of nerves, but my sense of conviction overruled my worries, which was why I was able to communicate freely with that person. A sense of calm washed over me as we said our goodbyes. The overwhelming surge of energy urging me to talk with the speaker had ceased, and I was able to focus on my family life for the rest of the evening.

Seeing this person's past life connection expanded my consciousness to now be aware of other people's past lives. However, I was confused as to why my experience had occurred at such an inconvenient time and place – the M25 is not the most ideal setting for dealing with major insights! Surely a more appropriate setting could have been found? Later I came to realize that because I was focused on driving the car, there was no mental energy left to try to fight and push the images away. If it had occurred at home in a more peaceful location, my mind may have ridiculed the images, not trusting myself to accept what was occurring and thus ignoring what I was receiving.

As word spread of my newfound talent, people started coming to my house, intrigued to find out who they had been in a previous life. I enjoyed this time of expansion in me, as I saw many different past lives and previous life situations. The information contained within a past life usually acted as a key to unlock an even greater understanding in each person.

Although it was a wonderful experience seeing all those different previous lives of people, I began to feel it would be more expansive for the individual if they could see and feel their own past lives for themselves. As this thought evaporated I became aware of a wonderful energy, that holds the key to past-life existences. Excited by the introduction to yet another wonderful energy residing in our universe, I began to explore gentle ways of taking a person back to a past life. I would keep my focus on the person who was going to be regressed with me, for at least a week beforehand. When the day arrived that had been booked for the regression, I would make sure my intent and focus was on the task in hand. Before the sitter arrived I would prepare the room that was to be used for the regression. I always lit three candles; one for my Angel, one for the sitter's Angel, and one for the energy that holds the key to past-life existences. (Who, by the way, has a name, or rather I should say; a vibration with which he resonated). As I lit the candle, I would call this energy by name and declare my intent, stating; "If Divine Will sees it is appropriate for the regression to occur, please can I have all the help from creation's highest beings of Light. But if it is not appropriate to perform the regression, then please block my way." Making this statement and repeating the name of the being 'who holds the key to past lives connected me to his energy. I would feel my bones and blood respond to the presence of the past-life energy. When I felt this sensation, I knew the session was going to be immensely productive.[2]

---

[2] Only on two occasions have I *not* experienced a connection to this divine energy. One occasion was when a sitter had traveled many miles to see me, having a week earlier booked to see me for a regression. Due to the time and effort she had taken to come to see me I felt almost oblige to opt for a past life regression, since this is what she wanted. It was only when I succumbed to the fact that the session was not working that I was finally given an explanation by the goddess Isis (historically known as an Egyptian goddess). Very beautiful and graceful, Isis came to explain to us that there would have been no benefit at all for the sitter to have experienced a past life regression. I didn't question Isis why this was. (When communicating with these wondrous spirits, one gains a quite sense of when it's all right to ask a question and when it is inappropriate to ask!). Isis then took over the session and spoke for around thirty minutes to the sitter, who was a young girl in her early twenties. Although the girl had

My other preparations before a regression include asking for all the help and guidance in the universe that is appropriate for the person who is to be regressed and for myself. Then I like to place something extra in the sacred space that has been created. This can be anything; flowers, an ornament, even a soft toy belonging to one of my children. Whatever feels right goes in the space. I then go through a process of questioning my own motives about why I'm going through with the regression. "It just feels right to do," isn't enough confirmation for me to do any spiritual work; regression or otherwise. I have to go through all my weaknesses until I touch my innate strengths – and then I have total faith and trust in myself and the universe for the process of regression to occur.

And when it does occur, it is with great ease. Using the wonderful universal energies and in particular the being who holds the key to past lives ensures a powerful session and a safe and transforming outcome.

It takes about five to ten minutes for a person to regress. They are fully aware of their physical body at all times. Many describe the experience as being like two people at the same time. It is like watching a video, except you are part of that video and the video is real life going on around you – it's a 3D type of experience.

The Angels know exactly how far back to take a person, to get right to the root of the problem occurring in their present life. Whatever

told me she was on a spiritual path, she had in fact become lost and confused, and tangled up with the many different rigid beliefs, ceremonies and ways that earthly spirituality has to offer. The young girl asked questions and Isis answered, bringing clarity to her much confused heart. When Isis departed and my will returned, the girl – looking extremely happy – told me:

"Through my confusing spiritual path, I have always been drawn towards the goddess Isis. I feel that no one else could have helped me the way she has helped me today."

I found it all quite amazing, as up to that point I had only met Isis once, and that had purely been an introduction to Isis' energy.

it is causing the problem or block they are experiencing now has its origins in a past life. They do not change what has occurred in the person's past life – I have not found it possible to change the past to suit the present. What the Angels do is encourage the person's viewpoint of an incident that has caused them pain and harshness to expand. They assist the person to become aware not only of their deep emotions and feelings born out of the incident, but also to become aware of emotions and energies of other people around them, to have a complete overview. Sometimes they are even guided to inhabit another person's body or – if need be – into the spirit of an animal, bird or sea creature, during the time span to which they have regressed. This can prove to be a particularly powerful experience, as I was to discover...

Flying to freedom

The lady in question had come to me feeling very worthless; her husband in this life was dominant and controlling. She felt she didn't have a life; she was only here to "serve" her husband. During the regression she was aware of herself repeating her present situation in a past life, this time as the wife of a Roman farmer. The farmer was her present day husband. She was aware of feeling trapped in this past life and had resigned herself to these feelings. She felt unacknowledged and unrecognized as a person.

My Angel encouraged her to journey deep into her spirit to see the abundance of beauty and freedom that existed there. She tried and tried, but because she had so completely resigned herself to her state of worthlessness her heart had closed down, and she found the process of true recognition impossible. The block on herself was very large indeed. So the Angels guided her out of herself – she needed to get out of her own way in order to experience the senses of freedom and joy. She was asked to imagine any bird, so she chose a dove. She was then guided to take flight with the dove. She did this with ease, because the emphasis was now on the dove and not herself. As she and the dove soared through the air, she was asked what her feelings were. Her face became softer, her body relaxed and her breathing was less restricted as she replied; "I feel I can go anywhere. I feel free, I feel light, with each dive and with each ascent. I feel stronger. I am becoming stronger and stronger in my person, its strange, I don't know myself. I feel so good!"

She was asked to "fly over" to where her husband was in this regression. She flew above her home area and watched her husband, who was talking loudly with other men. She was asked to observe what type of energy they were giving off.

"Raw," she replied. "They think they are better than others, they get their power and self assurance by walking over people, but they are weak; they could not survive on their own. They do not know how to live and be free. They are imprisoned by their self-created importance and brashness. They are not strong; they are weak. They are not even as weak as the weakest branch on a tree – at least the branch is part of the tree, no matter how weak it may seem. But they are only part of themselves, they have no strength."

The lady was guided once more to fly freely, to enjoy the person she truly was. It was explained to her that her husband's light was weak, and at times when his light became weaker he would project the sense of domination and controlling towards her and various life situations. It appears easier to blame or accuse others than to nurture what is inside. To acknowledge the light in her husband would free her spirit from its worthless sense, and as her spirit grew stronger, her physical being would also gain strength. She would be aware of more direction in her life, she would know where and how to live, and to remain free.

Before she was brought back to waking consciousness, she was asked to remember in her heart her journey with the Dove, and the freedom and strength it brought. My Angel explained that she would be able to recall those feelings at any point in her life.

When the lady opened her eyes she was astounded by the reality of what she had experienced. She looked stronger, and a touch bedazzled!

A year later, Adrian and I had taken my ginger tomcat to the vet.[3] We both sat in the vet's waiting room, looking at the other cats and dogs being brought in, Adrian smiled at a lady sitting opposite with her golden retriever dog. I figured she must be one of the patients he treated at his chiropractic clinic. She smiled back and so I smiled also. Adrian whispered to me, "That's Maria," speaking as if I should know who she was. She was a very smartly dressed, well-presented lady. She appeared to know me, given the way she looked and smiled at me, though at the time I had no idea who she was (although I didn't admit it!). We started chatting to pass the time whilst waiting for the vet. Maria was first to be called in to the vet's treatment room, with her golden retriever.

"You don't know who that is, do you?" Adrian enquired with amusement. "You regressed her a year ago – her husband was a bit of a rogue. I can't believe how much she has changed; she looks so different, so confident. That must have been one mighty big regression she had!"

I was stunned! "It can't be – are you sure?"

"Of course I am, can't you see?" replied Adrian. He was pretty excited. I was a touch speechless.

"Look, I'll ask her on her way out,"

When she came out of the treatment room Adrian asked how she was getting on. She explained that since her regression, her life had completely changed. She had got herself a job, she felt it gave her independence from her husband, and she had taken up some

---

[3] He had been fighting with other cats and had gone and got himself a large abscess on his head. Adrian had come with me – I had made up some lame excuse why I wanted him there. Actually, it was because I didn't want my ginger tomcat to blame me totally for his experience at the vets!

sporting activities. She was still living with her husband, 'but not as a doormat for him any more' (as she put it).

"I will never forget the freedom and strength whilst flying with the dove," she said wistfully, "I still recall that memory from time to time."

Sparkling and with confidence she thanked me and said goodbye. I remained speechless…

This was a wonderful example of how divine beings can help a person to unblock themselves and release new energies and capabilities that exist within them. These energies had been made inaccessible by some previous life (or indeed, present life) situations. Once the regression has released the blockage, dormant energies can rise to the surface and allow the person to be who they truly are.

Carol – mistress of Charles II

Carol was a successful desktop publisher, very well respected in her field. She'd had a number of previous relationships but was currently single, which was why she had come to see me. She felt she couldn't commit to any relationship that she had – a great part of her was being prevented from fully committing to any relationship, and this resistance to commit was probably due to that fact that she found it extremely difficult to show any emotions.

"Although I'm happy", she told me, "I can't laugh; nothing comes out of my mouth. I want to laugh, I want to let go, but nothing happens. It's the same when I'm sad; I just can't cry – never have for as long as I can remember. I know I want to cry; I can feel all the emotions building up, but when the point of release comes, whether it's tears or laughter, I just seem to freeze. It's so frustrating! I was wondering whether there was something in a past life of mine that had affected me so greatly – that perhaps it had scarred my emotions in this one."

Whilst Carol was explaining this to me, I didn't receive any inspiration or any great *eureka* that may have suggested her problem could be the result of a past life incident. Many people are quick to blame past life trauma as a convenient excuse for their emotional problems and unruly behavior in their current life. But there are many factors that can cause emotional, mental and physical blocks or restrictions in a person's life – to simply lump the blame on to previous life traumas is rather limiting in an unlimited universe! So I find it is best to remain as open as possible to the solution of the problem. Anyway, I agreed to help Carol regress – at least we would find out if there was anything in her past or not. Carol booked the appointment for a week later.

It was a beautiful early autumn day in late September. There was a clear sky, crisp fresh air – the sun was casting a soft glow, very different to the bright sunlight of midsummer. I love those days of late September; I can feel the energy of the Earth beginning to slow down. Everyone is still rushing around as they did in summer, seemingly unaware that the Earth is withdrawing her energy for the long winter sleep ahead. She (the Earth) knows how to rest, and then come to life once more when spring arrives. I love this feeling of the Earth slowing down.[4]

Carol arrived, she was very excited and eager to begin. I had already prepared the setting, half drawing the curtains to calm the

---

[4] Some time ago, I symbolically placed the four seasons of the Earth into age categories of our life. Spring is from birth to around the time when we are approximately twenty; summer is from twenty to around forty-five, and this is where our energy is feeling busy and productive – almost as if we don't have time to take for ourselves and remember how to live and how to be part of the world (and not just live in isolation upon it). Trying to meet each deadline, each bill payment, having demands put on us either by ourselves or by others…

Then comes autumn. We are beginning to accept ourselves, accept life, and realize we can walk or run. We begin to realize there is a deep beauty within our spirit. We have through spring and summer seen many different aspects of light somewhat, and then lighting three candles as I always do; one for Carol's angel, one for mine and one for "the being who holds the key to past lives" As I lit each candle a huge surge of compassionate energy soared through me – I knew we were in for an exciting time.

Carol made herself comfortable in a soft armchair. I began to guide her through the relaxation process, and then my Angel stepped in and took over the session, taking Carol back in this life to the age of around four or five years old. Carol was aware of a sense of freedom and play, fun and laughter. She was guided to stay awhile at this age, soaking in the memory, feeling and remembering the laughter and the fun. I watched her face moving with pleasure as she recalled these fond memories. My Angel reminded Carol that she could access these nurturing memories at any time. The remembrance of these warm memories would lift and empower her.

It was then time to move back further. My Angel very gently guided Carol's focus to begin going back through the rest of her childhood, back to infancy, back through her birth. (Sometimes if there is any trauma connected with the birth, my Angel will stop awhile whilst the healing process occurs. In Carol's case, her birth was without trauma or emotional resistance.) Back into the womb, being aware of her mother's heartbeat, being aware of herself as a fetus.

ourselves. We no longer fight against ourselves or try and be who we are not. We become confident and accepting of who we are.

Winter finally comes; our way of living slowly dies, and we begin to clear ourselves of any restrictions that have prevented us from living life to the full. We see how our life was a jigsaw puzzle, and how each event of our life helped us to complete our puzzle. We see how timing was so important for the puzzle to be completed successfully. If we tried to rush our puzzle we do not find all the pieces, and we are left feeling empty or robbed. But for most, it is a time to feel at peace with the wisdom that winter brings. We can see further spiritually and mentally – as the leaves that clouded our vision have fallen.

My Angel questioned Carol as to whether there were any particular feelings or sensations that particularly stood out for her, whilst her consciousness was recalling the time in her mother's womb. Carol explained that she felt safe, wanted and very loved. She told me she could feel her heart swell with the intensity of the pleasant emotions she was experiencing whilst in her mother's womb. My Angel took Carol back, further and further, and then asked:

"Who are you?"

Carol explained that she was a woman living in France. She described what the area looked like and where it was. She was aware she had two children, but was very surprised to report that they had red hair – this seemed to stun her somewhat. Even more surprisingly, she told me she was Charles II's mistress, and the two children (a boy and a girl) were Charles' offspring. She seemed to be quite shocked by this memory – not in a negative way, but shocked that she (Carol) could have been connected to royalty in the past, since she felt quite conventional within contemporary society.

Staying awhile and recalling this memory, my Angel soon realized that there wasn't anything scarring Carol at this point in her regressed life. So Carol was instructed to take a deep breath and move slightly forward. Carol responded: The scene around her had changed. She wasn't in France any more, she was now in England, at a large house in the country. By her description I could envisage a large stately home. Carol then began to become afraid. She told me that Charles was in this house also. Her panic increased as she breathlessly explained that some men were entering the house. Charles and his allies took refuge in one of the many secret passages within the house – the men in their clanking military armor unsuccessfully searched the many rooms and halls. There was a lot of tension in Carol's voice.

My Angel moved Carol yet again slightly further on in this life. Carol's tension and panic suddenly magnified hugely. My Angel very calmly asked where she was. Carol answered, her voice shaking with sheer terror;

"I'm in France – I'm in the tower."

She had been sentenced to death. She told me she was dressed in white. Her hands were restlessly moving, with scared determination.

"What are you holding?" My Angel asked.

"Rosary beads." She said, her voice quite breathless. My Angel became more focused and directed.

"Move forward," she said. "Where are you now?"

"I'm walking towards my execution. I am wearing white, and I am holding my beads very tightly." Carol answered.

As she spoke tears fell down her face; she was sobbing helplessly, and feeling utterly alone and frightened. She told me that everyone had come to watch her die. There was a large crowd jeering and shouting, calling her names. They were directing all of their anger towards her. She saw the guillotine – she saw her executioner. An air of quickening confusion and anger surrounded her. Her heart began to beat faster and faster.

As this scene unfolded I was thinking to myself; 'surely the Angels are going to stop this scene – surely they are not going to take her right through to the end of the execution??' Carol was sobbing and shaking uncontrollably. Surely they could see she can't take any more? But I was also thinking; 'Wow Carol, for someone who reckons they've never cried, you're certainly making up for it today!'

"What is happening now?" My Angel asked Carol.

"My head is being positioned onto the wood."

At this point I was feeling sick to my stomach, I was so concerned for Carol. I thought to myself; 'Oh my God – surely this is going to stop!.' I felt myself begin to start shaking at what was going to happen next. Yet throughout all this trauma I felt secure in my Angel's strength and focus. I knew my Angel was going to take Carol right to the very root of her problem, so that she could fully heal her past and move on.

There was a countdown to the release of the guillotine (myself still not believing it would actually happen) Carol was mumbling very fast and quietly, pulling all her energy in to deal with her death. The guillotine was released – suddenly my Angel clearly and firmly said 'STOP!' The whole scene froze; the guillotine halfway down, the crowd and their jeering, the officials overseeing the execution – *everything* froze. Carol's tears stopped immediately. A stillness beyond words entered Carol and myself. My Angel held out my arms and she instructed Carol:

"Hold onto my hands. I am going to pull you out of your body, so you can be aware of your life passing, and watch without pain."

Carol held onto my Angel's hands and she was very gently pulled out of her body, her spirit resting safely with my Angel.

"What is paining your spirit now?" my Angel asked gently.

Carol told her that she felt dirty and humiliated by the jeers and ugly taunts of the crowd. She was carrying a huge amount of distress. She had absorbed the raw emotion of the crowd; all her self-worth had gone. So, my Angel sent her spirit out into the crowd, and then the frozen scene came back to life. Carol was now in the midst of her tormentors. My Angel asked her to be aware of what fuelled their energy. She surprised herself by replying;

"Ignorance and boredom."

Her execution had simply given the crowds something to project their negative energy at. They were dull and repressed in their everyday life. She realized her vulnerability and humiliation didn't touch them – they were not aware of her as a person, they simply loved a good execution! It was their way of releasing their own built up frustrations. Relief and lightness speeded through her spirit. No longer did she feel helpless and attacked. She understood the crowd and their motives.

Before she passed over from that life into the Astral worlds, she asked if she could see her children. She explained to my Angel that she was concerned that they may have suffered the same fate as she. My Angel guided her to a large house where Carol could see her son, who was about eight or nine years' old, playing quite happily with his younger sister (Carol's daughter, who was about five or six years of age). My Angel told Carol:

"They have within them a strength and a knowing. Before they were born they knew they would not be with you for long – so they were well prepared to be parted from you at an early age."

As I watched Carol's children, I understood that they had good lives and grew to adulthood in peace.

Carol was now ready to return to this life. My Angel very gently brought her awareness back to the comfortable chair that she was sitting on opposite me. She slowly opened her eyes and looked at me in disbelief.

"I can't believe that all came out of me, and yet I know how real it was. I want to doubt my experience, but I know I can't. My head – my whole being – feels as if a great burden has been shifted. I am absolutely speechless…"

As she was speaking I could sense to the right of her head the burden of that past life memory being packaged and taken away from her. Amazed at the amount of tears she shed, she began to start laughing, only gently, but definitely a happy sound. She left my home still somewhat dazed by the experience – trying to find a logical explanation for it.

A few months passed. Carol was now in a happy relationship, which she felt she had committed to. She felt much freer and was talking of having children. She could at last laugh. She hadn't as yet had any reason to cry, but she could really laugh.

That past-life session as usual left me in awe. The Angels know exactly where the roots of a problem are and they will only take a person to that point if they feel the person is ready to face it. The regression then occurs with great ease.

A journey into my own past

As well as these fascinating insights in to the past lives of other people, I have also had cause to visit my own previous existences – a journey required to clear a blockage in my current existence. At many times in my life since first starting this journey I have doubted myself, allowing negative thoughts to cloud my mind. "What's the point of it all? Does anyone really care?" or "I must be the worst person on this planet, bringing in all this information that could upset so many people's belief systems." Many times I have wondered why am I doing this? Why can't I live an ordinary life – this work is never going to earn me a living or pay the bills! Constantly I have to work on myself, my attitudes, my vulnerabilities, my wanting to fit in somewhere – simply to feel part of the human race and not isolated from it. So many times I have wanted to give up.

One particular time, many years ago, I was feeling very alone and my life appeared to have no meaning (apart from being mum to my children, which I have to say was probably my main lifeline – being responsible for and able to give my love to my kids).[5] On this particular afternoon I began to grow very tired. An overwhelming sense of a past life began to engulf me. I knew I was being slowed down by the Angels, making me feel sleepy. They wanted me to be aware of a past-life incident that would help my present doubting mental state. If an Angel simply appeared and said: "Tonika, go and sit down while we take you through a past life which will explain to you why you doubt yourself – you will be able to release those

---

[5] The children really did keep me going. The love that flowed from the children to me and from me to the children was a constant reminder to me of how wonderful, how perfect and how unconditionally the universe works. To this day, the sense of wonderment I have for creation stays strong within me. But, being an ordinary human being, I guess I still get my "off" days – I used to get a lot in the earlier years. Not so many now, thank goodness.

doubts and become more understanding of yourself..." Well, that would be too easy. In fact, because of the doubting mood I was in at the time, I probably would have begun doubting myself even more! Usually, I took the hard route and would mentally beat myself up and get totally exhausted, until eventually I couldn't doubt myself any more. Next day I would rise up fresh and sparkling – until the next time my doubts surfaced. Yes, I was very tough on myself in those early days! But fortunately for me, the Angels knew all my tricks and foibles, so they would simply make me sleepy so that I *couldn't* fight myself. Then I would have to go and shut my eyes for a few minutes.

I became more and more tired, so off I went to rest awhile in my comfy chair. An Angel stood to my right and began to relax me, using breathing techniques. My consciousness was awake but my body and mind was completely relaxed. I began to be aware of myself as a Native American Indian boy.[6]

"What is your name?" the Angel asked.

"Little light in the sky," I replied. I was aware the name had been given to me after the passing of one full and one new moon – roughly one month after my birth. The Angels then moved me forward in time quite considerably. Now I was full-grown and fairly old, my body was very strong and I felt quite tall. I was now an Elder of my tribe and my name had progressed to "Great White Thunder". I felt it was a name I had earned from various situations and events of significance in my life.

It was dusk, and there was a huge fire in front of me. Three other Elders also stood in front of the fire. I stood to the east of the flames, the other three Elders stood south, west, and north. I was aware that the rest of the tribe had formed a great circle around us, and were chanting with great focus and passion. I knew what was going to hap-

---

[6] Previous lives can be of either sex.

pen. Each Elder had a vision that would affect our tribes – not in the immediate future, but generations later. The other three elders and myself were aware of a great tragedy that was to wipe out most of our people. We knew our people would only survive if we gave our vision of new life and abundance to the energy of the fire. The sacred fire energy would keep our vision safe and ensure the survival of our tribe. Each one of us had to walk into the flames holding our vision and offer our bodies to feed the fire. It was self-sacrifice – seen as the only way to save our tribe. My body shook with the terrifying prospect, but my conviction to perform this task outweighed the terror I felt.

Each one of us represented the four elements – air, water, fire, earth. All needed for a race (our tribe) to survive. I represented air. The tribe chanted louder and louder; I could feel their strength, passion and support, as myself and the other three elders focused on our visions as we very slowly entered the flames. Adrenaline rushed through me, replacing any fear. I desperately fought to hold onto my vision – it was so hard. I couldn't breathe, no air, my legs were burning, pain soared through me right to the depths of my soul. The tribe carried our pain through their chanting, their sound becoming stronger and stronger as if to drown out our cries of agony – and then silence. Stillness fell in and around me as I passed through the fire and into the heavenly realms.

The Native Americans refer to God as "Great White Spirit", and having died as a Native American, I would have thought that I would be carrying the belief of the title "Great White Spirit" with me. So I was very surprised indeed to be met by a being dressed in white, a male, with shoulder length hair, who I recognized as God[7]. This

---

[7] To this day I still haven't quite worked that one out. My confusion, is simply because I see God as the ultimate energy and therefore I do not see this Great Energy encased in a form. To me, God is Creation, is Divine Will, is flow of the Universe; it is the energy that flows through and unites everything and us all. It is not a person.

wonderful being dressed in white took my hand, seemingly unaware of my confusion, and turned to show me my tribe generations later, living well and living in abundance. He explained to me; "Just because you do not see immediate results within the work you do, never doubt the effects of your work. You may never see results in your life time, but every time someone gives of themselves, selflessly – mountains move." I do feel that message was not just for me, but for everyone who gives, and gives unconditionally. I left that life as a Native American, and returned to this one with a greater sense of peace and direction.

It was during the regression of John that I discovered that not all spirits who are given the opportunity of another life on Earth (so that their soul may grow and expand) actually want to come back. Sometimes the previous life(s) they had lived caused them so much trauma that they would rather stay within the cozy comforts of the Astral Realms.

When our individual learning has gone as far as it can within the Astral Realms, we are advised by Angels and higher sources to take another journey back in to the human dimension, and (hopefully) release blockages that are preventing our soul growth. We need to go back to the Earth, back to the dimension and reality where we first acquired our restrictions, limitations and blockages. We cannot do this in the Astral Realms, since we cannot understand the bigger picture of why our blocks and restrictions occurred. Armed with this knowledge we can then be guided to a life and life situations where we can release our restrictions, etc. without pain and trauma – or at least with as little as possible!

That's the plan, anyway. However, as said, some spirits in the Astral Realms are very resistant to the idea of returning to Earth. As a result, the mother of one of these reluctant Spirits (once they have been reincarnated) will probably not have a great bond with their child, and as the reluctant child grows into adulthood there will be very little contact from the grown child to the mother and father.

As children grow they can be seen to struggle physically and/or emotionally with themselves. This is because they are still resisting being on the Earth – and may have not walked within this dimension for a very long time. They seem to struggle with childhood, but in most cases will adapt to adulthood with a great sense of freedom.

The mother, more so than the father, would have been selected very carefully to carry and give birth to one or more of these reluctant spirits. It will be the mother's inner understanding of freedom and all that is associated with freedom, which will allow the reluctant spirit (whilst inside her womb) to grow and progress with maximum ease. These mothers are more likely to be much firmer and stricter than the father. The reluctant spirit will often try and disassociate itself from society, staying within the safety of its own world. It may start to rebel against their parents and society, which is their reluctance to being on the Earth coming out to the full. These children do not become offensive to society. They are watched very carefully indeed by Angels and their guides. They were given a shove back into a body – but they are never alone.

John's problem in this life was with his father. On the surface they appeared to get on and have a normal father/son relationship. But there was a strained type of respect between the two of them, an invisible barrier that neither of them could cross.

"I feel I owe my father, but not like owing a debt of gratitude or that type of feeling. It's like he's cross with me and blames me for something, I can't understand why. He doesn't look at life the way I do. I want the most that life can offer, but all he does is go to work on the building site, and then down to the pub, gets totally drunk, then comes home and falls into bed. The next morning he gets up and starts all over again. He seems okay with the way he is living his life; he certainly doesn't appear unhappy. He has plenty of friends, most of who behave as he does. But to me he seems fixed, and I have this overwhelming feeling that I am responsible for him. My mother puts up with him and gets on as best she can with her life

– she doesn't seem affected by his behavior. I feel the more I try and get close to him, the more distant we become."

John was a lovely man, very optimistic and enthusiastic with life. It seemed odd that he struggled with his father. So we began the regression.

John was taken back to a time around the sixteenth century. He was a sailor; a huge and foul-mouthed man who loved his beer. He caused mayhem wherever he went, and was arrogant and full of his own importance. However, John also had an older brother, with whom he was a very different person – caring and protective. His brother had been born crippled; very weak and frail. Fortunately for him, John had enough strength and stamina for the two of them.

John made sure his brother was well looked after whilst he was off at sea. And whenever he was back home, he took over his brother's care and needs. Although John had a feisty loud personality, he was always calm and reassuring to his brother.

John was guided to go back through this life to see if the root of his problem in his present day life originated in the life he was recalling. As he traveled back through that life, back through his teenage years, back through childhood and infancy, it became apparent that John's previous life (despite his brash and raw ways) did not hold the key to the problem he was aware of with his father at the present time. So he was guided to go back further, beyond his birth and up to the point of his decision to incarnate into this brash sailor's life. John was aware he was now spirit, no body and no form – a great sense of freedom filled him.

However, he could also sense the existence of a spirit who was very weak and in a great deal of stress, having had one or two very tough incarnations previously. The spirit found it difficult to trust, and because of this inability to trust in Creation, had closed himself off. (I refer to the spirit as male, because at this moment in time that's how the spirit presented itself). It was decided that the only way the spirit could regain trust in Creation was to be re-born into human form; and with help and assistance learn to accept there is a great deal of goodness within man. There would be people in physical form that would freely support him, and of course people and energy beings in the non-physical form also there to give protection and guidance.

John recognized this tired spirit as his present day father. John had chosen to be re-born solely to look after this weakened spirit, not to do so for his own growth – the purpose of John's incarnation was unconditionally to assist this weak and reluctant spirit, and constantly reassure him that he would take care of him, he would protect him. Now, one may wonder why the spirit could not be helped more while "between bodies". This spirit was indeed given immense help and healing whilst in the Astral Realms. But our individual souls are like flowers – flowers need water and sunlight to grow; the more they are nurtured the more they grow. Likewise, our individual souls are fed by the experiences we have on Earth. Often we arrive at our birth like race horses wearing blinkers – these blinkers can make us turn away from a situation that is created on our life's journey to help us. So we cloud our inner trust with fear, and our lives then become harder for us. On the other hand, the blinkers can also make us run too fast, wanting to get to the finishing line (the end of our life) – before tripping and falling or making a mistake. Either way we end up learning nothing, and our soul does not grow.

Life and the Universe are constant, ever flowing ever changing and evolving. For our soul to remain productive within the flow of creation, it needs the strength our experiences in life have taught us. John's father's spirit had, during a couple of unpleasant incarnations, lost his ability to trust – so he had to return back to the Earth in order to find that trust. He could not find it in the Astral Realms since that was not where he lost it. If he did not agree to incarnate, and through his future life experiences find his trust in creation, his soul would have withered, as would a flower deprived of water and light.

So it seems we can incarnate purely to help others to find their trust and to find love, and we may incarnate to support others as they find once more they are part of creation and that they are not separate, alone and forgotten. It was decided his father would incarnate as the older brother of John, and physically crippled. Although this may have seemed quite harsh, it was in fact the most gentle approach possible.[8] In this state, John's brother was not able to participate in life that much; but what he could do was observe, watch and be aware of everything around him. He could watch how people respond to various situations, watch what gives pleasure, watch what gives anger, watch how people interact, watch power struggles forming, watch great acts of kindness and watch what to be part of and what to avoid. He would be able to watch all of life, but at the same time not be aware of his observations. This therefore by-passed his logic, which would only try and analyze various conditions and in so doing break the larger picture down, so that the whole essence of the observation would be lost, thus depriving his spirit of the deeper level of understanding of why or where certain human traits stem from. When we truly understand and accept something, we feel it within our heart area and at the same time our heads go quietly silent.

John's father's spirit agreed to be reborn, knowing he would be supported by John – who followed shortly after. Unfortunately though, John, despite having given himself freely to be involved in this supporting role, met an early death in a drunken brawl. He thus left the planet earlier than intended, leaving his crippled brother

---

[8] I must add here that there was no judgment being made by Creation on John's brother. For him to be crippled in his life was a means for him to truly observe humanity and so learn to trust – nothing more and nothing less. That isn't to say this is the case for all people that have physical disabilities. For them there may be a million and one different reasons for their disabilities. But, one thing is for sure – creation places no judgment upon them as greater or lesser.

with no means of physical support. As a result, John had carried with him ever since a sense of letting his brother down, which weighed very heavily on his spirit. John had made a promise to his brother – a promise that he had broken. John knew deeply that he had lost his direction in life. He had succumbed to too much alcohol – and had paid the price.

It would seem reasonable to assume that if we do something completely unconditional for someone, then surely no harm can come to us. To an extent that is true, but if we do the ridiculous, i.e. reckoning we can survive jumping off a cliff because we lived our lives helping others and so the universe is going to protect us – well, that would be rather foolhardy! Although we may have a life plan, it is destiny in name only, for we have free will to subvert that plan at any time. And we often do! As was the case with John's situation. Although he had given himself unconditionally to be reborn to protect his crippled brother, this selfless action did not automatically constitute protection for himself to live a life free from wayward influences. The alcohol took hold of him and he left the planet, leaving his poor brother feeling alone and afraid. His brother died shortly after John, and the two did not meet again until this present lifetime, when the brother returned to be John's present-day father.

During the regression, John was guided by my Angel to understand that although he felt he had let his brother down, his brother had still grown stronger from the experience. His brother could understand that John, who had given himself freely to be of assistance to him, also had a weakness towards alcohol, and it was John's weakness that brought out the strength in his brother. So although John's brother was left alone and crippled, he found his strength to cope and be part of the society in which he lived. Finding strength in himself enabled John's brother to begin to start to trust once more.

John was reassured by the Angels that all was well. He was

reminded that although the promise he made to his brother in the Astral Realms was with the best intentions, the Earth is a wonderful place to learn from. There will always be pitfalls, which can be avoided if one stays true to oneself, and that is the challenge for every spirit who reincarnates.

Can we experience other people's past lives?

Occasionally, during regression therapy it is possible to tap into a past-life memory that actually belongs to someone else – someone we may never have met. (This is why there are lots of Napoleons and Cleopatras walking around!). The reason a person can access these memories is quite simple; we are all connected within the flow of Creation so, because no separation exists, we can wander into another's life memory. If we have a block in our psyche or spirit but we remain open and flexible to universal law, our spirit can be pulled towards a past life memory of someone in history. By feeling the positive traits in a historical life memory, we can gain clarity and freedom from our blocks. These historical past life feelings are so strong that it can leave the sitter thinking they *were* that historical figure.

Why does it always tend to be famous people? Simply because these are the people we've heard about! Significant people in the past become instilled in our memory, thanks to having heard about them, read about them or perhaps been taught about them. So as they are already in our memory, we can through our energy naturally create a link to their energy and therefore accumulate the strengths that helped mould their lives. Many people are drawn to or have an affinity with figures like of Nelson, Gandhi, Napoleon, Joan of Arc, Jesus, Saint John, Elizabeth I, Buddha etc. Indeed, it seems that on some occasions the past life of a certain historical personality will be transmit quite strongly. On one occasion, three people separately came to me within a two-month period, all feeling they were connected to the memory of Joan of Arc. These people knew intuitively that they hadn't *been* Joan of Arc, so they couldn't understand why Joan's energy was surrounding them – often insofar as getting a very clear sense of burning at the stake!

"I felt her energy leave her body, as the flames rose up her legs," one person told me.

"I knew her spirit left her body before she took her last breath," was another comment.

Another person found herself drenched in Saint Joan's memory whilst on holiday in France.

This is quite a hard one to explain – think of it as a 'spark of pureness'. This spark or energy was what gave Joan of Arc their strength – and if other people who are naturally open to Universal Law pick up that spark, they are able to absorb the lessons and strengths that were born out of the life that Saint Joan experienced here on Earth. The experience from St Joan enabled them all to feel subtly clearer, more solid and stronger. And one doesn't need to be regressed to experience this type of energy.[9]

As we can access a famous historical person's life experience, we can also access the life experiences of other individuals whose

---

[9] Entering the memory of another person's past life must not be confused with negative energy, which can take on the appearance of and mimic someone historically famous. Such a negative energy aims to convince and deceive a person into thinking that they were someone famous in a past life; earning their trust by flattering their ego. Remember that – just like anyone else you may have reasons to admire in history – you were created in perfection just as they were; no more, no less. See and feel that completely within your cells and then you will close the door within your persona that allows deceptive energies to enter.

An easy way to determine whether or not you *were* truly a person of great influence in a past life is look at how you react to this discovery. If it excites you or if you find yourself telling others about your previous fame – then you probably weren't that person at all. A real experience doesn't have to be exaggerated. If you were that person, then your spirit will have remembered that life and become empowered by the experience.

memory can also help us. It's as though there's a great universal bank of memories that can be accessed by our spirit, to help us clear a block or limitation that is occurring in the path of the life we have now. Some people may therefore recall memories of different lives that were not their own, which can bring understanding to them of the life they are in now.

An example of this occurred when a young girl called Elizabeth came for regression therapy. She recalled the life of a young Jewish girl in a concentration camp in Germany. She was just seventeen, very weak and emaciated, but she looked after the younger children and supported them as best she could. She spoke apathetically; all life had been drained from her, she now merely existed. She felt no emotions, no anger, no fear, no sadness, only coldness and emptiness came from her words. She had lost her identity when her head was shaven; numbness had spread over her and she had become completely withdrawn. She told me that she and lots of others were being herded towards the "showers". Holding two children close to her naked body, she bore a defiance in her being that left me humbled in her presence.

"They say we are *dirty*." But she and everyone else knew what was really coming. She died silently and with dignity, amid the sounds of terror as everyone slowly choked and fell.

Elizabeth was brought back to this life, confused as to why she had experienced this memory and what it meant, because she was absolutely sure that it was not her own previous life that she had just experienced. She left the session feeling as well as she did when she came in, but quietly confused. A few weeks later she phoned to explain what it was all about.

She had felt a desperate sadness; a pain in her heart for the people the Nazi regime had so callously killed. Like many people she couldn't bear to watch films or stories of the terrible atrocities that occurred throughout that war. She wanted to feel pain for those innocent people but her heart just couldn't carry any more pain, which was why she drew away from any remembrance of the concentration camp casualties. What the past life session had brought out for Elizabeth was a light shining through the darkness, in the form of the young Jewish girl who was about to meet her death, not with fear and terror but with a pride and dignity that she Elizabeth had not seen or felt before. The pain in her heart was slowly being replaced with an understanding of how great the human spirit can rise in times of absolute turmoil, and the experience had given her great relief and freedom.

Elizabeth knew that she had not been the young Jewish girl. But she was able to access the young girl's memory and death, because the memory acted as the right magnet to clear Elizabeth's pained heart.

*   *   *

As the experiences in this chapter make very clear, past life regression is a very powerful tool when used correctly and within the balance of the universe. For the individual involved, the ability to look at and understand a past life from a completely unbounded angle gives the spirit total freedom to unlock the present life situation that has been blocking their life's path.

However, because it is equally easy to connect to *other* people's past lives – especially those of figures of historical significance – it's not something that should play about with! Unless the person conducting the regression is connected to Divine Will and fully understands what they are doing, the results could be very misleading.

There is also the point mentioned earlier, that the whole concept of past lives carries a subtle block in energy in itself, and people are often far too quick to blame past life experiences for whatever might be happening to them in this current life. It is very easy to view any malfunctions of our current existence as a consequence of some deed we think we may have done in a past life. But this leads directly to the unproductive thought form of blaming others or ourselves for our present day situations. Which is a load of nonsense, as the universe neither blames nor judges! But our human form needs reasons for why we think our lives are a struggle, so a traumatic past life situation becomes a convenient excuse for our current situation and prevents the person from looking at themselves at a deeper level. Past lives are but one part of the universal picture – they should not become the basis of a belief system for anyone.

The universe is providing us with answers on a daily basis. Our struggle is that the universe flows one way whilst our belief systems struggle in the opposite direction, so we don't hear what the universe is saying. And as I have said many times already – to hear the universe requires total surrender and trust.

7

Time Travel

In this final chapter I am going to describe some of the most exciting, exhilarating and profound voyages of discovery that have played their part in my journey home – journeys back in time. These have not only provided breathtaking insights into the true story behind events that there is much popular interest in, but also shed more light on the way the universe works...

Time travel is really easy – so long as you are sensitive to time, all the elements in the universe, the restrictions in man, and do not hold deep or strong belief systems. This might seem quite a tall order, but it's not unachievable. Unfortunately though, it would seem that one cannot choose the particular time to travel back to. I would be the first to admit that I am no scientist, but from what I can understand, there is a scientifically valid process going on here. Time travel is all to do with what scientists term *wormholes* – a vortex-like connection between now and some moment in the past. Indeed, the theorists predict that at some time in the future there may be a way of creating these wormholes to order, and transporting a human through this wormhole into another dimension or time. However, apparently the energy required to achieve this is substantially more than the sum total of everything we can produce on this planet at the moment, so it won't be happening any time soon. Fortunately, my own experiences of time travel have not subjected the National Grid to any major strain at all. It is purely my consciousness – my energy body – that travels through the wormhole, while my physical body remains anchored in this dimension.

So why do these wormholes arise? It appears that interest in or a questioning by humanity of a particular historical event (an event of a profound nature that has affected or influenced that particular culture) results in creating a mass subconscious call for answers to that particular culture's questions and uncertainties. This call acts as a magnet to help draw a wormhole into play. Influences can then pass via the wormhole from that time in the past to our current time frame, to help provide answers regarding that historical event and /or belief systems held within their society.

Questioning occurs when the spirit is growing faster than mankind is evolving. The spirit therefore becomes stifled by the exaggeration or falseness that has molded his or her culture. When a lot of spirits become stifled their combined energy pulls the relevant wormholes towards their culture.

The whole process takes place over a considerable time. The first warnings I get that a particular wormhole created by past events is drawing close come in the form of inspirations connected to that particular time in man's history. These come in waves. As I understand it, the wormhole is not simply a parallel-sided tube like a hose connecting the two dimensions (then and now); it is more of a spiral structure. It is the beginning of the wormhole that I pick up first as it is spiraling in our general direction, the energy then draws away but gets stronger with each turn of the spiral, until eventually the energy reaches the bottom of the spiral and the connection is made. It is then that I travel back to that period in time, with the assistance of universal energies that help me safely and with ease through these wormholes.

So in a nutshell, that's how it's done. I will now describe some of the most exciting time travel experiences I have had, which shed some very interesting light on historical events which we've surely all wondered about at some time!

The birth of Jesus

My first experience of time travel occurred about a year after I'd had my fourth child, Atlanta- Rose. It was just before Christmas, and I was in the process of cleaning the house from top to bottom. Whilst stripping the settee covers off ready to be washed, I spontaneously felt what could only be described as a window "etherically" beginning to open. I was filled with a great rush, *eureka* – I suddenly became aware that I was being offered an opportunity to travel back in time and watch the birth of Jesus. Wow! It came completely out of the blue, and was the last thing I was expecting. However, I decided not to act immediately, but to wait so as to make sure that this calling had not come from my ego.

For the next few hours I kept quiet, wanting to be completely sure of what I was sensing. I didn't say anything about it to my husband – he would for sure be extremely excited about it, and this enthusiasm would have added extra pressure to me to respond to this calling. However, by early evening, with the feeling growing ever stronger, I decided to tell Adrian what was happening – as predicted he was very excited indeed! And by now the feeling was so strong that I would not have been affected at all by Adrian's excitement.

From long experience, I know that I am best and most comfortable doing my spiritual activities in a tidy house, so unless the house is tidy I do not do anything. However, having four children, as you can probably imagine the house is normally in a fairly messy state! But right now, I was buzzing so much with the energy caused by this imminent time-traveling experience that I couldn't concentrate on housework at all. Fortunately, fuelled by his excitement, Adrian had the place spotless in no time. My focus was kept on the time window, which seemed to be growing larger and larger. My children are usually late going to bed, which would not have been conducive to any major spiritual journeying, since I would have been too tired to focus. However, as luck had it, the kids had all taken themselves off to bed by 8.00pm, and baby Atlanta-Rose had fallen asleep by 7.30pm, having had her last feed.

(Another security device I use for working out whether I'm meant to do something is to look for reasons *not* to do it. On this occasion there were only "green lights"; the children in bed, the house spotless, nothing to distract). There was no reason not to go, so I sat down with Adrian, and turned the tape recorder on.

My head was very gently eased back; my will slipped out and in popped a strong and loving energy who introduced herself as the Great Mother Energy. This energy was not the Earth's energy, or that of Mary, mother of Jesus. This was an energy that encompassed every aspect of motherhood – not just for mankind, but also for everything: the birds, the animals, the sea creatures, plants, flowers, trees, etc. She seems to be the mother of all things in this dimension. The Great Mother Energy said to us (Adrian was to travel back also): "You must let go of all that you have learned of this most sacred of nights."

This in itself was a challenge. Having grown up in a predominantly Christian country, we had since our earliest childhood days been subjected to vast amounts of information regarding Jesus' birth. In fact, as I'm sure is the case for so many people in the western world, the first play we had both ever acted in was the nativity at infant school, and because this is such an impressionable age, those scenes from the play were ingrained in our memories. So to let all this go was going to be tough!

The Great Mother then began guiding us, through a series

of breaths, to loosen our consciousness and travel through the wormhole. The process took around five minutes, during which breaths were held and released in various ways, each time encouraged by her to go "back, back, back," until at last our energy slowed and then stopped.

"Now be aware – what is it you see?" she asked.

Bringing my awareness into focus, I thought I had come to the wrong place – it wasn't as I was expecting it to be. In front of me was a stone, cobbled track, while to my side were a number of small single-storey white buildings. The one I was standing next to had a small window and a wooden door. It was early evening; night was just falling. My initial response to this scene was confusion with regard to the cobbled path; in my mind I had expected some sort of dirt track. Sensing my confusion, The Great Mother reminded me, "Let go of any expectations." Calmed by these words we took another deep breath and moved slightly forward in time, to the evening. We remained in the same area as before, but now I saw in front of me a tall man and a very weary lady, who was quite small – just over five foot in height. Instantly, I knew this was Mary and Joseph. As I looked at Mary and Joseph I wondered, "Where's the donkey?" And even more confusingly, Mary was holding a young child, a boy who looked to be around the age of two and half years old. Intuitively, I knew this was Mary's son – but this didn't make any sense at all. Again I wondered whether I as in the right place. The Great Mother reassured us once again: "Let go of everything you have ever learned of this night – you must let go." This was even tougher than I thought it was going to be! There was no donkey. Mary already had a son. I had to let go of *everything* that I had been taught at school about Jesus' birth… The Great Mother drew a breath into me, and I started to relax and open my mind fully to the traveling experience.

Joseph and Mary had gone into the small building I was standing in front of. There was a seat near the door and Mary, looking very relieved, sat down with her young boy in her arms. Could this building be the inn that is traditionally spoken about? It was certainly packed with people. Joseph walked over to the right hand corner of the inn (I don't actually know whether it was an inn, but for simplicity's sake I shall refer to it as such). He spoke to a man who was standing behind a dark-colored wooden bar, and appeared to be in charge of the place. There were some rooms through a couple of doorways, sealed by curtains, which also had a number of people in them. But I could sense that these rooms were occupied by local people. The man shook his head – whatever Joseph had requested, it was not forthcoming However, as he walked back towards Mary he was joined by an elderly woman who, seeing Mary was exhausted, took the child from her and asked them to follow her. They went out of the inn, turning right up the cobbled path. I was aware of two or three dwellings opposite the inn and buildings to either side – these houses were detached from each other and appeared to be private homes. After passing a couple of buildings close by to the inn, the old lady (who looked about sixty years' old) turned right into what appeared to be the town square. We entered the courtyard, which had buildings on each of its four sides. On the left she indicated the town barn – they could rest there. We went in through two large doors and the barn was filled from top to bottom with hay – only hay, I couldn't see any animals.

My body breathed in again, following the instructions of the Great Mother, causing us once again to move slightly forward in time. It was now very late at night – whether it was the same day, I am not sure. Mary, Joseph and the old lady were inside the barn, the lady had the boy-child in her arms. Suddenly there was a lot of commotion, running footsteps and a sense of general panic occurring outside. Three men then ran into the barn and snatched the child from the old lady, who appeared panic stricken – it was a very frightening scene. The men, dressed in everyday clothing, ran out with the child. Soon after, they came back into the barn; it appeared that they were looking for more young children. Joseph stood in front of his very pregnant wife. Up until now, others had not been able to detect Mary's pregnancy as she had worn long loose fitting robes and had carried a small child into town. Joseph was shaking his head in determination, as the men were asking and looking for more children.

Mary was very frightened indeed – I knew the child they had snatched (Mary's son), was to be killed. This whole scene happened so fast and was unexpected in what was otherwise a very peaceful time, a time to rest, especially for Mary.

What was interesting for me at the time was how my emotions were somehow being kept under control. For this scene to be fully appreciated, it needed to be observed with absolute dispassion. However, as a mother of four I am very passionate about children, and would normally be desperately disturbed by any scenes of children being hurt abused or unloved. So I couldn't understand how my emotions were being kept from me. It was a very surreal situation.

My body breathed in and we moved slightly forward in time. Mary was giving birth behind a red curtain that had been erected in the Barn. Whether this was the same night or one that followed, I am uncertain. The curtain I felt was symbolic so that privacy could be given to the birth – even though I was observing purely in energy form (the same form as the spirits who watch and help us are adopting), it is decreed universally that some things are kept private. A young lady from the inn, in her mid-twenties, was assisting in the birth. The old lady was not visible in this scene.

We then moved forward slightly to the hours before dawn. I guessed that we were about to see the baby, and wondered whether he would have the halo with which he is usually depicted in pictures. I always felt it was rather fanciful, but I suppose it demonstrated his uniqueness. (I say unique rather than special, as of course all babies are very special!).

My time then came to look at this babe. My energy gazed down in awe as I looked at him. Oh! This was indeed a beautiful, child; so clear and vibrant, he was physically strong and obviously very healthy. Indeed, I was surprised by his size – for some reason I had expected him to be smaller. As I looked into his blue eyes, everything around me seemed silent. I marveled in the pureness and freedom he exuded. And to my astonishment the child did indeed have, emanating from his shoulders and over his head, a haze of white light filled with what appeared to be hundreds of stars; some bigger, some smaller, all shining away. Intuitively, I felt that the child was focused in his energy and seemed oblivious to the traumatic events that had recently occurred.

Mesmerized, I did not want to leave the purity and safeness of his presence. But slowly my energy drew away from him and I observed the wider scene. I cannot say if he was in a manger or not, although whatever he lay in was fairly small, filled with hay and then covered with cloth.

Three children then entered the barn through a small door on the right. These children, two boys and one girl, were aged between six to eight years. I was initially confused as to why they hadn't also been taken and killed – when the men had taken Mary's child from the arms of the old lady I had sensed their desire to kill *all* small children. However, I then realized that these children weren't so small, and that this had saved them.

I did not see any shepherds and I was not aware of any great star. However, in the next scene I did encounter the wise men. I was shown telepathically that two had traveled from the East together, and one traveled from the southeast.

"Do you see what they wear on their heads?" the Great Mother asked.

They wore a headdress of about eighteen inches in height. The Great Mother, with awe, reverence and honor towards the wise ones (that's how she referred to them), said slowly and deeply; "These wise ones are so wise, so great is their wisdom, that their heads must always be higher than anyone else [*hence the headdress*]. They are revered more than kings."

Her energy swelled in my heart when she said this, I could feel the enormity of their wisdom.

The next breath took me to the moment when the wise ones arrived at the barn where the babe lay. For me, this was the best part of my experience, and I could really sense their energy, since I had no physical body to restrict my feelings.

The Great Mother gently said; "So honored are the wise ones they bow to no one, but, do you see, in the presence of this child, they cannot bow low enough."

My whole being felt it would burst from the great and pure joy they exuded as they bowed low before the babe. In this moment, I realized that – although in my present life I have experienced happiness, peace and some joy – never had I experienced anything like this joy that these wise ones exuded; a joy that felt so pure, on such a high scale. It was the most wonderful and empowering feeling imaginable. I soaked it in for a few moments. Later one of the wise ones lit some incense and began to smoke it around the babe. "This is to cleanse the child's aura, as the child was born in traumatic circumstances," the Great Mother told us.[1]

I looked at the child and at his energy and thought how clear both were; the child's head and neck still surrounded by hundreds of stars. If only they could see what I see, they would know he was

---

[1] Two years after my experience, one of the national newspapers ran an article about the possibility that two of the wise men had come from one of the countries in the east where frankincense and myrrh originated. The article explained that a small community existed in the east, which are very religious, and for the past two thousand years have lit frankincense to cleanse around the aura of the new babes born within their community. Upon reading this I wondered whether I had observed the very first child to experience such a ceremony as this.

just fine. Another of the wise ones mixed some substance into a small bowl of water and began to bathe the child's feet.

Suddenly I felt the window beginning to close.

"We have to go back," the Great Mother said; "Take a deep breath and I will guide you back."

Following her instructions we returned to this present time. As I opened my eyes, a great sadness fell over me, which felt almost like homesickness. I wanted to go back! I felt I could have helped, that I could have been useful in that time. Even though I was there only in energy form, I realized that my physical body had also undergone some deep shift in perspective as a result of the experience and the energies that I had encountered. I couldn't talk about the experience for a few days, and even then I couldn't initially go in to too much detail about it – I needed time to settle and absorb all that I had seen and felt.

When I could finally talk about it, I described my experience of Jesus' birth to a close friend. I mentioned my confusion with regard to the cobbled roads – she explained that the main routes in and around the towns under the control of Romans were often cobbled. This helped to bring clarity to my confusion. For two or three weeks after the time-traveling experience, the memory of that night stayed with me – I could still feel the hay between my toes, the darkness of the night sky, and the brightness of the stars that shone.

Obviously one of the most profound observations from the journey was the discovery that Mary already had a son. However, as I was to find on another journey (detailed later in this chapter), this should not be in any way taken to reflect badly on her. She is an incredibly wonderful person and fully deserving of all the reverence paid to her by history and religion.

I decided to take time to light candles every day throughout the Christmas period for Jesus' brother who had been taken and killed. As I see it, the brother was a catalyst for Jesus' safe entry onto this planet.

Indeed, when considering the whole story of the nativity before this time-traveling experience, I had often wondered why Herod's men had not been informed that there was a lady about to give birth? Now I knew. When I first saw Mary walking in the streets with Joseph I hadn't even noticed that she was pregnant. I only saw her weariness and put this down to the weight of the young child she carried in her arms. Anyone would notice a heavily pregnant lady who was due to give birth at any time; but how many people would notice her pregnancy if she was carrying a small child and wearing loose fitting clothes?

One thing I often wondered about when I thought back to the experience was about Mary's emotions. Joseph was very easy to understand. He was in a state of terrible shock – shocked to the point that his feelings had closed down. He was numb with disbelief at the horrific fate of his first son – and then sorely confused to witness revered wise men bowing low to this new babe. It was all beyond his comprehension. However, with Mary – just as my feelings as a passionate mother were kept from me when the first child was taken, so too were Mary's emotions and feelings withheld from me. This felt strange, as I had free access to the feelings of all the people I viewed on that journey, except her. At the time I could not understand why this was, but all became clear a few years later, as I will explain further on in this chapter.

As the weeks passed, I began to feel strengthened by my experience, and the inner confusions left in my physical being slowly faded away. It now all made complete sense to me. However, I was left in no doubt at all that the Nativity was not in any way the scene of gentleness and harmony that we are taught in school – it was actually a time of terrible stress and confusion. Yet still the serenity and strength of the baby Jesus shone through.

Moses

My next time-traveling experience occurred just over two years later. For some reason I kept finding myself thinking about Moses, and not surprisingly just couldn't understand why – when already living a full life bringing up four children, working as an electronic gem therapist – there would be any extra capacity for wondering about Moses! Particularly since I have no interest in, nor can I relate to, any one religion. But drawn to Moses I was, and the feelings grew stronger day by day. Eventually I said to Adrian; "I think I've got to travel back to Moses' lifetime; it seems we need to understand more of that time." Adrian was predictably interested.

"When?" he asked.

I didn't know. I needed to see whether the inspiration I was feeling would grow stronger or weaker. All I could do was wait.

However, by a couple of weeks later the inspiration was incredibly strong, so I decided that the time-traveling journey needed to be made. We invited about eight people to the house to sit in on the journey, or hopefully also to travel back using the energy and influence entering the room at the time.

The day of travel saw me very excited indeed – I could only focus on the journey ahead. To prepare myself that evening, after eating a light meal I had a quiet and relaxing bath. Ensuring that my make-up and hair was OK, I went downstairs to prepare the back room, which was already full of fresh flowers bought specially for the night. I began to light numerous candles, dedicating each one I lit to particular universal Light essences, but then suddenly felt a presence urging me very strongly to allow it to communicate. So I sat down, feeling somewhat concerned as to the timing of this communication, since I was extremely focused on the journey ahead. As I sat and allowed my will to depart, energy entered my body that was very, very old. Extremely frail and weak, this energy did not have much light left in its flame. Telepathically (and very slowly), the energy told me that he was Moses, and informed me that he had been around me a great deal recently.

"My Light grows weak. Many stories have been told of my life, but they do not speak of my life as I lived it, and these stories are not as my life would have told", explained Moses.

The untrue stories written about his life were weighing heavily on his spirit; they were suffocating his Light, which was near to extinction. Moses, I realized, wanted the truth of his life to be known, so that his Light could grow once more and fill his soul.

When everyone started to arrive and had settled themselves comfortably, I shared what Moses had told me. This made them relax as they appreciated the magnitude of the evening that lay before them. Just before I was about to start I left the back room to check on the children, who were playing happily in the front room. I said to them, "Give me an hour and a half or so, then you can bring in the chocolate biscuits."

Leaving Toby and Atlanta arguing over who was going to take in the best chocolate biscuits[2], I returned to the back room, smiled at everyone and announced that I was ready…

---

[2] My children love these times; a sense of magic and inquisitiveness fills the air, topped with extra chocolate biscuits! It lends them to being as supportive as they can, in their own individual way. Toby, by taking extra care of Atlanta and making sure she's not too noisy, getting her drinks and keeping her occupied, giving me extra hugs filled with warmth and love. Atlanta throwing herself on me and squeezing me tight. Showing me her toothless front gum, framed by her fangs on either side (she knows I am so going to miss those gums when her second teeth appear). Offering me her favorite toy of the moment to look after. I know how much that means to her, so I am spurred on by the pure love in the smaller children. Lucy is usually dressed up to party and paint the town red. Lucy takes all that I do in her stride and wishes me a good night. James (you never know what James is thinking) wanders around the house, not going near the back room, and keeping away from Toby and Atlanta as their young playfulness irritates him – he retreats to his bedroom for the evening. I think he is aware of what's going to happen, but only James could answer that.

Adrian set the tape up to record the evening's discoveries. As always happens preceding big events like this, I spend a few moments belching like crazy to get rid of all the trapped wind that builds up before any "etheric" communication occurs, then my bones and blood confirm my connection to Divine Will. My head is very gently eased back and twisted from side to side, my will slowly leaves my body, for a second or two there is only emptiness in me, and then the appropriate energy steps in and strengthens and straightens my body. The first energy to enter on this night is the Energy of Truth! This energy settled into my body as always, by using my hands to move and cleanse my energy field and aura – keeping them flowing and unrestricted. After introducing herself, she says:

"I come now to share much of Light and expansion. Now is the time for only words of truth and wholeness to come forth. Within all your hearts has been placed a golden key. Imagine each one of you, that you are now turning your golden key and opening your heart. Only truth can enter a heart that is open. Remember to use this key when you are ever in doubt of truth."

Very gently she departs. The next energy to enter is Moses.

"I am Moses."

"Welcome Moses!" (Everyone present responds.)

"I ask for all Light Angels and Light gods and goddesses to come forth tonight. I, Moses, ask that my book be read."

Moses departs after voicing his request. Then a strong male energy enters:

"I am known to mankind as the voice of Saturn." (Saturn is often depicted as Old Father Time).

"Welcome Saturn." (Everyone acknowledges Saturn's presence.)

"My task here is to open the book of Moses and guide you all back to truth. I shall perform this task, I shall bring my Energy here." (Saturn indicates that his energy will stand to the right of those who come and speak.)

Saturn continues:

"I shall turn each page like this, " (Saturn demonstrates how he will turn over the pages of Moses life,) "so all present can witness what happened."

Saturn departs from my body to stand to my right. A feminine energy enters my body and informs us that her energy swims in the timeless seas of the universe.

"My task," she says, "is to take you all back to the time of Moses. To begin your journey just close your eyes make sure that you are warm and comfortably positioned."

The Energy then takes us through certain breathing techniques to enable us to alter our individual vibrations. After about five minutes we arrive where we are meant to. She says: "I shall now depart, but someone with great knowledge and wisdom shall enter and guide you through the land."

The Energy departs and is replaced with an extremely strong masculine energy. With emphasis he says;

"I am Rameses! I come because you are here in my lands. I come now to show you my lands. Through great knowledge and wisdom it is in my soul to say – there is much importance upon you being here and although I understand only a small part of this journey, I am open to share as much as I can with you. We may converse, do not fear me."

Rameses continued; "Now you are sitting in an area which is very comfortable to me. It is an area where I come when I need only my thoughts."

At this point I was aware of a heavily marbled room, fairly large, with a raised platform at the back where a gold ornate chair was positioned, which Rameses sat on. Apart from the marble, the room was accented in light blue and gold decoration; the room was empty, no statues or treasures adorned this simply decorated, yet elaborate room. There was a double door to the left corner of the room. A young woman entered – she appeared to be a servant, but a well-respected and loyal retainer. She did not appear fearful or restrained in the presence of Rameses. In her arms she carried a child, which she took to Rameses. An inquiring sense of what should be done with this child was projected towards him from her.

Rameses continues:

"Now I am being shown a child." Anger enters his voice; "This child is not of my blood. This child must be abandoned!"

"My strength," (Rameses pointing to his head/his logic) "tells me this child must go, and yet my soul tells me this child must stay. I ask you to be aware this child is small, but he is not of my blood. I have torment in my heart, so I choose to let the under people [*the servants*] care for him."[3]

(Group represents questions asked by the eight people who had time-traveled back to Moses' lifetime. Rameses and Moses respond to these Questions.)

GROUP: Where was the boy found?
RAMESES: This I cannot answer. The child has only been brought to me.
GROUP: How many years old?
RAMESES: He is maybe 15 moons [*15 months*].
GROUP: Are you holding the child?
RAMESES: I have not the heart to touch him. [*pushing acknowledge-*

---

[3] It is important to understand that neither Rameses nor Moses could literally hear the questions being put to each of them. They were not aware of the energies of myself and the group, around them. The questions appeared to them like thoughts in their minds, and the answers they gave were descriptions of their feelings. It appeared to them like they were daydreaming, but not in a dreamy sense, but one filled with realization to the particular environment they were experiencing at that particular time. For example, Rameses was in the room in which he felt most comfortable so that he could think with little or no distraction and allow his thoughts to manifest. During this time the group questions appeared as his own enquiring thoughts.

ment of the child aside.]
GROUP: Why do you have difficulty in touching him?
RAMESES: My strength [RAMESES' *head/logic*] says No!
GROUP: Does the child live with you in your home?
RAMESES: My eyes have turned.

RAMESES, *turning away from the child, trying to ignore the situation in front of him, indicated to the young woman to leave. RAMESES had become distressed; his logic and his heart were in conflict. From RAMESES energy it was obvious to all that his head and logic governed his strength. His head knew he should order the child to be killed, and yet so strong was the fight from his heart that his logic became confused. RAMESES was uncomfortable and unfamiliar with this sensation, and was wrestling with himself to come to terms with the situation. RAMESES departs.*

My body takes in a deep breath and my energy moves forward, and a young male energy enters:

MOSES: I am Moses, I am a very strong boy. I am around nine cycles [*nine years*]. I shall answer if you ask.
GROUP: What is your mother's name?
MOSES: My mother died. My keeper told me a story long ago. I am cared for by one of the ladies who look after the Queen.

MOSES, *at the age of nine years old, was looking at his home. It was a round dry mud building, with just an opening as a doorway to within, and to the right of the opening was a small hole of about a foot square that served as a window. A storage building close to the window was filled with hay. Many other similar mud dwellings surrounded MOSES' home. He was a slender boy, dressed in simple cloth material and sporting a mass of thick black hair. It was a hot day – the ground, sprinkled with stones, was dry.*

GROUP: Are there children with you?

MOSES: There are four, but I am not like them.

GROUP: Do you know where you have come from, who your people were?

MOSES: I only know those I am with – are they not my people? I know I am not the same, but that's because I have those things in my eyes. When I see, I see much.

GROUP: What do you see?

MOSES: I see great wars, great battles. I see much pain. I do not see nice visions. [MOSES *seems disturbed at this.*]

GROUP: Do you share what you see with anyone?

MOSES: I share with one person and she is my friend, she is of five cycles, she is much smaller, but she understands.

GROUP: Do you know her name?

MOSES: Her name is Toleta.

GROUP: What do you do during the day?

MOSES: I work – I have to tend the animals who give the juice. [MOSES *tended goats and their juice we now call milk.*]

GROUP: Do you know what will become of you when you are older?

MOSES: I suppose I will be strong and I will build.

GROUP: Do you see buildings now?

MOSES: Always are buildings, always buildings. [MOSES *began thinking of the many buildings going on nearby.*]

GROUP: Do you have a brother?

MOSES: Well I ought to have a brother, but I have no brother.

GROUP: What do you mean, you ought to have a brother?

MOSES: If I was like the others, I would have a brother, but I am not.

[MOSES *was not at peace with his visions, and although his adoptive family accepted him, he felt distanced, which prevented him from fully accepting his family. He was much freer in spirit when he was around his small friend, who was the youngest daughter of his adoptive family.*]

GROUP: Are you happy?

MOSES: Well, [*he takes a pause and a moment to think*]. I'm not sad.

GROUP: What makes you happy?

MOSES: My friend.

GROUP: Do you see the Queen very often?

MOSES: No one sees the Queen." [*I felt this to be because the Queen was ill, and had been for a long time. MOSES' thoughts were based upon rumors he had heard around his community.*]

GROUP: Is there much building going on outside?

MOSES: Our Pharaoh wants great monuments.

GROUP: And who does the work for the Pharaoh?

MOSES: So many people, but they are so sad.

GROUP: Where do they come from? Are they Egyptians?

MOSES: They are not the same as the ones with power.

GROUP: So do they work and get food, and do they work because they want to work, or do they have to work?

MOSES: Work?

GROUP: Doing all the building. You said they are sad doing the building – is that because they do not want to do it?

MOSES: I am not so sure.

My body took in a deep breath and moved forward to when Moses was now nineteen years of age, very strong in his physique and quite tall. His voice is much deeper, too. He seemed comfortable with himself and focused in his direction in life. He was observing all the building going on around him.

MOSES: I ask that you begin to be aware more of the surroundings. I can explain on the one side of the land [MOSES *points to the left*] there are great palaces. On the other side of the land [*pointing to the right*] is where many people are sheltering. These people are the workers. The land on this side [*the left side*] is for the mighty.

GROUP: Where are we standing at the moment – we seem high?

MOSES: We are quite high; we are looking down and around.

GROUP: You seem big and strong?

MOSES: I am fairly strong, I feel quite brave.

GROUP: Do you wear something in your hair?

MOSES: My hair has no garment around it. I wear cloth [*from the waist to the legs*]. Not so elaborate. I work, I work hard but I am fulfilled, I am not weak.

GROUP: What is your work?

MOSES: My work is a stone person; I carve the stones. I carve symbols into the stones, messages for future existences. I am also a visionary and this is why I carve the stones.

GROUP: Is that a position of privilege?

MOSES: Unfortunately! [MOSES *was not happy with his position of privilege, as it isolated him from many people. He was kept relatively isolated so as to encourage his visions.*]

GROUP: What is your vision at the moment – what have you seen?

MOSES: My vision on stone was carved recently – it was one of great disasters for many people. Great famines, great wars, great destruction.

GROUP: And of the people who shelter, what of them?

MOSES: They are weak; they choose to stay because they do not have to think. They have no thoughts. [MOSES *did not appear to be particularly concerned about the workers, as there was nothing to be concerned about.*][4]

---

[4] During my observations I could see very clearly that the workers, Moses' people, were not slaves. They were not held against their will. Food and shelter was provided by the Pharaoh in return for hard work. The people only had to work and payment was in the form of food and a roof over their heads. They did not have to worry about being hungry and they were with their own blood people. But when disasters came, the war and famine, and then disease struck – there was no food and so they had to go searching or they would not have survived.

GROUP: And what of the Pharaoh?

MOSES: He is mighty, but he is also broken with great illness. He has a spirit that is strong but he has great illness. [MOSES *answered with warmth toward the Pharaoh.*]

GROUP: Have you spoken with the people in the shelter?

MOSES: Only on a few occasions. This is because I am not allowed out. I have to stay where there is much grandeur. Much of what I have prophesied has already come to pass and so I have to stay much with the Pharaoh.

GROUP: Why is there so much disease?

MOSES: The Pharaoh is broken with illness, he is weak. There is no leadership at the moment. Neither here, [*indicating the rich on the left*] nor there [*indicating the workers on the right*].

There is no leadership, all is broken.

MOSES *was clearly aware that he was communicating with others from another dimension of time in their energy form, but he was comfortable with this – different from the young boy* MOSES, *who had not been aware of us in energy form. We then moved forward again, my guess was a year or two at the most.*

MOSES: Now I am being given much responsibility. This is not good for me. The great Pharaoh has now died, and there is the war that I prophesied. [*The war* MOSES *was speaking of was probably with the country that we now call Ethiopia.*]

There is no leadership at all. There is emptiness in both these people [*indicating left*] and these people [*indicating right*]. I have been told I do not carry Egyptian blood – my blood is from another land. It is written that I, Moses, take the workers from these lands into freedom. This was **not** so. I have no blood in Egypt; how can I stay in a land that is empty of my being? I, Moses choose to leave the land I grew up in, and with the workers, move and find my land. This is what I choose.

Great disease has fallen upon many in these lands; it is a very dark time. People all around me are dropping. They are crying, they are hungry, there is famine, and the lands are empty. I must go. [*Time moves slowly forward.*]

Now, do you feel all the workers leaving these lands? There is no more work, no more food, too much illness. We all move and search for a new life. Move forward slightly. I shall take you to where the lands were so dry. So much pain. [*We took another breath, and moved forward.* MOSES *left, along with others who were not of Egyptian blood.. Despair had replaced the bustle of what had been a thriving and developing empire – the spark of life had been taken from there. The next scene I saw shook me to my core; a vast contrast to the prosperity of the Egyptian culture.* MOSES *now speaks with a dry voice, his energy is very weak and he is close to death.*]

MOSES: I have not eaten for so long. The people want me to show them where to go. "You are a prophet, you have vision," they shout, but they shout in a way that is unkind. They mock me and yet they also demand of me.

The lands were dry and barren. MOSES *was strong in his spirit, but his body was weak and tired – he was very, very weary. The people around him were aggressive and demanding – they remembered* MOSES *as the prophet and they wanted answers and direction to salvation. He had almost relaxed into the prospect of impending death.*

MOSES: I have no more visions, no more. I am tired. Now we shall move forward. [*My body breathes in gently and we move forward once again.* MOSES *now speaks in a clear and gentle voice, with new life running through him.*]

Now I am not so tired. You are now sitting around lands that hold much knowledge. I grew weary on our travels to find new lands, food, and water. I grew so weary, there was so much hatred in the people who walked with me, only a few stayed. We were found lost and alone, tired and hungry by great tribesmen who through the cycles of many, many moons I have been taught by."

[*The tribes people* MOSES *spoke of were nomads. He continued.*]

They are carriers of great knowledge and wisdom. I have learned many ways, many ways to find peace. I would like you all just to be aware of one moment sitting in the company of great men, also of women. [*The feeling was of peace, calm and tranquility.*]

There are only a few of these tribesmen – where they come from I do not know, but they have great knowledge. They live amongst themselves. We cannot stay here. We have to go. We have learned all we can from them, and now it is with great strength that I raise my whole being up and I walk with great knowledge and wisdom in my heart. I will search out all those people who caused me great pain and showed hatred towards me, and I will share all that has been shared with me.

MOSES *did not particularly want to leave such a peaceful environment. The tribesmen knew peace in themselves and peace on Earth. It was difficult to leave, and* MOSES *needed to summon all the strength in him to do so.*

MOSES: Now I walk for many days. I have a vision for the peoples who worked within the lands where I grew up. These are the workers, but they are wild, they are crazy. If they shall listen, then I shall speak. [*We all move forward slightly in time.*]

Now they see me standing upright, they see me strong. They think I have had great honors bestowed upon me, and yet I tell them, this is what I have learned. I share all my wisdom with these people. But it is not enough; they are too wild, they have too many desires – simple words are not enough.

Wild in their ways, the ex-workers of Egypt did not listen to MOSES' *simple words. His reappearance after they had left him and others for dead caused them to think a great miracle had occurred.* MOSES *tried to reassure them that his recovery was due to the simple ways and wisdom of the tribes people, who had found and saved him and the others who had stayed with him.*

Now I walk until I find land and abundance, a land that I can call mine, where I can live my truth. You may ask any questions of my life, any which has been written or otherwise.

GROUP: When you left Egypt, it is written that a sea was opened up enabling you and all the people to walk across the sea. Did you cross any seas? [MOSES *had no idea what the* GROUP *was referring to, indicating that the story of the sea parting was probably pure fantasy.*]

MOSES: My life was blessed by the tribes people who saved me. My life holds no magic.

GROUP: When you went to search for lands, after you shared some of your wisdom and insights, did many people go with you? Did many people listen?

MOSES: There were more than a few, but not all. But the ones who shared my life with me became family.

GROUP: And did you find the lands that you searched for?

MOSES: The land I found was so. My blood was not Egyptian. My blood was of the workers, this I only knew when I learned much from the tribesmen who saved me.

GROUP: When you found the lands, were there people already on that land or was the land free?

MOSES: The land was free

GROUP: I know you said there was no magic in your life and this I understand, but it is said in writings that there was much encouragement and many visions, which encouraged you to lead the people out of Egypt. Was there such a vision or was it out of necessity that you left?

MOSES: My journey from Egypt was because of famine, of illness, of a need to find new life. Everything was being destroyed.

GROUP: When you left the land did the Egyptians try to stop you?

MOSES: Not really – there was slight confrontation because for the Egyptians it was right to have many servants, and they were going also, which was not easy.

GROUP: How did you manage to escape them?

MOSES: The Egyptians were weak, but many of the people were weak also. It was only the strong that could leave.

GROUP: The Egyptian's revered certain idols and Gods. Who did you revere?

MOSES: I always search, to revere was not so.

GROUP: Were you aware of the existence of Angels and other Light beings?

MOSES: I had guidance. In my visions a voice would talk, it would show me a way, it was clear.

GROUP: When did you write the Ten Commandments? Was it the voice that told you to write those Ten Commandments?

MOSES: I came from the tribes people who found me, who saved me, and it was their knowledge and wisdom that I passed on to my people. But I do not know what you speak of, and this was not so.

Moses had shared the wisdom, knowledge and ways of living of the tribes people with his people. These were the people who had left him for dead, and then many months later, found him strong and vibrant in life, yet peaceful with the words he shared. Unfortunately, the people – seeing such a transformation in Moses' physical and personal manner – thought that he must have been touched by the hand of God, since he appeared so different from the Moses who had lived close to the Pharaoh. For they had witnessed the Pharaoh, who had great wisdom, see fit to have one of their blood honored in the way Moses was while living in Egypt. Yet Moses told the people that it was the tribesmen who had told him which people he belonged to; and that it was the tribesmen's wisdom he now shared with them, but many of his people did not listen.

The wandering tribe – or nomads as they are known – lived their lives by community rules. They relied on and supported each other in their everyday living. For example, it was not acceptable to go off with someone's wife or husband. This would weaken the strength in their community, as would killing and stealing. The nomad tribes people honored the Earth, the sky, the air, the sun, the waters; all was equal to their support system. And as long as they remained strong in their bonds of trust and support to each other, harmony, balance and abundance would fill their lives.

Moses learned many simple ways of living whilst with the tribes people. He had gone from not belonging, to being part of his adoptive family, to then having reverence unwontedly poured upon him whilst in Egypt and with Rameses, to feeling the hatred which man can inflict on his fellow man. A fairly turbulent journey by any standards! It's no wonder then, that when saved by simple folk who could survive in the barren lands, thrive and enjoy life, Moses was so eager to learn of their ways, simple as they may have seemed. He saw and lived off the fruits of their wisdom and knowledge. On his return from the tribe, a few of his people listened and were touched by his words and, as he explained: "came with him, shared his life and became family, and went on to become more family". But, where the idea of the commandments on stone came from I do not know, and it seems neither does Moses.

The next questions refer to the later life of Moses.

GROUP: Did you live long in the land you found?

MOSES: Long and wisely. But one can only gain access to such wisdom when one has experienced such pain and disaster.

GROUP: How would you best like to be remembered? [MOSES *thought deeply. Slowly and meticulously he answered.*]

MOSES: I would very much like to be remembered as an old man who found his God. [*As he spoke, peace touched every word. The following group questions* MOSES *answered with care and precision, choosing each word carefully to portray his answers.*]

GROUP: Out of everything that you have learned what can you share with us, out of all the many experiences in your life, as to our life on the Earth now?

MOSES: My experiences were so different and yet one thing we all have in common is the need to belong and be part of, and so I would say; remember you are part of God. I do not have so many wisdoms.

GROUP: How do you see God?

MOSES: My God is the only God; one who knows life, who knows pain, who knows the smallest prayer. My God holds everything, but your group asks me to say how do I envisage him. As everything – in everyone, in every light, every thing!

GROUP: What happened to the people who didn't follow you or who didn't travel with you?

MOSES: Oh, I expect they found something.

GROUP: Did you have any further visions in your old age?

MOSES: Only one and that was of my death.

GROUP: And how did you die?

MOSES: I died peacefully in the arms of my child's child.

[*I saw* MOSES *being held by a young lady, burning oil lamps had been placed around him as he lay in a tent-like shelter. She was kneeling on the floor, cradling* MOSES' *head in her lap, comforting him gently. The daylight outside did not affect the softness of light created by the oil lamps.*]

GROUP: Who did you marry?

MOSES: I shared my life with a fine woman, she was known as Marian, she bore me four children, but she grew weak before me.

[*Zipporah is the documented name of Moses' wife, which gives way to confusion. Moses' answer to her name was given from his intimate memory. Therefore is it possible that, like today, a person can be given more than one name?*]

GROUP: We spoke earlier and you said your light grew weak. Was that also because of the adoration that occurred in your life or more from the writings that have followed?

MOSES: My light became weak because of falseness.

GROUP: And your people, did they flourish in the new land?

MOSES: Life was good. [*I could see the people had settled near water on flat land, which had vegetation, with mountains behind.*]

GROUP: At what age did you die? [MOSES *considered the group, and not knowing how many cycles / years he was before he died, he touched his beard and with his hand showed how long it was. It was very, very long!*]

MOSES: Oh! My hair [*beard*] was long… Old!

GROUP: "Did you ever see the tribesmen again?"

MOSES: [MOSES *shook his head indicating no.*] But I always remembered.

GROUP: When you went into the wilderness it has been written that there was no food. What did you live on?

MOSES: There were only animals from the ground. Maybe some sap. Many perished.

[*Everyone went quiet, then* MOSES *announced*] Now, I shall depart [*and off he went*].

The energy of Saturn then returned to speak:
"I am the voice of Saturn. Now the book shall close. I shall say, do not depart with a heart that is still wondering. As you can see, so much is an illusion."

Saturn leaves, and the energy that had taken us back to Moses' lifetime returns, this time to bring us back to our own time span. Again using certain breathing techniques she helps us all very gently to return.

We all opened our eyes. Moved deeply by our experience, no one wanted to speak. For a few moments the group sat quietly each catching another's eyes, and sharing smiles of unity between us, grounding more with each breath, until finally I spoke and asked Adrian and Jan to put the kettle on. That was the signal to everyone that they should share their experiences.[5] Our chatter filtered through to the living room, where an excited Toby and Atlanta eagerly waited their opportunity to bring in the chocolate biscuits. Much as I like a nibble, I found I didn't want anything at all – my whole being was full and energized with the adventure.

The following day, with the memory of Moses still deep within me, I kept thinking of the time when he appeared most focused and strong. It was before his big journey, when he was a craftsman carving his visions on stone. He exuded a lot of physical strength and stature in that persona. However, as I recalled the memory throughout the day I continually sensed an old man around me. Eventually I realized why I was sensing him; my memory flashed back to the question asked of Moses; "How would you best like to be remembered?" and his reply; "As an old man who had found his God." I had been trying to remember him as *I* wanted, but Moses was having none of it! So, now I remember him in the way *he* wanted.

During the following week after this time-traveling experience, everyone in the group (including myself) reported feeling numb, and I couldn't understand why this was. Surely we should have felt elated – perhaps even on a high! Being shown the truth of an existence should surely cause us to feel brilliant – so why were we feeling this numbness?

Clarity eventually arose from my confusion. In our journey the illusions had fallen from us, and truth was healing the space where

---

[5] Although I am describing here what I experienced during these time-traveling sessions, the other people in the group would also usually see or feel something fairly similar. Sometimes they would see other aspects more clearly than I – a good analogy would be that I was driving the bus, and thus seeing everything ahead of me, but everyone else was looking out of a different window and seeing certain things in extra detail. Some people would see the buildings really clearly, others would see the workers – it depends on their particular sensitivities. But everyone would feel the same principle emotions of each scene; the confusion, disharmony, rage, etc. The conversations after the time-traveling experiences were great for completing the picture, as everyone recounted what they saw or felt.

the illusions had been. To use a metaphor, if you have a diseased tooth removed from your mouth, the mouth remains sore until the wound heals, even though the diseased object has been removed. This is what was occurring to us all, and why we were feeling so emotionally numb. And indeed, a week later we were all feeling brilliant and hugely free and empowered – it was as though we had been given a forward thrust in our lives.

I was still confused, though. I wouldn't have expected to be affected by the illusions of Moses' story, since I do not follow any particular religion and it did not bother me in the slightest as to whether or not Moses did part the Red Sea! Then I realized that – although consciously I wasn't concerned as to what really happened or didn't happen in Moses' life – sub-consciously there *was* a belief buried in me that the story in the Bible was true. Before my birth, when I was all sparkling and clear (as are most soon-to-arrive babies), I was gradually picking up belief systems held by my parents, either from their conscious or subconscious mind, depending on the intensity of their thoughts. My parents were pretty open and simple in their thought forms, but although they were not practicing Christians, Christianity was the belief system they adhered to. So I picked this belief system up, and even before I was born I already had a whole load of baggage to carry with me. Unfortunately, the same goes for most of us. These comforting little stories actually burrow deep in to our mind and tie us down. But if they turn out to be false – so what? Yes, the truth does set us free! We lose a touch of magic that the illusion had created, but what do we want, freedom or magic? I know what I have chosen for my life, and that is freedom.

Mary

I absolutely love time traveling. What I don't enjoy is any insecurities that I may have rising up to reveal themselves to me, which always tends to happen in the weeks before any time-traveling experience.

I find myself filled with doubts, usually about myself and my sanity, so I really go through some hard times! My mind tries to convince me that I don't *need* to do this journey, that my life would be so much simpler without it. (Believe me, it gives me no pleasure to be the one who is told things that fundamentally contradict belief systems followed by many millions of people!). But all the time this is happening, deep within me, I know that to ignore this "etheric" call is to deny myself, my true essence. So I go through this internal struggle time and time again; what pushes me forward is the inspiration to time travel, which grows stronger and stronger as time goes on. Finally, the inspiration is so strong that I have no choice – I set the date and make the decision to travel back. Then on the day communications stop it is as though no one is at home and I'm left hanging in mid-air – pretty scary. An hour or so before I am to travel, the inspiration returns and this time it's really strong (thank goodness!), and by the time I'm ready to go, I'm really buzzing.

About nine months after the Moses journey, I began to feel Mary (mother of Jesus) round me. I tried to ignore her presence since at the time I was going through one of these self-doubting periods. Nevertheless, her energy – her presence – grew stronger. As Mary is the mother of Jesus, I started to wonder whether she was around me to prepare the way for me to conceive another baby. Not good news – that was the last thing I wanted! I really did not feel I could cope with baby number five, and physically, knew that my body wasn't meant to have another child. If I had told Adrian of Mary's presence, his excitement would have made it difficult (if not impossible) for me to discern clearly enough as to what to do. So I remained in quiet contemplation of the situation.

One day, as we pulled out of our drive, Adrian suddenly slowed the car and looked around in shock.

"What's up?" I enquired.

After taking a moment to compose himself Adrian said, "I've just seen Mary standing by the gate, holding a baby in her arms." He was in shocked surprise. Then laughingly he said, "Maybe you're going to have another baby!"

He then saw my concerned face, and became more serious. "What do you think seeing her means?"

"I don't know," I shrugged. "You're the one who saw her…"

I tried to dismiss Adrian's question as unimportant, just in case he sensed that I'd already felt her around recently, which might cause him to get in to his stride about me having another baby. Well, my quick rebuff of his question was the end of that conversation, although as I found out later Adrian silently still wondered what it meant!

A few nights later, just as I was drifting off to sleep, Adrian suddenly jumped up. "I've seen her again!" This time he was really excited. "Something is definitely going on here Tonika, she was so clear – are you sure you haven't seen her?"

"No." I replied, vaguely.

"I'm sure this means something." Adrian said, "She was still holding a baby. How would we cope with another baby?" He was now starting to get concerned.

"Adrian, we are definitely not going to have another baby!" I replied with some vigor.

A few days passed with no further visits by Mary. But then, again just before Adrian went to sleep, he jumped up very excited, but this time with understanding. He said, "I've just seen Mary again – she came very close. She wasn't holding a baby, but I knew from her projection that she wants you to travel back and relive her life. And she's really determined!"

Now it all made sense. My concerns about having a fifth child passed quickly, as I told Adrian I had indeed felt her presence for a number of weeks.

"So when are you going to do it?" He asked, in anticipation.

My reply was to allow some time to filter the information received, though the reason for her presence now appeared pretty obvious. A few weeks later Adrian saw Mary again – she was holding an Arum lily and he felt Mary wanted me to have the lily, which I gladly accepted. This inspired me to make a date to travel back to observe her life three weeks later, which felt the right time to do it.

The day to travel came and as usual I had invited a number of people to my home to share the journey with me. Unfortunately though, the day couldn't have had a worse start. The postman had delivered a letter from my stepmother, which wasn't very pleasant. She was to send to me the following year her final letter of rejection of me. If I had not already performed a final process to clear any remaining restrictions regarding my relationship with her, the letter would have caused me to become extremely upset. The day's weather was very dramatic, gray clouds, high winds, and heavy rain – "a good day for cleansing", I thought to myself.

As a family, we decided to go into town to have scones and a cappuccino, something I always like doing. We all arrived and made ourselves cozy in Howard's café. Then suddenly, a big commotion occurred outside. A woman was running along the high street screaming and shouting, slamming shop doors, going absolutely crazy and generally causing havoc. After about thirty minutes (a long time!) she was calmed as best she could be, and taken away from the town centre. This seems an odd day", I thought to myself, and began to wonder whether I had got my timing wrong for the forthcoming journey. I decided that I would have to watch how the day develops and be prepared to cancel the evening if necessary.

Well, the day certainly developed! A few hours later, on a shopping trip to Chichester, I managed to get a massive splinter of fiberglass from the car embedded under my thumbnail. To cut a very long story short, after visiting two hospitals, spending a lot of time in casualty departments, suffering a variety of anesthetic injections into my thumb so that the doctor could dig it out, I was home again, feeling very weary and sore – and extremely uncertain about the whole time-traveling thing. Surely I must have the timing wrong?! But I had never got my timing wrong before. And that very morning I had placed a dozen white roses in individual golden tubes onto a golden mini tree. I had wanted to create something beautiful for the memory of Mary and I strongly felt this would be the perfect offering. The joy I had felt in creating this rose tree for her suggested all would be well; and yet there I was, just out of hospital with only a few hours to go before the beginning of the journey. I had pretty much made up my mind that I would have to cancel the plans, and in my head I was preparing what I would say to everyone, and how I would now spend my evening. I felt very disappointed indeed.

Suddenly, whilst thinking and feeling all of these things, a burst of determination entered me. "I am going to time travel tonight. I *know* my timing is right and I am going to do it!"

But there was still work to be done. My house was in a real mess, and as I have already said, I like my home spotless when I time travel. There is nothing worse when coming back from a journey back in time to a home that is untidy – it causes a disturbance in one's energy. Traveling back in time is like going on a two-week holiday for me. I want to enjoy the memory – not clean the house!

Fortunately, my son James – not normally renowned for his attitude to tidiness or helping out – working alongside Adrian to get the house spotless. I shall never forget the invaluable help he gave! Meanwhile, I quickly cooked dinner, we sat down to eat, and then I got into a nice deep bath to relax. Whilst dressing, I began to feel really good. Focused and calm, I went to prepare the back room with candles and smiled with gratitude at the rose tree created for Mary. Without the rose tree I would have cancelled the evening – it was a glimmer of light in an otherwise very dark and confused day.

As everyone began to arrive, I gave myself a few moments alone to go through any blocks I may have had in myself and surrender my will – the process was easy. The events of the day had released a layer of strength in me, which up until then had been dormant.

Everyone came into the room and settled themselves. It doesn't matter who comes to the house, providing they have an open mind. Whether they have a belief system or not, or whether they have read a lot on the subject or not – even if they have never attended anything remotely similar to what I do – it doesn't matter. Providing there is openness there, that is all that matters.

As everyone relaxed in the back room, touched by the serenity given off from fresh cut flowers in their prime and softly lit candles, I slipped into the front lounge to make sure Toby and Atlanta were OK. As usual, they were both looking forward to handing out those chocolate biscuits after we had finished time traveling! Returning to the back room, I briefly outlined to everyone the evening's agenda, reminding everyone that when one works to Divine Will it is important to remain open to the unexpected, and that something completely unplanned may occur. Everyone understood.

I settled into myself, giving thanks to everything in the universe that had helped me to go ahead with that evening and travel back freely in time. I closed my eyes and felt my bones and blood begin to respond. My head was gently tilted backwards and rocked side to side as my will slipped out. An energy stepped in that hadn't been in my body before, and said;

"I am known as the one who walks inside your minds. I am the one where light meets dark. I say on this most sacred of nights that you must allow your logical mind to cease."

With these profound words, the energy departed. I could tell this was the energy we all use to create a balance within our minds when we are wrestling with an unproductive thought. Well, it was this energy (probably amongst others), which works to assist that balancing process.

My head is pulled back, another energy enters, and my head is brought forward to an upright position. This is the energy of Truth, who I have spoken of before. The energy speaks:

"Many cycles past, much has been unread, much has been kept

quiet, and this quietness has in many ways distorted the Light and existence of a being of supreme grace. Her energy comes forward on this very sacred night to ask that those gathered here listen with non-judgment to her life. Her life as she lived when she walked on this planet." And the energy of Truth departs.

Next to enter and communicate is the energy of the Keeper of True Identity. He says: "I come because a call has been placed upon the life existence of a very fine energy that once walked your planet. Her life now needs to be shown as it was. I come to bring forth all her records and I say to you all do not judge." And he departs.

I began to wonder as to why we should judge her life anyway – it seemed odd. The next energy to enter was the universal energy that lives in the timeless seas of the universe. Using breathing techniques, (which are a different set of procedures each time we travel) the universal energy escorted us through the illusions that had been created of Mary's life and back in time, back to observe Mary's life as it truly was – the energy then departed.

Mary's energy entered my body. The first scene I am aware of is a small home; a two-storey building, very simple and basic in structure with fields behind the house. Mary was young and was slightly breathless when she spoke.

MARY: I am Mary. I come now and say my task on this night is to share my life with you. You have become part of my existence. I am fifteen. I am a child who has many brothers and one sister. We work hard in my father's fields. I am not the strongest of young girls. I have a condition in my chest that causes my breathing not to flow as it should, and so I work in my father's field and this a fine place for me.

GROUP: How many brothers do you have?

MARY: I have four.

GROUP: Is your sister older or younger?

MARY: My sister is much older than I am. I am the youngest of us all.

GROUP: Is your mother still alive?

MARY: My mother is so strong and her heart is like an Oxen. She has a spirit that is enough for us all. [MARY's *mum was well built, with lots of energy and very practical and efficient.*]

GROUP: Do you have any dreams of what you would like to do when you are older?

MARY: "I fear my life shall be one of loneliness and this is because of my condition here in my chest.

[MARY *feared that her chest weakness would prevent her from being chosen as a wife. Her health would be a hindrance to whoever wished to marry her, she continues.*]

MARY: I would not be strong.

GROUP: What is your mother's name?

MARY: My mother is known as Terea.

GROUP: Do you have any religious teachings?"

MARY: We have a...[MARY *stops to reconsider the words she is to use*]...I feel I must not be too harsh in my choice of words. But I feel I can tell you how I feel. We have a man who preaches much, and many listen. But I feel he somewhat talks words that have no meaning. He is a strong character, but he is also very domineering and I am uncomfortable around him. People listen to him because they feel he makes some sense, but to me he is unpleasant. I keep much inside me."

GROUP: What is your father like?"

Mary became light and joyful to be able to talk of her father; they were alike, and there was a strong bond between them.

MARY: My father is also very strong. My father is not like other people in this village. He does not listen to that man.

[*The preacher who preached of judgment, doom and gloom, was projecting a sense of fear into the people that listened. It seemed Mary was free enough, along with her father, to determine that he actually spoke a lot of rubbish!*]

GROUP: Although you are not strong in body, are you as strong as your mother in will and mind?" [MARY *thought about this, and could not see how she could have the strength and practicability her mother possessed. She answers,*] I am not sure. [*At this point my body breathes in deeply and time moves forward. MARY, now a few years older, and not so unsure of herself and the future says*]

Now I am of an age of more wisdom. My age is now twenty-three cycles [*23 years old*]. I am not at home any more, and the condition of which I suffered is not so much in my chest. I am freer. [*She was a lot stronger mentally and physically.*]

GROUP: Where are you now?

MARY: Now, I have a home, I work, and I make cloth. I weave and weave, but my condition in my chest is much clearer. I am not near my mother and father. I am away from my brothers and my sister, my sister I miss.

GROUP: Why have you left home?

MARY: When we find a partner we then travel to their land, and so this is why I am not with my first family.

GROUP: What is the name of the place where you are now?

MARY: "Where I live is above a sea. It is a land that is flat, but it does not have a name. [*I guess that was because where MARY was now living was not too populated, or a place where everyday business took place, therefore it did not warrant being given a name*].

GROUP: What is the name of your partner?

MARY: My husband is known as Joseph, he is strong but he does not have time for me."

[*I could feel Joseph had come from a good and well respected family, and I felt him to act as was socially expected, according to tradition. He appeared a strong character and committed to his particular lifestyle. MARY seemed to have a sense of duty to her husband. But there did not appear to be love between either of them, although there was a silent respect for each other.*]

GROUP: Are you happy?

MARY: "I am comfortable.

GROUP: Do you have any children?

MARY: "I do not, but I have one growing inside my body." [MARY *felt so happy and peaceful to be pregnant with this child*].

GROUP: Have you experienced in your dreams, or have you experienced the existence of Angels?

[*The question did not resonate with her, but she took the underlying meaning of the question to be; had she experienced wonder? This is how the question became translated in her being.*]

MARY: I often wonder of all the simplest things that occur in life, and in my wonderment I know I have touched peace. My child shall also know this peace.

GROUP: How do you know this to be the case?

MARY: Because I shall teach my child this. I shall show him to find peace in the simplest of gifts in nature. I shall show my child while youth is on my child's side.

Mary's answer was spurred on by the memory of the preacher, who talked only of heaviness and darkness and judgment. His preaching of fear took many away from the joy and wonderment that life and the Earth held. It made people aggressive and fierce towards each other, judging each other's actions in a negative way – after they had listened to this man. Mary wanted to fill her new child with a wonderment of life, to gain strength in simplicity, so there would be little room for others to come along and fill him with fear.

GROUP: Joseph seems restless?

MARY: He is a good man, but he does not hear my heart. But he is a good man.

[*My body breathes in and we move forward.*]

MARY: Now I have my son.

GROUP: What is his name?

MARY: His name is Thomas and he is a fine boy. My son, my child of light." [MARY *spoke with such joy, and pleasure in having such a beautiful son. She was at her happiest.*]

GROUP: Do you have any help?

MARY: The folk in the village, we all help together, we are a close community. We have a closeness I feel because there is none trying to dictate, like that man of my earlier years. [*The preacher*] There is much freedom in our village. We share all together, but I feel in my heart of a disturbance which I am not comfortable with. I look at my child and in my heart I have tears and this confuses my Soul. And so I spend many days with him and yet I cannot shake off this pain in my heart.

GROUP: Have you spoken to your husband about this?" [*MARY shakes her head; these were her deepest private feelings and ones she would not express outside of herself.*]

GROUP: Do you know why you hold so much pain?

MARY: My husband and I are not close. My husband is good, this I know, but he does not acknowledge my essence. Maybe I am not good for him – I have many confusions in my heart. [*There was obviously an emotional distance between Joseph and MARY, and as a result she devoted her time and love to her son Thomas.*] [*My body took a deep breath and we moved forward again.*]

[*MARY is now withdrawing into herself for protection.*]

MARY: Now people are shunning my presence. Now I feel alone. People say I am a disgrace, people say I am unclean, people say I am a woman of not good morals. I have another child growing inside, but I do not know how this came to be. People say I am crazy. People say I make stories, people say so many things that hurt my Soul.

GROUP: What of Joseph, what does he say?

MARY: He is good, he stands with me. He has not deserted me, he stays by my side, and yet his heart is more distant than ever before. I am so frightened. I do not know what is happening." Mary was very frightened, as her tummy was growing so were her fears as to what lay ahead after the birth. She had no idea whatsoever as to how she became pregnant. Feeling so alone and afraid, so unclean and worthless, she began to absorb the taunts and accusations directed at her. She became weak – her only 'light' at that time was her son Thomas.

GROUP: What of Thomas?

MARY: Thomas stays with me, he never leaves my side. I hold him tight, he does not judge me. I am confused. I am so frightened.

GROUP: How many more months before the baby will be born?

MARY: I have around four to go, four moons that are full, and then everything shall be. I fear I shall die, I fear I shall go to the deepest, darkest place in all eternity. But I have done nothing wrong. I am so frightened.

Mary's fear shook through my whole being. I could feel the blackness in the taunts thrown at her, the disgust being projected at her. People writing her off as crazy, their frustration not being answered as to how she became pregnant. So much hatred was towards her that her identity was becoming lost, as her essence was constantly sapped by these negative attacks. Because she was married to Joseph, who was a man of substance and came from 'good blood', her body was protected from physical attacks and aggression – it was her mental and emotional body that was under attack.

My body breathes in deeply once more and we move forward. Mary is now very weak and very tired. She has almost given up, resigned herself to the worst – defeat now taking the place of fear.

MARY: Now I am tired, I do not feel I can fight any more. I do not have the strength left in me. I am so weak, and also we have walked so far. We have to go and declare ourselves for some type of order. I am not sure which, I am so tired, and I am so cold and weak."

They were walking on foot. Mary slowly dragging herself, every step sapping more and more of the little strength left in her, desperation and despair overwhelming her mind.

GROUP: "What of your child, do you know any more of the child you carry?"

MARY: My Thomas is with me, but I do not know of what I have inside me, I do not even care if this is a child or not. I do not care, I am so tired and so weak. My only concern is that Thomas shall be safe. I feel I have no more left to give [*it was her son Thomas that really kept her going – just*].

GROUP: Where are you now?

They had arrived at the town they were traveling to, I began to recognize familiar scenes to those I had observed three years before, when I had time traveled back to watch the birth of Jesus.

MARY: "I am now hoping that someone will take this weight from my feet and lay me down, but nobody will let us in anywhere. I am becoming very weak – very tired." [MARY *was now sitting down in the inn building I had seen before.*]

MARY: I am aware a fine lady has taken Thomas from me.

Mary is now desperate and struggles to catch her breath – I realize her labor has started. My body moves us slightly forward to the intensity of Mary's contractions and to her giving birth. She cannot communicate. So intense was the energy pouring out of Mary (who in turn was using my body), that my own energy began to alter. The best analogy I can give for what I was feeling is when you pull the TV aerial out of its socket and the picture 'snows' – this is how my energy felt, as though it was fast fading. I knew deep within me there was a potent reason for me to experience such intensity of energy, but I felt that I could not take much more of this. Having complete faith in the workings of the universe I knew I would be taken through the birthing memory of Mary, to the absolute point of release. I could feel immense emotional pain connected with this birth.

One of the group was very concerned for me because of the intensity of what was happening, and opened their eyes. Some time after the journey, they told me that the blood vessels in my neck were hugely distended, like inflated balloons and they had been most worried about me!

Just before breaking point, relief and immense stillness suddenly came. Mary and I had moved forward. The atmosphere and its calmness was a million miles away from the intensity moments earlier. Someone asked gently, "Mary, where are you?"

We had now moved forward to the point immediately after the birth of Jesus. Calmly, and with confusion Mary answers;

"I am now in a place in my heart which I do not understand," She fiercely struggles to retain her great anger and grief. "I am feeling pain, anger and yet there is something inside that shines. I feel I must be declared insane, I am so angry. I am so angry at life."

Mary's son Thomas had been snatched from the arms of the older lady who had been looking after him. It was clear the men who snatched Thomas were carrying out a murderous order of some type. She, Joseph and the old Lady were powerless in the face of this aggression. Shock and trauma were ringing through her as she was giving birth. Yet around her newly born son she experienced an amazing light and peace. She had at that moment experienced (and this is the only way I can explain it) a journey from one end of eternity to the other. She had touched both ends, and her mental and emotional body simply could not cope. For me, I could see an incredible lady, so pure and so light in her being. But others declared her insane. It was as if she had now become 'untouchable'; only the light from her new child could touch and bring nurture to her. Now I knew why I was not allowed access into Mary's feelings on my journey three years previous to watch the birth of Jesus. Had I known the enormity of her experience and its emotional affect upon Mary, I feel pretty sure that I would not have subsequently traveled back to observe her life!

Someone asked tentatively, "How did Thomas die?" But Mary was too traumatized to answer.

We move forward. Now, as Mary spoke, a few years after the events, her voice trembled with determination and strength. It was as if for the first time since she 'lost' her sanity that she had been given an opportunity to share her innermost feelings.

"Now my second child is four. He is a fine boy, but I feel I cannot reach him. I feel I have lost my mind. My husband has abandoned me, he became so distant."

I could see that Joseph had left Mary. Mary was speaking in isolation in what felt like a shelter, with a small opening.

"I now live with my child, but I am declared unworthy to bring him up alone, so other women from our village talk with him."

At this point I could see the young boy Jesus close by, interacting with three other children. A familiarity surrounded them in what appeared to be a friendly household.

Trembling still, Mary continued, firmly and with control.

"I am declared insane. But I know my son sees something in my heart that others do not, and so my strength comes from his light. I know he has a strength that is unrivalled and I know he will shine, and I know also that he will touch many; and I also know that if giving birth to my child caused my sanity to become lost, then I have strength in that knowledge. I have no fears anymore."

I could feel completely the insanity Mary spoke of. Yet she had gained so much strength in her realizations and the recognition of the purity contained within her son, Jesus. Alone and unacknowledged by the people in her community, Mary watched her son's inner strength and freedom grow and grow.

Time moves on once more. Now at peace with herself, Mary feels to be in her mid-fifties. A great stillness and compassion flowed deep within and around her. My eyes shed so many tears, I feel they were hers and mine also. With determined clarity she says:

"I am Mary. I am old but I am not insane. My son has, through his strength, shown me that to walk a path of truth and destiny, with clarity, is one of the finest gifts that can ever be given. And I Mary, give many thanks to all the pain and suffering that I endured. I know now they were my finest lessons and they were my greatest lights, they were never my darkest days. And I ask that whenever anyone considers placing my essence higher than their own, I ask they place my heart into theirs and they will know my sufferings can be lights for them. I do not wish for praise, reverence and glory. All I ever performed was my task."

Love and compassion, for all of us present, filled her heart, as she slowly and gracefully departed.

Another energy enters my body, pure light and the most 'finely tuned' energy I have ever had in my body.

"I am known as the Holy Spirit. My essence only comes to your existences when truth in all its surrender needs to be performed. Only very rarely has my essence manifested. I ask for humanity as a consciousness to move forward, that you do not forget the words that you have heard tonight, and if you cannot speak those words from your heart, do not speak at all."

The Holy Spirit departed, and the universal time energy enters to bring us back to our time. Everyone slowly opened their eyes and looked at me, concerned that I was okay. Well, I am always OK. I know people think I should be exhausted after my experiences, but I never am. As I have already said, I could run a marathon! (Well not literally, but I am incredibly energized by the many different experiences). This time though, it was different. I wasn't exhausted – far from it. I looked back at everyone and smiled reassuringly at them. But my heart was so pained for Mary. "I'm just going for a pee", I told everyone. I knew I was going to break down in tears and I didn't want to do that in front of them; I did not want them to be concerned.

It was Mary who had suffered so much, not me. I did not want their compassion to move towards me. It was Mary who needed the acknowledgment, whose traumatic life needed to be understood, whose essence up to now had been denied. I cried all night and became angry at the churches for denying her true life. I felt she had been kept in a cage; she was a prisoner, trapped and alone in the denial of her life. Only very rarely do I get angry, but now I was furious! Being angry is just not part of my personality, so as my anger started to subside I realized that the way the religions portray Mary was not actually untrue. The Church portrays an aspect of her essence to us. The holiness in her portrayal was an aspect she had truly earned. But, her persona, her wholeness, was asking us to see her life and to see it without judgment. Mary could never be free when all the while she was being denied. To explain this more fully – you may feel you know someone from seeing them on the TV or in a theatre, but you are only ever seeing that person as an actor. But then after the show the actor comes over to you and says: "You have accepted one aspect of my life, the one which has just been projected, but that is not who I am. I want you to see the real me, I want to show you who I am, how I really live."

Well, the reality is never like the myth, and as so many people are secure in myth – reality does not need to feature.

Just a note to finish on. Two days after the time traveling to observe Mary's life and the intensity of the birth, my menstrual period was brought on twelve days early. That has never happened before or since.

I have thought long and hard as to whether to share these experiences from my time traveling, especially with reference to Jesus' birth and Mary's' life, since I have absolutely no desire to upset people's belief systems. However, I cannot deny these incredible experiences, and knowing what I know, I can only share. I appreciate that it may be hard for people to accept what I am saying. After all, I fought for many years against myself! I'm merely asking people to realize 'the picture is not flat, it has many sides'. Mary was indeed an incredible person and deserves her adulation, even if the actual immense suffering she underwent is not recognized. Likewise with Jesus – even if the nativity didn't happen the way it is portrayed. And indeed with Moses – the detail may be different, but the fundamental focus of the story is that Moses did leave Egypt in search of a new land, and he shared good advice to live peacefully by.

Whether my insights are regarded as deluded or amazing is the choice of you, the reader. What I do is time-travel, and I report what I experience. I am merely someone 'doing my job'. My aim is to sleep peacefully at night and to retain an openness to everything in creation. I have no interest in changing people's beliefs.

The next wormhole that appears to be opening up, is to travel back and observe the pyramids being built. I'm in the waiting room, waiting for the window of inspiration to grow stronger!

* * *

I truly believe that the whole of humanity will one day be able to travel back in time as I do now. They will be able to observe history as it happens. They will see and sense all the emotions and feelings that are connected to the time span they are traveling back to. When we all can do this, there will be no more wars, no more controlling beliefs. Confusion and illusions will pass, and conflict in families, communities, and countries will be no more. Humanity will know and feel history and evolve positively into the future, filled with wisdom and knowledge.

The journey home, which is a journey back to our true essence, is one we are all undertaking, whether we are aware of it or not. I for one, feel that I have only scratched the surface of what is out there to experience and discover.

My experiences of traveling into many different dimensions and the communications that I have had to date with numerous universal beings has left me not only in absolute wonder at the power of creation, but also marveling at the diversity of every individual I meet. For it is these individuals who, on a daily basis, teach and help me to discover and unveil more of my true self.

I am so very proud to be part of the human race and to have been given life – the most wondrous gift this planet could give.

I am filled with an excitement that says:

"You've only just begun."